Dimensions in Salvation

Dimensions in Salvation

by

WALTER RAYMOND BEACH

AUTHOR OF
We and Our Children
Eventide or Morning Glory?
South to the Mascareignes
Light From God's Lamp

REVIEW AND HERALD PUBLISHING ASSOCIATION
WASHINGTON, D.C.

PAINTING BY RUSSELL HARLAN

The unrest and turmoil among nations threaten to upset our peaceful way of life, and are topics for serious discussion on radio and TV and across the garden fence.

DEDICATION

I owe a very great debt to my daughter, Jo Ray Beach Cotton, without whose talent and constructive observations this exploration of the deeper dimensions in salvation would not have been possible in the present form. Together we dedicate the pages that follow to all who would seek resolutely a permanent solution to life's problems on planet Earth.

While the Christian believer and conventional churchgoer will find many things in this book that coincide with his traditional faith, *Dimensions in Salvation* was written to challenge that faith and to appeal to the rational thinker and honest doubter. It will prove provocative to those who share the growing cynical feeling that Christianity has failed.

Thousands of world leaders scan the political, economic, and social horizons of this contemporary hour and see no real solution for the perplexities and confusion of the times. Despairing of redress of the world's ills, countless numbers of these endeavor to isolate themselves and their small cosmos from the tide of rising evil, salvaging such contentment and satisfaction as they can from a precarious prosperity and a submission to whatever fate may prescribe. It is to these and to all who are fighting a losing battle with life's complexities that Dr. Beach directs his eloquent and persuasive thesis.

That Christianity has not failed, but rather that most of its proponents have only superficially grasped its tremendous potential, has led him to attempt this breakthrough into the deeper dimensions of salvation as outlined in the gospel story. If the ethics of Christ so stirred the world of the Caesars that it led men to martyrdom for its ideals, a discovery of its Spirit-borne dynamic is conceivably the solution for the current ills of humanity, providing a new hope in the midst of the growing fear of doom.

Dr. Beach is eminently qualified to underwrite the ideas he expounds in this volume. His education in liberal arts was received in Whitman and Walla Walla colleges, and in law from the Chicago Law School. He holds the Master's degree from the Sorbonne in Paris, and an honorary doctorate in laws from Walla Walla College.

But above these academic credentials, the author speaks as a highly successful spiritual church leader and administrator of forty years' experience. From secondary school teaching he went under appointment by the Seventh-day Adventist Church in 1926 to become an administrative youth leader in Switzerland. His qualifications for leadership led him to successive responsibilities, from president of the Belgian Conference to president of the Franco-Belgian Union, and eventually to the presidency of the Southern European Division. These appointments afforded him extensive travel during which he became conversant with the cultures and ideologies of varied peoples. In 1954 he was elected general secretary of the World Conference of Seventh-day Adventists, which position he currently holds.

His urbanity and sympathy with diverse national needs are reflected in his books, among which are *Vers les Claires Mascareignes, Crépuscle ou Aurore, Nous et Nos Enfants,* and *Light From God's Lamp.* The reader will find his propositions not dogmatic, but graced with the disarming invitation Isaiah used in times of disquietude not unlike our own, "Come now, and let us reason together."

H. M. TIPPETT

INTRODUCING THE THEME

Were you to ask me what I aim to accomplish in the following pages, I would answer without hesitation: to lay the ground for a religion of experience. It is not enough to know the truth conceptually, although certainly that is a beginning. The truth must be known experientially as well, in a full commitment to God as He is disclosed in history and in the heart of every believer.

Salvation is undeniably our need—now more than ever before. We are living through the greatest revolution humanity has known. Everything is exploding—population, knowledge, material goods; and man himself is bursting out into space. Men are hungry for a savior. Perplexity has driven them to reach out for security beyond human limits. At such a time the messages of God face the supreme test of relevance.

The challenge is heightened and complicated by other factors. For instance, non-Christian religions are experiencing an unprecedented upsurge as they tighten their grip on the minds and hearts of people. Defective Christianity has become involved in false revivalism, bringing the apocalyptic fulfillment into ever sharper focus. Strife and tension strike countless areas. The nations are churning in unrest and turmoil. Arnold Toynbee calls this era a "time of trouble," in which he re-echoes the words of Saint Paul: "You must face the fact: the final age of this world is to be a time of troubles." [1]

With disappointment we note that Christians are often

---

[1] Second Epistle to Timothy, ch. 3, v. 21. *The New English Bible*, New Testament. © The Delegates of the Oxford University Press and the Syndics of the Cambridge University Press 1961.

poor examples. We are not all inwardly content nor outwardly radiant. Many regular churchgoers are as fretful and anxious as their church-neglecting neighbors. It behooves all of us—Christians and non-Christians—to seek resolutely a satisfactory solution to the problems of life on our planet.

Our conclusions must be based first on reason, then on faith, hope, and love. We must use faith accurately and aggressively. A faith not grounded in reason is a weak faith, vulnerable to devastating attacks and to subversion. A religious faith without reason actually breeds defective character and evil conduct.

I shall endeavor to make such a reasonable search in the pages of this book, believing that the deeper dimensions in salvation will answer our questioning minds and will lead us in faith, hope, and love to set aside the anxiety, care, and insecurity that have become so much a part of us.

Mind you, the process of salvation itself is simple—wondrously simple, as we shall see—but in total commitment and devotion the contract leaves no loopholes. The God-centered solution requires all there is of us. Our dedication must be sure, constant, and enduring. It must equal in earnestness life itself.

In this context let us through the following pages dedicate ourselves to a fuller, a more satisfying comprehension of God's "Dimensions in Salvation."

THE AUTHOR

TOPICS

CHAPTER 1

Truth

a MAN TRUDGES down Main Street of a large city. He wears a faded suit, almost as faded as his blue eyes. His shoulders lead his body in a discouraged slump. He no longer has a wife. His children are ashamed of him. His life has been a classic failure. Up from the steaming pavement, down from the towering skyscrapers, and thundering from within his human heart comes a voice: "Whence have I come? Why am I here? Where am I going?" These three questions are pressing for an answer.

The deepest thinkers, the brightest minds, have grappled with this same threefold giant. For most of them there has been no easy answer. In fact, everyone who has tried to think systematically about the universe has reached impasses and impenetrable walls.

Now, of course, no human being, limited as he is, can know everything about everything. He cannot even know one thing exhaustively. Why then bother to know anything? Why not let life take its natural course, allowing the fittest to survive and the weakest to fade away? Or, if we insist on being intellectual about it, why not take one

PAINTING BY HARRY ANDERSON   © 1963 BY REVIEW AND HERALD →

During the trial of Jesus, Pilate, the Roman governor, asked Him the significant question "What is truth?"

specialist's view of man? Why not, let us say, go either
to the psychologist, sociologist, anthropologist, or econo-
mist in order to get our information? After all, the empirical sciences have spent years of intensive study filled with
every kind of behavioral and theoretical experiment to get
man straightened out so that he could be understood and
he himself understand what goes on around him.

The trouble is that science, brilliant as its career has
been, has never managed to reflect to us a composite picture of man, but only a surface filled with different images,
rather like a contemporary cubist painter who splits up the
whole of whatever he is painting into dislocated facets
and planes, each reflecting a different angle. This system
is unsatisfactory to our inborn thirst for truth.

The quest for truth is not a contemporary emprise. It
is as old as the universe itself. It began the moment God
created beings with intelligence. Everywhere, in countless
different languages and with varying shades of emotion,
the question has been repeated, "What is truth?" One of
history's most dramatic queries for a definition of truth was
presented by a Palestinian magistrate employed under
the Roman eagle. Sitting in judgment on a young Jew
who had been accused of rabble rousing and undermining
the government, he asked, "Art thou a king then?" The
Jew gave a straightforward reply: "To this end was I
born, and for this cause came I into the world, that I should
bear witness unto the truth. Every one that is of the truth
heareth my voice." Then Pilate posed the age-old question
"What is truth?" [1]

According to the Record, Pilate never waited for an
answer to his question. Perhaps he had only asked it in
jest. Perhaps his sophisticated life had made of him an
embittered cynic who had already sorted all the answers

---

[1] Gospel according to John, ch. 18, vs. 37, 38.

and found them vain. Or, perhaps the young Jew had already given more answers than Rome's civil servant knew how to deal with. Be this as it may, the fact remains that Pontius Pilate asked the most significant question of life.

Pilate's world, as the world before him and the world since, was one in which truth wore many masks. It was a boiling pot of riddles, ideologies, doctrines, facts, and private prejudices. Men who tried to approach truth often gave up in despair because it seemed impossible to justify all the paradoxes and to make rational decisions between alternatives. Using the easy way out, many clutched an idol or a piece of inherited dogmatism, relying on these artificial crutches to keep from losing balance. Others refused to compromise. They kept searching until they formulated some sort of personal philosophy or over-all picture to serve as a backdrop for their daily tasks.

Of the many frameworks developed, let us look at five that have affected history most profoundly. All of them deal with the three fundamental questions stated at the beginning of this discussion: "Where from?" "Why?" "Where to?" They endeavor to analyze and assess what is important or valuable within the scope of these questions.

1. *The idealist* attempts to answer the question What is truth? by stating that whatever we see in the material world is but a fleeting, imperfect reflection of a realm that is perfect and eternal. Plato, for instance, declared that if we clear our minds of the images of all particular things, we shall be able to contemplate the universal ideas in all their pristine purity, unaffected by matter. In other words, instead of thinking about one tree in particular, we ought to think about what is common to all trees. This, he felt, would allow man to focus on the ideal tree, which exists only in the spiritual realm.

Immanuel Kant, another leading idealist, was of a different opinion. While, like Plato, dividing the world into two realms, he maintained that we could have knowledge of the material world, but that the spiritual world was beyond our knowledge.

2. *The realist* stands in direct opposition to the idealist. His main thesis is based on Aristotle's view that whatever we perceive is real. To him the world we apprehend with our senses is not an illusion but something that really exists. Every blade of grass, mountain crevice, and gust of wind is there. Realism does not exclude religion. Thomas Aquinas was a realist, yet he believed that both matter and spirit were created by God, and that God's creating the universe is proof of its reality, for anything divinely created must be real. So, too, the evidence of the senses is not a fraud, says the realist. What we see is really there, although it is possible for us to make mistakes and interpret what we see to be other than it really is.

3. *The pragmatist* has been regarded as a more modern addition to the pursuit of truth. He agrees with the realist that matter indeed exists and is not simply a projection of man's mind or a reflection of something more spiritual. But when this is acknowledged, what then? There still remain scientific problems, wars to reckon with, and social problems to solve. Thus William James, the great pragmatic philosopher, advocated that man must always be prepared to alter the way he has been doing things. His means and purposes must remain flexible, constantly open to change and revision. The pragmatist emphasizes particularly man's social environment, contending that the happiest man is one who has learned to operate thoughtfully and deliberatively among other men. According to pragmatism man does not simply receive knowledge, he *makes* it.

4. *The existentialist* represents a rather recent revolt against traditional thinking. He declares that the center of all truth must be the thinking, feeling individual. Noth-

ing makes much difference unless it refers to the personal life of men. The existentialist feels that too often seekers after truth have moved in the thin air of abstract speculation instead of addressing themselves to such important issues of human existence as love, anguish, sickness, death, and the decisions of each passing hour. The existentialist says that man must never submit himself to any regime, not even religion or science. He is a free moral agent, therefore all of his acting and thinking should be his own.

5. *The logical empiricist* has recently come to exercise considerable influence in thinking circles. He contends that most problems can eventually be reduced to problems of language and meaning. Our main task, therefore, is to clarify the meaning of propositions and statements. When this is done, says the logical empiricist, we shall find that problems are either scientific and mathematical, or meaningless and nonsensical. The logical empiricist is perfectly happy to sit in an attic room solving isolated, individual problems without attempting to create from them a system of truth.

Centuries of creative thinking and careful analysis have gone into the formulation of such frameworks as the five we have just described. To ignore them would be unthinking. We cannot deny that each of these schools of thought presents some aspect of truth. Man *is* primarily a spiritual being; matter *is* real; man's mental processes *should* remain flexible; we *should* give thought to grievous social problems; statements *ought* certainly to be crystal clear. Yet, no sooner have we admitted this than we realize with a sinking heart that we are no happier than before, and that if this were all there is to life our hunger for truth would keep on gnawing at us and we would remain empty and miserable.

One day a peasant of India asked an old traveler as they stood together under the shade of a tree, "Where are you going, holy man?" The old man answered: "To a city far away."

"In India?" the peasant queried. The answer was, "Farther."

"In Asia?"

"Farther, farther, friend, farther; for that city I seek is Truth, and Truth is hidden in the heart of God."

In this answer the old wanderer expressed wisdom that has bridged time. On this fundamental position we must build all branches of knowledge. Because this is so vital to our correct thinking, all our ideas must harmonize with the larger idea of God.

We say that life is a gigantic jigsaw puzzle that forms a correct picture only when all of the pieces fit together harmoniously. If there are pieces that do not fit into the picture, the question is immediately raised concerning the truth of the whole or at least of the parts that do not fit. Such a theory of truth is the cornerstone on which we must build if we are to find satisfaction in our search. The Holy Scriptures urge us to progress in that way. The prophet Isaiah, for instance, said, "To the law and to the testimony: if they speak not according to this word, it is because there is no light in them." [2] This actually means that if a certain claim to truth does not harmonize with all truth previously established the disparity is enough to reject the claim.

Those deeply concerned with truth have found in the Scriptures the source of genuine harmony that explains man's three crucial problems. They have been amazed time and again at how consistently both the Old and the New Testament delineate a plan for man's salvation from sin and restoration to perfection. The harmony of the Bible, despite the varying cultural and emotional back-

---

[2] Book of Isaiah, ch. 8, v. 20.

grounds that each writer brought to it, is to them irrefutable proof of its truth. With amazement the reader sees each little bit take its appointed place in the formation of the whole.

According to the coherence theory of truth, when Jesus, in the New Testament Gospels, tells us what God is like, then this description of God must harmonize with the Lord of the Genesis story in the Old Testament, else one or the other or both must be untrue. In the New Testament, Jesus tells us that God is a God of love, whose children are meek, kind, patient, and peaceful. He also tells us that God is a God of justice, a rewarder of men, whose children acknowledge His requirements and obey. This likewise is taught in the Old Testament. Jesus propounded nothing inconsistent with previously accepted truth. He only emphasized concepts that had been rejected or neglected. In the Old Testament and the New we find a composite revelation of God as Creator and Redeemer.

But along comes a thinker such as the German philosopher Friedrich Nietzsche. He looks at humanity and observes only one aspect of life. He sees people destroying one another in a horrible battle for the survival of the fittest. And he jumps to the conclusion that the Bible God is a God of fierce, inflexible force arbitrating the struggle for existence. His children must be supermen in order to withstand the tooth-and-fang war among them. Thus, Nietzsche considers Christ's teachings a "foul trick played on humanity." "Truth," he cried, "has been stood on its head."

Nietzsche was wrong. His narrow, partial view is refuted by the complete picture. The god of Nietzsche and of the evolutionary ascent of man cannot be reconciled with the Creator-Redeemer God of Holy Scripture. Modern attempts to do so result only in confusion and in untruth, according to the coherence requisite. Man's fierce, sinful struggle, which so impressed Nietzsche, is not the making of the God of the Bible. This escaped the philosopher's limited view. On the contrary, the God whom Christ presented is committed to a restoration of His creation to its original state, in which man thinks God's thoughts after Him—thoughts of love, mercy, and righteousness.

Now, let us say that we accept Christ's description of God and reject the evolutionary theme. Have we attained? Can we sit back and rock in perfect contentment because we have made a pleasant discovery and a worth-while decision? We cannot. Truth on any human level is incomplete. It lacks finality because the most perceptive mind is still only human and therefore incapable of seeing all. Our knowledge of truth is partial. However, we have the fortune to possess minds that grow. We can add new information, new experiences, and new comprehensions to our present framework. Our duty, then, is to continue the search for truth to the end of our life. But we must make sure that the new insights gained do not conflict with previous revelation. In other words, we must not conjure up novel ideas and think to replace a portion of the Bible with them. Rather, our growth must be part of the architecture of our already cohesive truth. Jesus Himself said, "Think not that I am come to destroy the law, or the prophets: I am not come to destroy, but to fulfil." [3] Christ came to "magnify" the law and "make it honourable." [4] New truth does not deny old truth, but simply expands and enriches it, much like sugar and salt bring out the natural taste of fruits and vegetables.

I wish to submit that precisely such a concept of unfolding truth is the basis for contemporary truth. Indeed, nothing is more disastrous to Christianity than a mind unwilling to explore new experiences, a mind content to

---

[3] Gospel according to Matthew, ch. 5, v. 17.
[4] Book of Isaiah, ch. 42, v. 21.

ossify alone, untouched by the thousands of new and exciting nuances God holds in reserve for every one who diligently seeks truth.

Note this passage from the pen of Ellen G. White:

"God intends that, even in this life, truth shall be ever unfolding to His people. . . . Whenever the people of God are growing in grace, they will be constantly obtaining a clearer understanding of His word. They will discern new light and beauty in its sacred truths." [5]

Truth at the human level is either ever expanding or gradually suffocating. Once we accept this axiom, our search for truth becomes a lifelong growth, like that of a tree. The tree never stops growing; it keeps right on pushing upward, stretching its limbs toward the golden sun.

Some Christians have the idea that truth is whatever grandfather handed down to father and what father taught his own son. They are content to swallow a ready-made opinion without waiting to taste it and see whether it is good or bad. This is not to say that a son or daughter ought to go against his parents' faith and practice. The past has had its glorious moments. Each generation gratefully stands on the shoulders of previous generations and from this vantage point is able to see a little farther. The pity is that too often the last generation shades its eyes with fear of what the view will disclose and becomes thus a useless paralytic, unable to function in the emerging present.

Granted that our progress in truth seeking is geometrical; that we open our minds to new and everlasting vistas. Is that, then, enough? If it were, any avid scholar would stand in no further need. But experience as such is not enough. Once opened, our mind may still be only an empty cave through which the cold winds howl. We can spend a

---

lifetime running from a terror in which we would not believe, toward a safety in which we have no faith. Or, like a slave who has finally been freed, we approach any river thinking that it will be our Jordan.

Note well that the old man of India was looking for a truth hidden in the heart of God. How wise he was! Pilate was not so wise. He never learned the answer to the most important question ever raised. Had he only stayed close to Jesus a little longer, or had he become acquainted with Him sooner, he too would doubtless have heard the now famous answer, "I am . . . the truth." [6] Had Pilate searched a little further, he too could have found truth at its deepest, most sacred dimension, that is, in the person of God Himself as revealed in Jesus Christ.

All our studies about God are useful. We are helpless to communicate Him to others without these. We need to study Him more. We need also to form a cohesive structure of doctrine and religion. I shall say more about this later in our discussion. But we cannot and must not attempt to reduce God to a set of propositions about Him. This is sheer blasphemy. God is a person. To make His acquaintance in truth is to encounter Him in the person of Jesus Christ.

A survey of human history reveals that whenever man truly knew God, this involved a personal encounter with Him. The children of Israel spent half a century wandering across the arid and lonely wilderness in search of God's purpose in their behalf. At times they faltered and became estranged from God; but they came closest to divine truth whenever they met God personally. Moses could have handed them a set of dogmas or some pertinent information about God; but this would never have sufficed. Only when the Israelites felt close to God as He hovered over

---

[6] *Gospel according to John*, ch. 14, v. 6.

them in the cloud by day and in the pillar of fire by night could they manifest in their daily deportment that they were in contact with Ultimate Truth.

Let us not ignore the empirical sciences, or the complicated philosophical systems of East and West. Let us simply realize that beyond them lies the living, loving God whom we can learn to know personally because He has revealed Himself to us through Christ. This truth was what Saul of Tarsus met in a blinding flash on the road to Damascus; what Moses heard in the soft wind on top of Mount Sinai. For each of us truth may be found in a different place. We may find it as we dig the earth to plant corn or as we speed along the freeway at midnight to answer a sick call or as we build a bridge or paint a kitchen. No profession is excluded from the possession of truth. Nor is truth confined to any certain period of history. We need not think of Christ only in terms of a long white robe and Roman sandals. He is not a figure of the first century. The historical Christ belongs to all ages. In the words of Albert Schweitzer:

"He [Christ] comes to us as One unknown, without a name, as of old, by the lake-side, He came to those men who knew Him not. He speaks to us the same word: 'Follow thou me!' and sets us to the tasks which He has to fulfil for our time. He commands. And to those who obey Him, whether they be wise or simple, He will reveal Himself in the toils, the conflicts, the sufferings which they shall pass through in His fellowship, and, as an ineffable mystery, they shall learn in their own experience Who He is." [7]

Happy are they who have this perception of the truth. They can then set their minds to high intellectual achievements, and their progress will prove fruitful. They will

---

[7] Albert Schweitzer, *The Quest for the Historical Jesus*, p. 403.

not disintegrate into a depressed state of mind, wishing they were dead so that the complexity of modern life need no longer be faced. Having surrendered their hearts in love to God who is the ultimate truth, they will allow truth to unfold before them. They will possess truth—and truth will possess them.

CHAPTER 2

Faith

REPORTER WENT to a wedding to cover the event for his newspaper. When the editor asked for his copy he pointed to a blank piece of paper in his typewriter, saying that he had nothing to report because the bridegroom had not shown up. From this incident I should like to draw "The Parable of the Sophisticated Philosopher." This modern philosopher goes in search of God and returns empty-handed because, according to him, no one showed up. He finds himself in a terrible plight with respect to faith, a plight that those who find faith easy to come by will not only misunderstand but also denounce.

Not all of us think alike. Some Christians feel no need to justify their beliefs. That God created the world and at a specific point in history sent His Son in human form to redeem the world from the curse of sin they never dream of doubting. Such believers go to bed at night thoroughly at peace and fully convinced that all affairs are in God's hands and that no matter what happens, it will be for the best. Their slumber is not interrupted with tormenting questions that keep the mind in a turbulent state. Resting on the bosom of unwavering faith they are genuinely satisfied.

There are others, however, who cannot share this experience. I am thinking in particular of the modern man who has problems with his faith. He wants desperately to believe, but for him religion and faith must not advance beyond human reason. He has found no final satisfaction in the purely philosophic view of the universe, nor in the evolutionary theory, yet he is constitutionally incapable of a leap into the dark without rational support. To him I wish to speak now, because I am firmly convinced that it is entirely possible to take a proper rational approach to faith—furthermore, that such a rational approach is stronger and more lasting than a blind faith. My assertion is that the intellect can take us far enough along the way to faith that it justifies our accepting the rest on trust.

The plight of many today with respect to faith is complicated by their training. They have inherited a century of religious doubt. For the past hundred years educators, theologians, and scientists have moved consistently toward the left of the fundamental religious center. Today it is relatively uncommon to find a product of higher education who is a committed Christian. In Great Britain and France only one in ten citizens has an active church membership. Even more to the point is the fact that the majority of the 10 per cent are elderly people.

Also, the climate of the times is hostile to faith. The modern generation is taught to make no assumptions incapable of being supported by scientific evidence. People are ridiculed and intellectually rebuffed if they champion religious ideas that do not pass the empirical tests. How can a body be resurrected? Why is there suffering and evil? How can you escape annihilation through atomic warfare? How? Why? How? Why? in endless repetition. Can we find an answer? Is faith a possibility in the querulous and scoffing age in which we live?

I wish to propose that indeed there is an answer to contentious doubt, and that faith is more justifiable than skepticism or agnosticism; moreover, that faith is the life-blood of our civilization. Once we lose faith we lose everything worth clinging to. The fact that our generation has lost faith in such a large measure is exactly the reason it finds itself in such a wretched state, with suicide, dope addiction, and other desperate measures for escape mounting at a mad statistical pace. We fulfill Biblical prophecy of our time in every respect: "This know also, that in the last days perilous times shall come. For men shall be lovers of their own selves, covetous, boasters, proud, blasphemers, disobedient to parents, unthankful, unholy, without natural affection, trucebreakers, false accusers, incontinent, fierce, despisers of those that are good, traitors, heady, highminded, lovers of pleasures more than lovers of God; having a form of godliness, but denying the power thereof." [1]

So, let us get back to faith, the one great need man feels keenly but rarely acknowledges. What is faith? One way to answer this question is by telling first what faith is *not*. At least this seems a plausible start toward a definition.

First, faith is not knowledge with a low degree of evidence. To believe that the value of the American dollar will decrease because competent economists predict it after having studied the dominant trends of the international market is not necessarily to have faith in the economists. We believe authorities and we trust their judgment, but that is not faith. Faith involves more than trust, although trust does feature in the whole of faith. Faith is based on truth.

Second, faith is not an act of the will. If you corner

---

[1] Second Epistle to Timothy, ch. 3, vs. 1-5.

yourself and tell yourself a thousand times, "I'm going to believe and be obedient to my beliefs," you are not showing faith. For instance, you may have doubts about a life after death. Now, the church dogma states that Paradise is assured to those who live righteously. The promise is inviting. You want to believe this, so you make up your mind that you *will* believe; you will simply put aside all other possibilities and concentrate only on the belief that life can go on. Such an act does not produce faith. At best, it is only a haphazard decision that could have seized on some other assumption with equal justification. No command to believe and no will to believe can create faith.

Third, faith is not a delirious state in which one's emotions burst with ecstasy over some inner, intangible delight. Certain religious sects equate faith with jumping up and down in a sort of calisthenic euphoria. They prove and sustain what they think is faith by emotional demonstration. In this way they rid themselves of the responsibility of thought. Thinking is painful. It is so much easier to scream, "Praise the Lord, I'm saved!" than to think through God's great plan of salvation. But faith cannot be restricted to this kind of subjectivity. Faith must be committed to persuasive truth and not rest on emotional moods.

Many attempts have been made at defining faith. Paul Tillich says that faith is the state of being "ultimately concerned," as expressed in the Old Testament: "You shall love the Lord your God with all your heart, and with all your soul, and with all your might." [2] In other words, this definition makes faith the total surrender to the subject of ultimate concern. [3] The Bible is full of concrete examples of how this faith is to show itself. For instance, men of faith will serve Jehovah and no other

---

[2] Book of Deuteronomy, ch. 6, v. 5, R.S.V.
[3] See *Dynamics of Faith*, pp. 1, 3.

God. In His name they will do acts of kindness and mercy and will refrain from vulgarity, dishonesty, or brutality.

Note that faith as a definition is not restricted to belief in God. Faith may be placed in something totally disassociated with God. You may have faith in the formulas for worldly success, or in the potential achievements of laboratory sciences, or you may even have faith in blind fate —that whatever is to be will be. Whatever commands your deepest convictions—that is your faith. That by which your total being is grasped is your faith. It may be a demonic force leading you away from reality and truth. It may be a philosophic snare, by its sophistries obscuring the light of true reason. What we believe matters infinitely but does not offer the definition of faith as a motivating force.

Another point of importance is that an act of faith is a conscious act, not an instinct or a drive, although it may be a response to the latter. At the basis of faith must be the conscious, dynamic individual. The apostle Paul recognized this, and added: "It is God who works in you, inspiring both the will and the deed, for his own chosen purpose." [4]

Immediately we come to God as the object of religious faith. How can man, who is so finite and so easily frustrated, come to terms with the Infinite? Is not this like stretching a rubber band to its breaking point? The answer is simply that God transcends the cleavage between Himself and man. He is the only source of faith that gives one-hundred-per-cent satisfaction. All other sources sooner or later prove to be a disappointment. Indeed, their failure is inevitable. The thesis of this exposé is that any man who misplaces his faith—a faith that deserves to be placed only in God—will find misery compounded.

Man has always craved God. The ancient psalm is no

---

[4] Epistle to the Philippians, ch. 2, v. 13, N.E.B.

less adroit today than it was when it was written by the psalmist: "O God, thou art my God; earnestly will I seek thee: my soul thirsteth for thee, my flesh longeth for thee, in a dry and weary land, where no water is. So have I looked upon thee in the sanctuary, to see thy power and thy glory." [5] But sometimes we forget that the search is two-sided. God seeks us as diligently as we seek Him. "The Lord looked down from heaven upon the children of men, to see if there were any that did understand and seek God." [6]

Well, then, if God is seeking man and man is seeking God, why do they not get together? How does one find God? How does one uncover the faith without which no man can live a full life?

There are three avenues along which man can find God. None of these avenues alone suffices; rather, man must travel along all three in order to find the God in whom he may place his faith as we have defined faith.

GOD IN THE PHYSICAL UNIVERSE

Open your eyes. Look around you. Neither Wordsworth, nor Shelley, nor any of the nature poets have adequately described the wonders of the universe. The stars, the multicolored birds, the multifarious animal and plant life all inspire confidence in a Creator-God. To view the world as the product of blind chance is inconceivable without blotting out reason. Prof. Edwin Conklin, biologist at Princeton University, has repeatedly said that the probability of life originating from accident is comparable to the probability of the Unabridged Dictionary's resulting from an explosion in a printing shop. Everything in the universe shows design, intelligence, order, and purpose. The universe is not an illusion. It is real.

---

[5] Psalm 63, vs. 1, 2, A.S.V.
[6] *Ibid.*, 14, v. 2.

Our universe was created in space and time. As Job put it: "He . . . hangeth the earth upon nothing." [7]

The rotation of the earth on its polar axis, with its alternating night and day and its yearly revolution around the sun, makes it habitable for human as well as plant life. This is not just chance.

The atmosphere protects the earth from the deadly impact of twenty million meteors that daily enter it at speeds of 30 miles per second. It also maintains a temperature within habitable limits. If the earth were the size of the moon, it would not be physically possible for it to hold both the atmosphere and water, thus the temperatures of the planet would be fatally extreme. On the other hand, if the earth were the size of the sun, any kind of human physical equilibrium as we now experience it would be impossible, and intellectual life would be out of the question.

Myriad facts in nature suggest that an organizing intelligence is behind the universe. If physical phenomena can be expressed by mathematical law and formula, it is because such order is the result of an orderly mind which has prearranged it. [8] Think, for instance, of the intricate design of human and animal bodies. Think of a brain with its unbelievable abilities—who can explain the functioning of this marvelous organ? All the combined intelligence of the world cannot reconstruct a brain.

Think of the mysterious chemical reactions that control the human body so that it is capable of producing neutralizing acids and antibodies that fight off harmful invaders of the system. They astound the most educated chemists.

In nature we confront miracles on every hand. A spider spins a web. A salmon swims from the sea upriver to its birthplace. Tiny ants work in an amazing kingdom. Flow-

[7] Book of Job, ch. 26, v. 7.
[8] See Louis Vialleton, *L'origine des Êtres Vivants* (Plon, Paris); Jean Rostand, *La Formation de l'Être* (Hachette, Paris).

ers absorb moisture through osmosis. Birds fly through the air and fish swim in the water. Take a walk down a sunlit lane. Note the marvelous detail of a flower; listen to the beautiful song of the robin; inspect the intricate nest of the Baltimore oriole. Did the flower just chance to form sweet nectar that attracts the insects, which in turn ensure the production of more flowers next year? Is it just accident that small pollen grains germinate the ovary of the flower and cause a seed to be produced?

J. B. Leathes has taken a look at the mystery of proteins. They are made from long chains called amino acids. The way these are put together matters enormously. If arranged in the wrong way, they will not sustain life, and may be poisonous. Leathes has calculated that the links in the chain of quite a simple protein could be put together in millions of ways. It is impossible for all of these chances to coincide in building one molecule of protein, let alone place in it the spark of life.

If one refuses to look through a microscope or glance at a photograph of an amoeba, he may be able to argue at length that an amoeba does not exist. But the minute he sees one, or its photograph, the basis of his argument is gone. So it is with God. As long as one refuses to look for Him or to acknowledge His handiwork with an unprejudiced eye, one can argue long and loud that God does not exist. However, once the unbelieving man glimpses God, then he can no longer argue against His existence. Ultimately this must be an individual experience. William Thomson Kelvin, one of the world's greatest physicists, has made the following significant statement: "If you think strongly enough, you will be forced by science to believe in God." Lord Kelvin is right. Logic requires belief that the unseen hand of God arranged all the phenomena of flora and fauna and stellar space by laws we must learn. All is so astounding and inexplicable without a divine

Creator. Albert Einstein spoke of "the illimitable superior reasoning power which is revealed in the incomprehensible universe." Max Planch, one of the scientists who probed the inner secrets of the atom, said this: "Religion and natural science are fighting a joint battle in an incessant, never-relaxing crusade against skepticism, against dogmatism, and against superstition; and the rallying cry in this crusade has always been, and always will be: on to God!"

Then, beyond nature as a sort of fantastic show place where every second something unexplainable happens, there is that in nature which commands our attention because of its over-all grandeur, beauty, and power. Perhaps we are sitting on a mountain peak overlooking rolling hills and flowered meadows. Perhaps we are standing at a window opening up on the ocean at sunset. Or maybe we are taking a solitary stroll at midnight while the moon is high. In these or similar circumstances each of us has at some time been atremble with the grandeur, the beauty, and the power of nature. We have lifted our eyes and have seen a little higher than ourselves. We have looked higher even than nature, toward the sublime.

Tragically, modern life affords diminishing amounts of time for the development of our sense of awe in nature. Students are taught to read, write, and calculate, with little time devoted to reverence. We are almost ashamed to admit that sometimes we see things that are beyond our ability to describe. We think it is weakness to admit that our scientific categories, our mathematical symbols, and our classified forms cannot apprehend everything. But our real strength is in the admission that the universe is directed by a Spirit greater than man, and that this Spirit accounts for all that is inexplicable to the human mind. Man can only stand and say with the psalmist: "Shout unto God, all the earth; sing praises unto the glory of His

name, make His praise glorious. Say unto God: 'How
tremendous is Thy work!' " [9]

REVELATION

The physical world teaches us much about God, but
we still have many questions to ask. Are they to go un-
answered? Is a knowledge of God like some sort of treasure buried in a rocky cave, which we have to excavate without benefit of a map that would show us where the cave is
situated? Certainly not. God has made provision for man's
faith in Him. Remember, He is seeking man as well as
man is seeking Him.

The God of nature alone could be a God with many
faces. As a matter of fact, He has been interpreted from
nature in many ways by philosophers, scholars, and theologians—each holding a different view of Him. Many men
admit God's existence, but refuse to admit that anything
definite can be said of Him. They make of God some sort
of inanimate cosmic symbol. Their only definition is that
God is something indefinable.

Faith is based on God's revelation of Himself in human
history. The Bible is the authentic record of this revelation.[10] The Bible is the history of the deeds of God toward
man. It tells how God created man, how He guided Abraham, how He chose Moses to deliver the Israelites from
slavery, how He came into the world to reveal God's love,
how the Holy Spirit worked in men's hearts to bring together God's community. Furthermore, the chronicle is
still being recorded. We live today in the fullness of sacred
history.

The Holy Scriptures are different from other historical
records because they present a history with a beginning

---

[9] Psalm 66, vs. 2, 3 (Holy Scriptures, Masoretic Text, Jewish Publication Society of America).
[10] See Chapter 4, The Bible.

and an end. The historian's view of the world is a never-ending recording of past events. Not so God's Book. The Bible tells the story of salvation from its dramatic beginning to its glorious end. This plan is being fulfilled stage by stage as told by the prophets chosen of God to be His mouthpiece. It is in the Bible that man can best learn to know God's character.

The weightiest claim on us by the Bible is the life of Jesus Christ as recorded in the four Gospels. His manhood revealed a holiness, wisdom, and power that are far removed from the life pattern of the ordinary person. No one can help recognizing in Him the ideal manhood. After we read His story—how His enemies despised Him and treated Him like a fanatic, and how His disciples acknowledged Him as the Son of God—we find it insupportable to think of Him as an impostor. It is reasonable to believe Him when He tells us that He is the Son of God. Believing that, it is reasonable to commit ourselves to Him.

To place our faith in the revelation of Jesus Christ as God made flesh, to dwell among men, is formidable indeed; but every true Christian has done this and his life has been deeply affected. Many people are afraid of such a faith—a faith that puts them at the mercy of someone higher than themselves. But it is richly rewarding. Christ discloses the hidden things of history. His appearance unlocked the prophecies of the Old Testament. Before Him history was depressing and inexplicable. Without Him humanity was doomed. But when the veil in the sanctuary was rent at Christ's death, the veil that had shrouded the future was lifted. Christ declared Himself the resurrection and the life. The meaningless death of innocents and martyrs was no longer confounding, for Christ had made provision for the eventual triumph of justice over evil.

Holy Scripture assures us of the covenant God has with

His people. His faithfulness stands regardless of man's unfaithfulness. Man can choose to withdraw from the covenant; he can choose to withhold his faith, but God never withdraws His contract. We can lean on Him with absolute surety.

The Bible tells us that God is both *in* history and *above* it. It refutes any mere historical approach, such as that of Darwin, which implies that the human race is progressing toward perfection. The Bible regards God as the Lord of history who alone gives meaning to all events. To each man God gives some light upon his own task and role as agent in history. If he accepts the challenge of his role with faith, he then is convinced that history has a purpose. He will not know all the answers because no human being can comprehend God's ways, but he will not be in terror or in a state of bewilderment.

Herbert Butterfield explains the human situation by using the metaphor of a symphony orchestra. The individual members of the orchestra have their own scores, but they do not have the conductor's score for the entire symphony. Nevertheless, they play as the conductor directs because they assume that he does have the complete score and knows precisely how each instrument fits into the composition. Similarly, the Christian faith, based on revelation, is not depressed by history but rather sees flashes of meaning in history which indicate that such faith is well placed.

MAN'S RESPONSE

Unless we learn how to respond to God's love for us, we shall never learn to know Him. This is where trust takes precedence over knowledge. If God were a neat little theory, then memorizing the proper theological facts would

When we contemplate nature in all its grandeur let us lift our eyes to glimpse nature's Creator and our God.

be enough. We could say, "My God is one, two, three, et cetera." But God, being a living Person, is in need of our personal response to Him. His name must be honored, His kingship recognized, His will performed.

Faith in God requires that we do all that the Lord has told us to do. We must do it *before* we can completely explore it. Those who decide that first of all they are going to do some research about God to see if He fits into their abstract thinking have missed the point that in the case of God—who is abstraction, principle, and rule all mixed into one—the response must be given antecedently. No one learns to understand music if he consistently abstains from listening to it. Knowing music and being grasped by its magic presupposes that you listen to it. Likewise, knowing God presupposes that you live with Him.

Supreme acquiescence is the beginning of faith. You commit yourself unhesitatingly to God's way of life. You enter a partnership with God that has high requirements. You do not rebel. You give God a chance. Certain things you must do, others you must leave undone. When God speaks, you listen. If you do not, no vacuum is left, for the power of evil immediately takes hold of your will. He who does not respond to God, responds to another power, that of God's enemy.

God asks for more than good deeds and kindly acts. He asks for our heart. What counts the most is really not the impact of what we do on the world, but the impact of what we do on our own hearts. This is the basis of faith. When man participates thus in God's plan, his faith is strengthened; however, when he separates himself from it, he begins to doubt. In this respect love and faith are the same. When you love you desire to be united with the loved one; if separation continues, love eventually deteriorates. In faith also you desire to be united with God, and when you remain separated, then deterioration of faith sets in.

This union with God gives birth to man's desire to respond—his desire to act in faith. How does this happen? The link between faith and action is love, and love always shows itself in action. You cannot possibly be fully concerned about someone without having compassion on him and the desire to actualize your concern. The Jews of Christ's time misconceived this aspect of faith. They thought response meant a system of rituals and laws without really caring on the inside. Their emphasis was on the mechanical execution of a response. So much so that faith became a stumbling block to them. Eventually they strangled it completely. Then nothing but a corpse was left of what once was, and still could have been, a living faith.

The Christian response to God is one of courage—courage to be and to do for God. Time and again God's Book calls for this courage: " 'Walk before Me, and be thou whole-hearted.' " [11] "Thou shalt be whole-hearted with the Lord thy God." [12] "Keep yourselves in the love of God." [13] "My son, give me thine heart." [14] "Thou shalt love the Lord thy God with all thy heart, and with all thy soul, and with all thy mind." [15]

Job of old[16] was the kind of man who responded whole-heartedly to God. His faith was not a matter of convenience or calculated investment. In the face of the most dreadful suffering imaginable he kept his faith; he responded with all his humanity. He had the courage to be. He responded before he asked any questions.

---

[11] Book of Genesis, ch. 17, v. 1 (Holy Scriptures, Masoretic Text, Jewish Publication Society of America).

[12] Book of Deuteronomy, ch. 18, v. 13 (Holy Scriptures, Masoretic Text, Jewish Publication Society of America).

[13] Epistle of Jude, v. 21.

[14] Book of Proverbs, ch. 23, v. 26.

[15] Gospel according to Matthew, ch. 22, v. 37.

[16] See Book of Job.

In conclusion, let me say that faith is the active acceptance of God's kingdom for now and for eternity to come. Disregarding all empty promises and the accepted status symbols, we must live the life of faith. A good American citizen does not only talk about patriotism, he lives the Constitution of the United States. A citizen of God's kingdom does not mouth platitudes about Christianity. He lives his allegiance to God. He has faith.

CHAPTER 3

Doctrine

*L*ISTEN TO an adolescent praying: "Nobody understands me, and it is hard to believe that You do. Since the world's future is too terrible to contemplate, let us find our consolation in jeering and jiving, rocking and rolling. In spite of the mess made by all previous generations, may we build the Kingdom of God on earth through scientific knowledge and technical skill." [1]

Shall we leave it at that? Shall we drift on while the coming generation cannot address God as the Creator because the idea of creation confounds them utterly? Shall we shrug our shoulders when they refuse to see God as the Judge because He has no courtroom, wig, or jury? Shall we smile indifferently because more and more the world denies any father except one who brings home the pay check at the end of the week?

The popular thing nowadays seems to be a friendly compromise. The skeptic says to the religious man, "I won't say a word against you. Just let me go my separate way, and you go yours. Whatever we do, let's not mix religion with knowledge or facts." This compromise has be-

---

[1] David Head, *He Sent Leanness*, p. 41.

come, quite extensively, a way of life on the public school level. Educators there claim that the crop of students coming up are more precise than ever, that the body of knowledge taught is vaster than ever. They seem to believe that the banner of knowledge is flying higher than ever. But this brings us to the question, Do religious beliefs matter? Can one be reasonable in his faith without holding claim to specific truths?

I wish to assert that it is impossible to pursue truth as a whole without pursuing religious truth in particular. The moment we accept the fact that God is intimately knit to the length and breadth of the universe, we cannot leave religious knowledge out of our lives if we ever expect to make the slightest sense out of the universe. If religious truths exist, we cannot shut our eyes to them without doing damage to our whole truth structure. Nor is it possible to understand the good life, much less to live it, without studying the individual arteries leading to the main stream of piety.

In a sense, to find salvation at its richest dimension, each of us must be a theologian. Oh, I do not mean that we must study Hebrew, Greek, or Aramaic, although those who have done so are to be commended; rather, I mean that everyone must understand the Person he worships and serves. He must put the truths he knows about God into a system, just as astronomers have a science of the stars and the geologists have a science of the crust of the earth. We cannot let our ideas of God dangle before us haphazardly, for He Himself is an orderly God. Thus it is extremely important that we know about our God. It is important that we know God experientially too. We must, for instance, understand that He is Lord of the universe, always ruling it according to the eternal rule of right and wrong. This poses the problem of man's freedom to obey or reject His rule. Then, we must decide whether or not man is capable of escaping his earthly plight on his own; or whether he must rely completely on the acts and the grace of God. Is it possible to please God by charitable works void of faith, or does God prefer only the acknowledgment of our undivided love, freely bestowed? What is man's future beyond death? And why does he suffer? These and other questions form the core of what we call doctrine. Their purpose is not to *ensure* our salvation, but to help us to *understand* it more fully.

Someone may quickly retort that he cannot tolerate the superstition and gloom in Christian doctrine; that he cannot bear the idea of intermingling concepts such as the cross with the crown, penance with heroism, Paradise with hell. In short, he does not find Christian doctrine pleasant enough. He says that if we are going to be good, let us be so simply because it is more graceful, more charming to be so. Let us be virtuous because it is plainly more rewarding. But, you see, righteousness as a matter of convenience will not work. True, the Bible speaks of a people who prefer one another, who abstain from rude speech, who avoid self-conceit, who are calm and grave, cheerful and happy, who make peace with all men, who are just, true, courteous, and gentle. Performance is important. But were this enough, then Harvard University possibly could turn out better Christians than any church. The point is that the church aims at the heart of a message of truth. She encourages men to keep striving toward central truth. To her the outward niceties cannot replace the inward convictions. The good life requires the solid foundation of doctrine. Without this foundation goodness becomes a matter of opinion rather than conviction; of prevailing custom rather than principle. After a careful study of history Arnold Toynbee wrote: "Practice unsupported by belief is a wasting asset."

Obviously true. But why is it impossible to profess

truth without having it couched in church terms? I think it is possible to give a very rational answer to this question.

First of all, we must understand that truth has two vital attributes: first, it is beautiful; second, it is powerful. If you pursue either line to its conclusion, you are led by either to the eternal and infinite. But when you make the decision that you will find truth on your own, disregarding revelation as given through the prophets and providences of God in history, you will—perhaps even unknowingly—gradually measure and proportion all your ideas by earthly standards, restricting them to the things you see, hear, smell, taste, and feel. Instead of pursuing either beauty or power to its infinitude, you will be satisfied with surface beauty and mechanical power. This is the tendency of all those who have denied revealed doctrine. They truncate truth in this way. A sense of propriety, order, and scholasticism replaces miracle and mystery. First, truth is faintly tainted, later it is adulterated, and finally it is rejected. These are the inevitable steps taken by those who refuse to be guided by doctrine.

I have another consideration to add. It applies particularly to those who wish to have a scientific explanation for everything in the Bible. Let us note well that the physical sciences—astronomy, physics, chemistry, et cetera— came into being *before* the introduction of moral evil into the world. It is no wonder, then, that they are distinct in scope from revelation and doctrine. Physical science describes power, fact, and order, even sharing in their excitement. But what can the physical sciences know about mercy, goodness, and the plan of salvation? Is it any wonder that physical structures can give no explanation for these? They were never intended to cope with moral error. Lord Bacon once said, "Sacred theology must be drawn from the words and the oracles of God; not from the light of nature or the dictates of reason. It is written, that 'the heavens declare the glory of God;' but we nowhere find it that the heavens declare the *will* of God; which is pronounced a law and a testimony, that men should do according to it." True, doctrine and revelation must be in harmony with natural law; but it does not follow that if you study natural law you will eventually happen on doctrine and revelation. As a matter of fact, if you rely on nature as it now is to supply you with revelation, your imagination may be seduced into paths of error from which there is no recourse.

Doctrine has another vital purpose. It stands at the inlet of all knowledge, be it science, literature, or practical arts, and it allows only those things to pass for truth which indeed are truth. It fears no knowledge, but it purifies all knowledge. The principle of doctrine is not to prohibit truth of any kind, but to ensure that no knowledge passes for truth without coming under the name of truth rightfully. Because we believe that doctrines are revelations from God, we hold that only they have the authority to be such a screening laboratory. "To the law and to the testimony: if they speak not according to this word, it is because there is no light in them." [2] We should bear this in mind as we proceed to study in depth some of the great doctrines held by God's church.

The study of doctrine has been placed in disrepute by some. I have heard it said that its evil lies in the fact that once you hold certain religious doctrines as indisputably true, you are trapped for the rest of your life. You are like a wasp buzzing against a windowpane. The wasp is unflagging in his determination to get through the glass, so he keeps bumping against it time after time in endless monotony. His failure makes him only more violent in his insistence. So it is with the study of doctrine, says the

---

[2] Book of Isaiah, ch. 8, v. 20.

skeptic. You have engaged in a quest which, even if continued into eternity, cannot reach its goal. The more you fail in finding appropriate answers, the more you are determined to keep looking; so you plunge forward against your windowpane—a miserable sight—joining a vast segment of human beings who, each in his own way and in his own church, butts his head against a private windowpane. All such is fruitless speculation, says the unbeliever. Christianity, he pretends, has turned man away from what he *can* know to the things that he *cannot* know.

These arguments do not need to be refuted because they have not as yet been proved correct. Were it true that religious knowledge cannot be ascertained with certainty, then, of course, it would be wrong to try for it. But, as we shall continue to see, the defenses of revelation and doctrine are too numerous and solid to allow of a moment's doubt. Religious certainty can be found at depth dimensions. God's prophets and leadings throughout history and the personal testimony of Christians across the centuries have been irrefutable evidence for faith in church doctrine. It is with complete confidence that in the chapters that follow we shall focus upon those doctrines that make faith the greatest possession in today's world.

CHAPTER 4

The Bible

SIDE BY side with the decline of religious life, the neuroses grow noticeably more frequent. Everywhere the mental state of European men shows an alarming lack of balance. We are living undoubtedly in a period of the greatest restlessness, nervous tension, confusion and disorientation of outlook. . . . [People have] the feeling that our modern religious truths have somehow or other grown empty." [1]

So wrote C. G. Jung more than thirty years ago. He had the people of Europe in mind principally, but he was describing the predicament of large segments of the human race. Men are confused and restless, because they have strayed from a firm belief in religious truth and the authority of Holy Scripture. This generation has diluted its faith with cynicism, negation, and indifference. Men have belittled confidence in the authority of Scripture to concentrate on conduct and behavior. Should it not seem at least a little strange that such an age should suffer an increase in misconduct and misbehavior?

In man's search for answers to today's desperate questions, he must turn to God's Word—the Bible. The Bible

---

[1] C. G. Jung, *Modern Man in Search of a Soul*, p. 264.

alone points unerringly to a consistent, infallible rule of faith and practice. It alone can reveal what men ought to believe and do, providing full assurance for those who would dare affirm, "I know what I believe." Today, we must stand unequivocally for the divine inspiration and inerrant authority of the Scriptures.

Down through the centuries Christians have taken this view of God's Book. More than one hundred years ago, in Geneva, Switzerland, Louis Gaussen could proclaim: "With the single exception of Theodore of Mopsuestia (c. A.D. 350-429), that philosophical divine whose numerous writings were condemned for their Nestorianism in the Fifth Ecumenical Council . . . , it has been found impossible to produce in the long course of the first eight centuries of Christianity a single doctor who had disowned the plenary inspiration of the Scriptures, unless it be in the bosom of the most violent heresies." [2] From Saint Paul to our day, "plenary inspiration" is the main stream of historic Christianity and has found expression in the great Christian creeds.

However, with the arrival of the age of science and discovery the classical conception of Biblical authority came under attack. The findings of astronomy, geology, and biology led to a protracted struggle in which numerous theologians bluntly rejected the centuries-old claims of Holy Writ. Actually, the findings of science did not disprove the teachings of the Bible; they only disproved some views held by churchmen who had interpreted erroneously the Bible. On this point we quote from Frank Lewis Marsh of the Geophysic Institute:

"[The] tendency to impute to the Bible, teachings that its literal text does not support has been prevalent for many centuries. . . . During these centuries [the Middle

---

[2] Louis Gaussen, *The Inspiration of the Holy Scriptures*, pp. 139, 140.

Ages] men in general and even leaders in the church, believed that the Bible taught (1) a flat earth with four corners, (2) a geocentric solar system in which the earth stood still at the center while the sun revolved around it, (3) spontaneous generation which continually produced living forms from dead organic materials, (4) extreme fixity of species, (5) prenatal influence of the sight-transfer type, and (6) a worldwide Noachian Flood. . . . History easily reveals the fact that church leaders of the Middle Ages did present these interpretations as the teaching of the Scriptures on these points. But in our evaluation of the Scriptures it is extremely vital that we distinguish between what the church leaders thought the Bible said and what it actually asserts." [3]

Add that Bible history and fact have remained unscathed, and you have the reason why "higher criticism," at the apex of development, literally fell apart, giving place to neo-orthodoxy. Karl Barth's experience illustrates this disillusionment and change. He relates how, in the early days of his ministry, he became disheartened with the "good advice" he had to offer his parishioners. He mounted the pulpit with "frothy palaver" and "superficial guesses." He stood before his people with a man's wisdom. The "table of the Law" slipped between his fingers, and he stood without a message.[4] He, with others, looked with nostalgia to the strong note of authority in the Christian heritage. Wrote he: "Our grandfathers, after all, were right when they struggled so desperately in behalf of the truth that there is revelation in the BIBLE. . . . And our fathers were right when they guarded warily against being drawn out upon the shaky scaffolding of religious self-expression." "We live in a sick old world which cries from its soul, out of deepest need: Heal me, O Lord, and I shall be

---

[3] Frank Lewis Marsh, *Evolution or Special Creation*, p. 17.
[4] Karl Barth, *The Epistle to the Romans*, Author's Preface, p. 5.

healed! In all men, whoever and wherever and whatever and however they may be, there is a longing for exactly this which is here within the Bible." [5]

So much for the rise of neo-orthodoxy. Now, what do we mean when we claim that the Bible is God's Word? For instance—how was it written? Even the casual reader of the Scriptures recognizes that the style and vocabulary differ greatly from one writer to another. The prophet Amos' book is very different from the writings of the prophet Isaiah. The first was a shepherd, a horticulturist; the second held forth at the king's court. Then, compare the Epistle to the Romans and the Gospel of Mark. They are different in mood and character. What explanation is there? Ellen G. White formulates it this way:

"The Bible is written by inspired men, but it is not God's mode of thought and expression. It is that of humanity. God, as a writer, is not represented. Men will often say such an expression is not like God. But God has not put Himself in words, in logic, in rhetoric, on trial in the Bible. The writers of the Bible were God's penmen, not His pen. Look at the different writers. It is not the words of the Bible that are inspired, but the men that were inspired. Inspiration acts not on the man's words or his expressions, but on the man himself, who, under the influence of the Holy Spirit, is imbued with thoughts. But the words receive the impress of the individual mind. The divine mind is diffused. The divine mind and will is combined with the human mind and will; thus the utterances of the man are the word of God." [6]

God chose the men who wrote the Bible. These men wrote within the framework of their character, personality, and culture. Revelation in this form involves problems of communication and translation. Modern studies in

---

[5] Karl Barth, *The Word of God and the Word of Man,* pp. 44, 50.
[6] Ellen G. White, *Selected Messages,* book 1, p. 21.

these areas have pointed out the complexity of getting across ideas when people supposedly speak the same language. Any two individuals listening to the same sentences or reading the same material will differ in their understanding and interpretation. The problem, of course, is more complex when a foreign language is involved. One of the marvels of the United Nations is to observe the translators in action at their earphones. A delegate speaks in his language while the translators give his message in English and other languages with amazing agility. Even so, occasionally the translator is at a loss to render certain fine shades of meaning with precision. Sometimes this is impossible. One cannot but wonder what diplomatic problems might be avoided or solved were exact translations possible.

Actually, these problems are not restricted to the United Nations. How often we make statements that to us are perfectly clear, yet these statements are misunderstood by the one listening. You can point out a passage of Scripture to someone with the sense of confidence that the language is plain and compelling. But, have you never been perplexed when the other person said, "I don't understand the meaning of that passage the way you do"? In fact, the multiplicity of contradictory teachings on religious subjects, all claiming to be substantiated by the Bible, is a loud witness to the possibility of variant interpretations. Should we then say that God's Word is contradictory?

This question is crucial, and to answer it we must explore the nature of revelation and inspiration further. Let us recall a Biblical story that may help to illustrate our discussion.

In Daniel's book we have the account of King Nebuchadnezzar's dream.[7] In a dream the king had seen a

---

[7] Book of Daniel, ch. 2; see our Chapter 11, pp. 125-127.

great image: the head was of gold, the chest and arms were
of silver, the belly and thighs were of brass, the legs were
of iron, the feet were part of iron and part of clay. When
Nebuchadnezzar awoke, he could not bring the dream
back to memory. Try as he would, it hovered indistinctly
on the horizon of his mind. He groped for a solution—
and it came. Since he had in state employ a staff of wise
men and sorcerers, he felt these men should be put to use.
He called them in; but they failed the test; they could not
reveal the dream. Nebuchadnezzar's disappointment was
bitter—so bitter that he determined to massacre all the
wise men of Babylon. It so happened that the prophet
Daniel and his companions were counted among the wise.
Daniel asked the king to reconsider his decree, and pro-
posed to give him the dream and the interpretation of his
dream.

Daniel did not know, of course, either the content of
the dream or its interpretation. However, he believed this
dream had been given with a divine purpose. He communed regularly with his God, and he sought in prayer a
revelation of the mystery and the purpose. The record says
that the dream was revealed to Daniel in a vision of the
night. He went at once to the king and not only revealed
the dream to him, but followed it with an interpretation.[8]

Notice this: the king's dream was a secret—hidden
and unknown. The dream was also unknown to Daniel;
but through a "night vision" the veil of mystery was removed, and that which was unknown and mysterious came
to light. Daniel was inspired by the Spirit of God, and in
this experience a disclosure was made. This disclosure came
through Inspiration.[9]

For purposes of discussion, let us suppose that Daniel
had revealed Nebuchadnezzar's dream but that he had not

---

[8] Book of Daniel, ch. 2, v. 36.
[9] Book of Numbers, ch. 12, vs. 5, 6; Book of Hosea, ch. 12, v. 10.

given the dream's interpretation. How many interpretations, do you suppose, would have been offered by the wise men? Several, at least. Let us further suppose that a wise man and Daniel come to the king and propose to give him the interpretation of the dream. Mind you, they are purporting to interpret God's revelation—in this case the dream which God gave to Nebuchadnezzar and revealed to Daniel. The wise man is first. We can imagine him saying that the statue of the man represents the kingdoms of the earth; that the stone that crashes into the statue represents the armies of Nebuchadnezzar which will conquer all other kingdoms. Since this stone was to fill the earth, the kingdoms of the earth will be under the rulership of Nebuchadnezzar.

Then Daniel follows with his interpretation. He says that the statue represents the kingdoms of the earth, but the stone represents God's kingdom, not Nebuchadnezzar's. Here Daniel tells the king that God graciously gave him the dream so that he might understand that God Himself is ruler of the earth; that Nebuchadnezzar should cooperate with God, and be part of His kingdom which would indeed last forever and ever. Which would be correct? Daniel's interpretation, of course. He understood the true meaning of the dream, because in communing with God he came to understand God's purpose in it. God had unveiled something of the kingdom to come and of the future of man in relation to his Creator. The wise man would have been mistaken in his interpretation. The dream was given by God; so Daniel communed with God that he might be instructed to understand what God had in mind in giving the dream.[10]

When we open the Bible and read, this is analogous to hearing Daniel's description of the dream. One who

---

[10] Book of Daniel, ch. 2, vs. 27-29.

reads the Bible is reading the content of a revelation from God. The question arises, How shall we understand or interpret the Scriptures? Like Daniel, we are dependent upon the Spirit for a correct understanding, a right interpretation of Scripture.[11] The Spirit that inspired the prophet and illumined his mind to understand will illumine our minds and disclose to us the scriptural meaning. This is why we must pray for guidance when reading and comparing passages of Scripture. This is why we speak of having a mind that is receptive to the Holy Spirit's instruction. When such a mind approaches the Bible in full vigor, revelation is dynamic: God reveals Himself. Rich rewards accrue as the Spirit of God holds communion with the human mind. Then the Bible begins to live. When we read the book of Genesis we see the God with whom we commune pictured as Creator. The call Abraham received to depart into an unknown land is also our call. The loving Father who tried to save His children from destruction in Noah's day is our Father. Elijah, Samuel, Isaiah are our brothers—they responded to the divine call. God revealed Himself to them for all men.

With the aid of God's Spirit we see that history discloses God's search for man and man's response to God.[12] The Old Testament becomes the anticipation of God's revelation in Christ. By signs and symbols God attempts to reveal Himself to men. He yearned after Israel. He sent the prophets messages of courage and hope, with warnings and rebukes. God revealed Himself and is still revealing Himself to men in the affairs of mankind. In the fullness of time God Himself fulfilled the anticipation of the Old Testament in the Person of Christ, the Messiah. Thus, as the student continues to study the Word of God, as his mind exercises its highest function and the Spirit of truth

---

[11] Cf. First Epistle to the Corinthians, ch. 14, vs. 6, 26; ch. 2, vs. 13-15.
[12] Book of Deuteronomy, ch. 29, v. 29.

illumines it, mysteries are unveiled, Jesus Christ is disclosed as the fullness of God, Christ becomes the key that unlocks the mystery of human existence.[13] We cannot know the world about us, nor can we know the purpose of history, except as the secrets are disclosed in God's Word made flesh in the Christ.

We shall have more to say about all this. But, as we continue our way, let us recognize the following points:[14]

1. The Bible is not merely a book that contains the word of God; it is God's written word, and can bring a contemporary experience in the knowledge of truth to all men.

2. Biblical revelation is the unfolding of God's grace in behalf of sinful man. This revelation culminates in Jesus Christ, with this distinction: others besides Jesus spoke the word of God; but He was in truth God speaking.

3. The Bible reveals God as a Person.

"All revelation," writes Dr. Kantzer, "has God for its object. The Bible does not present man with a set of universal truths like the propositions of Euclid in geometry. It does not set forth in formal fashion the arguments and counter-arguments of a theological textbook. . . . The ultimate goal of revelation is not so much to make man wise as it is to bring him into a direct encounter with God as a Person, and to evoke from him a response of love and obedience to God. The apostle Paul sets forth the goal of all revelation: 'that I may be personally acquainted with Him' (Epistle to the Philippians, ch. 3, v. 10)." [15]

4. Biblical revelation includes a disclosure of divine

---

[13] Epistle to the Colossians, ch. 2, vs. 8-10; Epistle to the Ephesians, ch. 1, vs. 17-23; First Epistle to Timothy, ch. 4, v. 6.
[14] See "Authority of the Bible," by Kenneth S. Kantzer, in *The Word for This Century*. Also Bernard Ramm, *Protestant Biblical Interpretation*.
[15] Kantzer, *op. cit.*, p. 34.

purpose and teaching. In the Bible, God acts and speaks.[16]

"Revelation," writes Edwin Lewis, "means that God is categorically affirmed and that He bears a certain character and that He is working for certain ends; and what these ends are, likewise, is included in the revelation. God utters His word, but the meaning of what is uttered is still to be conveyed and this is the work of the Holy Spirit. Revelation brings a disclosure of truth which would otherwise have remained at best only a speculation." [17]

"The Biblical writers," explains more fully C. H. Dodd, "were not philosophers constructing a speculative theory from their observation of events. What they said was 'thus saith the Lord;' and they firmly believed that God spoke to them. The interpretation of history which they offered was not invented by process of thought; it was the meaning which they experienced in the events when their minds were open to God as well as open to the impact of outward facts. Thus the prophetic interpretation of history and the impetus and direction which that gave to subsequent history were alike the word of God to men." [18]

5. The Bible reveals its authority.

When we accept the claims of the apostles and prophets regarding the divine origin of their message, we concurrently accept their conclusions with respect to the authority of their messages. The apostle Paul spoke clearly to Timothy, "All scripture is given by inspiration of God, and is profitable for doctrine, for reproof, for correction, for instruction in righteousness: that the man of God may be perfect, throughly furnished unto all good works." [19] Thus, the Master rebuked His disciples for not believing "all that the prophets have spoken." [20] In controversy with

---

[16] Book of Isaiah, ch. 46, vs. 9-11.
[17] Edwin Lewis, *The Philosophy of Revelation*, p. 256.
[18] C. H. Dodd, *The Bible Today*, p. 51.
[19] Second Epistle to Timothy, ch. 3, vs. 16, 17.
[20] Gospel according to Luke, ch. 24, v. 25.

the Jews He argued, "Scripture cannot be broken [dissolved or discarded]." [21] Once Jesus quoted an isolated passage from the Old Testament with the words, "God says." [22] By this it is understood that what the Bible says is not merely the opinion of a sage, "but it is the truth of God coming with the authority of God Himself. This unshakable conviction that in the Bible God has spoken and, therefore, that the Bible message possesses divine authority, transforms the Christian evangelist from a purveyor of good advice into a divinely commissioned ambassador of Jesus Christ." [23]

6. The Bible must be correctly interpreted.

This we have discussed previously, and repeat ourselves here in summary. Certainly, the origin, authorship, date, and authenticity of the various books of the Bible need to be investigated. Every effort to ensure the original text of Scripture is laudable. A faithful interpretation supposes a completely authoritative original. Furthermore, to understand the Scripture we must go to it to discover and obey exactly what it teaches. The divine pedagogy is that "he that doeth truth cometh to the light." [24] He who would learn of God must stand ready to obey Him.

7. Biblical authority is the foundation for doctrine.

Truths flows from deep within the structure of Biblical authority. Truth and the authority of the Bible stand or fall together. This goes for the Old Testament as well as for the New. Jesus believed unequivocally in the inspiration and authority of the Scripture held by the Jewish people of His day; and the apostles shared this view. [25] We can conclude, then, with Dr. Kantzer:

---

[21] Gospel according to John, ch. 10, v. 35.
[22] Gospel according to Matthew, ch. 19, v. 5.
[23] Kenneth S. Kantzer, "Authority of the Bible," in *The Word for This Century*, pp. 44, 45.
[24] Gospel according to John, ch. 3, v. 21.
[25] *Ibid.*, ch. 5, v. 39; Gospel according to Luke, ch. 16, v. 31; ch. 24, vs. 25-27; First Epistle to the Corinthians, ch. 15, vs. 3, 4.

"Genuine evangelical theology is based upon the teaching of the whole Bible received as the authoritative, written Word of God. Its theology rests solidly upon the Holy Scriptures, for they and they alone are not only able to make us wise unto salvation but are also possessed of God-given authority and are profitable for doctrine. Not a jot or tittle of Scripture can be set aside as void by any true follower of Jesus Christ." [20]

In this sense the Bible is indeed a "dimension" of salvation.

---

[20] Kantzer, *op. cit.*, p. 51.

CHAPTER 5

God

ONE COULD exhaust his mind trying to define God. Numberless questions crowd the consciousness, forming an unyielding riddle. Can He be here when He is there? Does He see all? Does He know all? Can He do the impossible? If so, then how can He still remain a personality with a physical form? Is God simply a vast spirit trembling or hovering over the earth? The Bible opens with the words, "In the beginning God . . ." By virtue of its cardinal rank, we cannot postpone the problem of God. We must confront it and think about it.

In our consideration of faith we discussed three reasons for man's faith in God. First, we found that nature—cause and effect in the physical universe—points to God's existence. This we call the cosmological argument in favor of God's existence. Second, we found a universe so filled with purpose and design that we are forced to consider a designer. This we call the teleological argument. Last, man himself has a moral nature. The moral law within him makes him yearn instinctively for union with an eternal law. This we call the anthropological argument. All three arguments lead to the unavoidable conclusion that the universe cannot reasonably be explained without God.

Michael Faraday, the renowned English chemist and

physicist, had been theorizing and speculating and building thought structures all his life. One day in 1867 he lay
on his deathbed. A friend and colleague asked the great
scientist, "Faraday, what are your speculations now?"
"Speculations!" repeated the dying man. "Speculations. I
have none! Thank God, I am not resting my dying head
upon speculations. I know whom I have believed, and am
persuaded that He is able to keep that which I have committed unto Him against that day."

We believe that the type of logical process which leads
the scientist to Faraday's sublime conclusion will become
apparent often and convincingly through the pages of our
discussion. For now, however, we shall be satisfied simply
to inquire into the Biblical detail in which God is revealed
to us. In doing this we shall not discuss the csientific
outlook, the historical perspective with its critical interpretation, nor the spirit of the modern age with its lofty
confidence in man. I think these viewpoints will be clari-
fied as we move along. For the present, then, what does
God's Word have to say about GOD?

The first word for God in the Old Testament is *Elohim.*
This occurs some 2500 times, and is a plural noun. However, this plural word when applied to God is coupled
with a singular verb form. This combination is possibly
an anticipation of further teaching on the Trinity. *Elohim*
could indicate a plenitude of power, the root signifying
"strong."

Another word for God in the Old Testament is *El,*
which occurs more than two hundred times, chiefly in the
Psalms and in the books of Job and Isaiah. Often this word
is accompanied by a descriptive expression which taken
together means "God Almighty" or "God Most High."

In contrast with these general terms stands "Jehovah."
This is an artificial English word developed from the Hebrew *Yahweh.* The basic significance of this name is given

in the second book of Moses, where we find the divine proclamation, "I am that I am." [1]

In *Elohim* and *El* we have God's relationship to His creation: "In the beginning God." In the second book of the Bible we find the story of God's special care for men who by Adam's fall were in need of redemption. There the great "I am" appears. These two names summarize what the Scriptures teach about God. *Elohim* is God the Creator, whereas Jehovah is God the Redeemer.

The Bible opens with the account of God's creating the heavens and the earth. Out of a brooding darkness "upon the face of the deep" all existing things were created. God is declared to be self-existent; nothing else exists of its own right, independently, or that has not had a beginning. This initial teaching is corroborated by later writers, of whom we may cite Nehemiah: "Thou, even thou, art Lord alone; thou hast made heaven, the heaven of heavens, with all their host, the earth, and all things that are therein, the seas, and all that is therein, and thou preservest them all; and the host of heaven worshippeth thee." [2]

The word *create* means "to cause to come into existence." God created all things out of nothing—*ex-nihilo*. Before any natural processes began, God created absolutely. In the beginning He made no use of prior-existing materials to fashion the earth and the planets, as does a sculptor when he carves a beautiful statue out of a formless block of stone, but "by the word of the Lord were the heavens made; and all the host of them by the breath of his mouth." [3] This is called "first creation," which does not mean that after bringing the universe into existence God did not use previously created substance in completing His creation. As a matter of fact, the Bible specifically states,

---

[1] Book of Exodus, ch. 3, v. 13.
[2] Book of Nehemiah, ch. 9, v. 6.
[3] Psalm 33, v. 6.

for example, that "God formed man of the dust of the ground." [4]

In creation, God speaks and acts. This speaking and acting are voluntary; they therefore proclaim the personality of God. God is not an inanimate, mechanical "First Cause." Nor is He a "descriptive principle," abstracted from the phenomena of nature. God set the pattern of the universe with a purpose. Intelligence and volition imply a personality. Moreover, a universal creation presupposes the unity of God.

But there is more. Since God created all things simply by His word, He is omnipotent. And the Bible contains countless assertions of His omnipotence. Note some:

"I know that thou canst do all things, and that no purpose of thine can be restrained." [5]

"Whatsoever the Lord pleased, that did he in heaven, and in earth." [6]

"He doeth according to his will in the army of heaven, and among the inhabitants of the earth: and none can stay his hand, or say unto him, What doest thou?" [7]

He "worketh all things after the counsel of his own will." [8]

Likewise, omniscience is involved in creation. All power and all knowledge cannot be separated one from the other. Here is the point: If an omnipotent God could be thought to be ignorant, He still would be able to correct this ignorance, otherwise there would be something He could not do and He would not be truly omnipotent. But even a momentary ignorance would be a momentary limitation upon omnipotence. Therefore, omniscience and omnipotence have to be inseparable.

---

[4] Book of Genesis, ch. 2, v. 7.
[5] Book of Job, ch. 42, v. 2 (A.S.V.).
[6] Psalm 135, v. 6.
[7] Book of Daniel, ch. 4, v. 35.
[8] Epistle to the Ephesians, ch. 1, v. 11.

Omnipotence is more particularly related to creation in that the works of creation follow a plan existent in the divine mind. In fact, the act of creation implies a pre-existent plan of action. Likewise, control of all things presupposes knowledge of all things. "Known unto God," declared Saint Paul, "are all his works from the beginning of the world." [9] This knowledge includes the minutest details: "The very hairs of your head are all numbered." [10]

Furthermore, this volitional and purposeful action, initiating as it does a series of concatenated events, requires a knowledge of the future. Thus, Isaiah speaks of God as "declaring the end from the beginning." [11] Centered in God's creative and redemptive power is what the apostle Peter calls the "sure word of prophecy." [12] Hence, all the predictions of Scripture stem from God's omnipotence and omniscience and are substantiated by the very existence of our creation and redemption. This we shall see more fully and significantly in the pages ahead. [13]

Creation exemplifies another of God's prerogatives: He not only was Creator of a physical universe but also of moral distinctions. When God created Adam and Eve and placed them in the Garden, He gave them freedom by offering them to eat of the tree of life as a choice of harmony with God, and to eat of the tree of the knowledge of good and evil as a choice of rebellion. It was a loving God who warned that rebellion would result in death, for separation from God is separation from life.

The prohibition to eat from the tree of the knowledge of good and evil displays the inmost essence of moral obligation; a request for obedience to divine authority is for the benefit of the creature. Had God commanded

---

[9] Book of Acts, ch. 15, v. 18.
[10] Gospel according to Matthew, ch. 10, v. 30.
[11] Book of Isaiah, ch. 46, v. 10.
[12] Second Epistle of Peter, ch. 1, v. 19.
[13] See Chapter 11, Time.

Adam, "Thou shalt not murder Eve," Adam might have obeyed because Eve was fair, or he might have disobeyed because she was not. In either case, Adam's actions would have been wrongly motivated. But the tree was quite different. No motive could be involved except his relationship to the Creator.

God could have allowed him his freedom to separate from God and die, with apparent justice. No condition left upon Him the obligation to talk to Adam again; nor did Adam seek God and beg for a visit. On the contrary, Adam tried to avoid a meeting. The psalmist was right: There is none that seeks after God, "no, not one." [14] This leads to a thrilling truth. God's initiative was prompted by love, another divine attribute emphasized in both the Old and New Testament. God does not love anyone because of what he is; He loves in spite of what man is. While "we were enemies, we were reconciled to God." [15] "God commendeth his love toward us, in that, while we were yet sinners, Christ died for us." [16] And this is perfect love.

Some have been inclined toward drawing an antithesis between a "wrathful God" of the Old Testament and a different, "loving God" of the New Testament. This evinces ignorance of the actual words of Scripture. In the Old Testament divine love is shown to be benevolently indulgent to human unworthiness in these passages of Scripture: "The Lord thy God hath chosen thee to be a special people. . . . The Lord did not set his love upon you, nor choose you, because ye were more in number, . . . but because the Lord loved you." [17] "In his love and in his pity he redeemed them." [18] "Yea, I have loved thee with an

---

[14] Psalm 14, v. 3. [15] Epistle to the Romans, ch. 5, v. 10.
[16] *Ibid.*, v. 8. [17] Book of Deuteronomy, ch. 7, vs. 6-8.
[18] Book of Isaiah, ch. 63, v. 9.

th all man's knowledge he is incapable of measuring
d's greatness. But God's love is revealed in His Word.

everlasting love." [19] For the Old Testament, as well as
the New, God's attribute of love is summed up in the
statement, "God is love." [20]

In both the Old and the New Testament God's love is
depicted in two figures of speech. First, God is called the
"Father" of His children. Jesus taught His disciples to pray
"Our Father . . ." [21] Like all important Biblical concepts,
the fatherhood of God has been distorted and misunderstood. By man, God has been regarded as the Father of all
men. This is a misnomer. He is their Creator, not their
Father. Natural birth is not sufficient for entrance into the
family of God. Rebirth through acceptance of God's redemptive acts alone is the basis of man's sonship with God.
The Epistles make use of the idea of adoption: "Which are
the children of the flesh, these are not the children of
God." [22] "For as many as are led by the Spirit of God, they
are the sons of God. For . . . ye have received the Spirit of
adoption, whereby we cry, Abba, Father." [23] Jesus rebuked
the unbelieving Jews, "Ye are of your father the devil." [24]
We are, then, adopted sons and daughters of God by virtue
of our conversion to Him. In fact, the idea of a universal
fatherhood of God independent of the new birth experience is inconsistent with Scripture and subversive of the
work of grace and redemption. Through creation and the
grace of re-creation, God is the Father of mankind.

Second, when the children of God are described in a
collective sense, God is designated as the "husband" or
"bridegroom." [25] This figure, with that of God's fatherhood,
sharpens the concept of God as a personal, loving,

[19] Book of Jeremiah, ch. 31, v. 3.
[20] First Epistle of John, ch. 4, v. 8.
[21] Gospel according to Matthew, ch. 6, vs. 9-13.
[22] Epistle to the Romans, ch. 9, v. 8.
[23] *Ibid.*, ch. 8, vs. 14, 15.
[24] Gospel according to John, ch. 8, v. 44.
[25] Book of Isaiah, ch. 54, v. 5; ch. 62, vs. 4, 5; Gospel according to
Matthew, ch. 9, v. 15.

jealous Person. Said He: "Thou shalt worship no other god: for the Lord, whose name is Jealous, is a jealous God." [26] This idea is embedded in God's ten commandments. To be sure, the marriage contract reflects the love of the parties; but at the same time it is an obligation to fidelity if happiness is to be maintained.

The Christian concept of God, the plan of redemption, nor the love of God can be understood apart from His attribute of righteousness. God's forgiveness must in no wise partake of a whimsical or capricious nature, for that kind of forgiveness would be unrighteousness. When a human judge frees a criminal, the act of mercy may in some sense be justified by extenuating circumstances. Then, however, the strictness of the law has been ignored in favor of other considerations—including man's inability to understand and his indication of his intention to give up rebellion. But God is righteous. He knows and understands all things. Therefore, His plan of redemption must and can maintain the majesty of the law. Righteousness and sin are incompatible. This must be demonstrated to the universe. This great principle involved the life, death, and resurrection of God made flesh in the plan of redemption. It confirms forever God's righteousness and the immutability of His law.

God of the Bible is both immanent and transcendent, or supernatural. The true child of God will see no conflict between immanence and transcendence. The sovereignty of God's creative power is evidence of transcendence, that which is beyond comprehension. Because of creation, God's power extends everywhere; this is His immanence. In fact, instead of saying that God is in the world, it is better to say that the world is in God, for in Him we live and move and have our being.

---

[26] Book of Exodus, ch. 34, v. 14.

Such is the God of the Holy Scriptures. He is one God, self-revealed as God the Father, God the Son, and God the Holy Spirit. This signifies that in God we distinguish three persons which are neither three gods, nor three parts or modes of God. He is the eternal God, manifest in Essence, Presence, and Action. This God is the triune God.

Objections to this concept of God appear wherever one insists on interpreting the Creator in terms of the creature, the unity of God in terms of mathematical unity. The Christian learns to know God from God Himself, as He has acted for him and attested His action in Holy Scripture. He is not surprised if an element of mystery remains which defies ultimate analysis or understanding. The Christian realizes that he is only man, whereas God is infinite. Moreover, the ultimate in his relationship with this God will be to know Him *personally*.

One day in Paris a religious procession wormed its way down a crowded street, a crucifix at the head. The procession passed Voltaire and a friend. Voltaire raised his hat. The friend exclaimed: "What! Are you reconciled with God?" The philosopher, with his characteristic irony, replied: "We salute, but we do not speak."

This is a description of the relationship of many to God. Philosophically, they cannot explain the universe without Him; they must acknowledge the existence of God to make sense in the universe. They believe in religion, too, in a general way. They must admit that it is good for humanity, for society. In moments of subdued reverence they themselves are moved with the dignity and beauty of the services of the church. They may even attend church, be enrolled as members; but they have no personal fellowship with God. They salute, but they do not speak. They recognize the existence of God, seeing His handwriting in the sky, in the constitution of matter, in the mystery and wonder of His providence, in the intricacies of their own personal need; but they do not wish to know Him personally. He is not, for them, Creator and Redeemer.

Yet, only when God has become Creator and Redeemer can He be what He must be; namely, the answer to the problems of man's origin and destiny—the basic dimension in salvation.

CHAPTER 6

Christ the Lord

$\mathcal{O}$UR SOCIETY is infiltrated by people who try to convince others that one religion is as good as another so long as it is packaged under the label "God." The point is not that they ignore Christ, but they simply place Him on the history shelf along with biographies of Mohammed, Moses, Confucius, and Buddha.

A most destructive view! Christianity is the one religion that is destroyed the moment it starts borrowing; for to borrow is to admit that somewhere something is lacking that must be supplied. Christianity's existence is dependent on the truth that it is the complete, perfect, and only way to salvation. Negate this concept and Christianity lies withered and defunct at our feet. Christ must be the center of the plan of salvation, or He is nothing.

Men with the urge to unify religious belief under one heading, neatly organized, on occasion recommend a universal religion, synthesized from the best elements of all the world's religions. This suggestion is based on the hypothesis that Christianity, as well as other religions, is partially adapted from types of worship of an earlier date. The idea of the virgin birth, for instance, has been hinted to be a copy of the story of Buddha's birth, or even taken from Greek mythology.

In the face of such rather vague claims, we must assert the uniqueness of Christianity. Nor can we go along with the suggestion that one over-all blanket concept is good enough. Plane and spherical geometry use the word "triangle," but it does not mean the same thing to both fields. In plane geometry a triangle is a figure that contains 180 degrees. A spherical triangle must contain more. Though both triangles are bound by "straight lines," still the term "straight lines" does not carry equivalent meaning in both cases.

So it is in religion. Several religions (or denominations and sects within one religion) may use the term "God," but this "God" may be as different as night and day within each system. For instance, Christianity, Judaism, and Islam all speak of the God of Abraham and Isaac. On the surface this may seem a point in common, but further study immediately reveals that the God of Christianity, with Christ (God made flesh) as the second person, and the Holy Spirit (God's presence and power) as the third person, is widely divergent from the God of Judaism or Islam. Then, when we move into the area of propitiation for sin or even of the meaning of sin itself, or the concept of salvation, the differences between the aforementioned religions become even more poignant. The more one tries to harmonize these beliefs, the more the differences become apparent, until we reach the conclusion that, after all, Christianity cannot be described as consisting of ideas culled from eras prior to the incarnation leading to Christ's ministry on earth.

Those who have attempted a merger of religions found it an impossible task. Christianity remains unique. The more important question to study is whether or not Christianity is true and profitable, therefore the best. And here, of course, we must encounter Jesus the Christ. He has dominated the centuries. He has stood the test of time in

the minds and worship of men. Why? Simply because in Him chaos is exchanged for cosmos, disorder is resolved into order. Each object finds its place without marring the harmony of the whole, whereas without Him the world could be described by the words of Milton:

> "The pillared firmament is rottenness,
> And earth's base built on stubble."

Thus our main problem is to point people to the overwhelming truth of Christ. They must become acquainted with this central figure of history without whom they are doomed to a life of frustration and the constant feeling that nothing is seasonable. Until men are prepared to accept and encounter the personal Christ, they will keep producing beasts instead of men, disjointed shambles of body as well as mind. Note these thoughts from the great Blaise Pascal:

"When I consider the brief span of my life, swallowed up in the eternity before and behind it, the small space that I fill, or even see, engulfed in the infinite immensity of spaces which I know not, and which know not me, I am afraid, and wonder to see myself here rather than there; for there is no reason why I should be here rather than there, now rather than then."

True, when the heart has been carved out and thrown away, then it no longer makes a difference whether it is now or then; here or there.

But the great drama of life lies not in marking time, letting the clock tick itself to silence, but it is in finding the pre-eminence of Christ and giving Him first rank of honor and dignity as the Creator of life, the Sustainer of life, Head of the church, and man's Mediator of salvation. We must see Him at all times as the representative of

od's power, goodness, mercy, and love are revealed in e Person of His Son, Jesus, who linked heaven to earth.

God's dealings with men. He is veritably the image of the invisible God. He was ordained of God to be the unique expression of God among men.

It was this that Saint Paul tried so hard to convey to the church members at Colosse when they kept bringing error into the church.[1] Never again, he felt, would they apostatize, if they accepted the truth that God bridged the huge gap between Himself and man by becoming flesh to dwell among fallen men and to redeem them. No other way could have made God more accessible to men. That is why Christ the Lord always must occupy the first place in man's heart. He cannot be denied without denying our next breath.

One would think that during the two thousand years of Christianity, thinkers have had time to examine Christ enough to catalog Him correctly; yet errors concerning Him increase and multiply in proportion to the passing of the years.

The major problem to set straight is why Christ came to earth in human form, or why He came at all. Strange views have been held on this subject. Some have tried to promote the idea that God had a difficult time loving human beings, thus finally He sent His Son into the world so that He could learn to love humanity by virtue of the fact that His own Son had become human. We cite this view because it is precisely an inversion of the truth. God sent His Son into the world not so that He could love men; but God loved men, therefore He gave them His Son. "God so loved . . . that he gave." [2] In other words, Christ's coming to earth added nothing to God's eternal dimensions. His love was present from the foundation of the world. God was made flesh only to reveal what always has been true about God. Nor did the Incarnation

---

[1] See Epistle to the Colossians.
[2] Gospel according to John, ch. 3, v. 16.

suddenly effect a spectacular union between human beings and God. This union has always been; Christ simply revealed it fully in human flesh.

A crucial war had taken place in heaven.[3] Satan had made the claim that God's actions were arbitrary and did not flow from love. This falsehood had to be disproved, so Christ came to earth to show that God's love is never arbitrary, but flows forever from His nature, and that nothing was ever created without His love.[4] Jesus came to reveal the nature of God's connection with men. Ellen G. White notes: "The King of the universe summoned the heavenly hosts before Him, that in their presence He might set forth the true position of His Son, and show the relation He sustained to all created beings."[5]

"Was Jesus like the ordinary mass of human beings?" some ask. To answer we must come to understand that He clothed His divinity with humanity, remaining fully God and fully man. In other words, Christ did not masquerade as a child would masquerade and pretend to be an Indian, a cowboy, or a prince—an erroneous interpretation bordering on Docetism. As a matter of fact, we have no illustration to simplify the concept of how Christ could be so fully God yet fully man, because nothing in human experience equals this magnificent role. It is difficult even to discuss a subject so fraught with mystery. However, the mystery need not paralyze us. An earnest study of the Scriptures reveals all that is necessary to achieve spiritual fullness.

It is fully revealed, for instance, that Christ succeeded where Adam, the first man, failed,[6] and in this way He meets each of us today on every level of our human ex-

---

[3] Book of the Revelation, ch. 12, vs. 7-17.
[4] See Chapter 21, Atonement.
[5] Ellen G. White, *Patriarchs and Prophets,* p. 36.
[6] First Epistle to the Corinthians, ch. 15, vs. 21, 22, 45, 47.

perience.[7] Through Him we have God-given potentiality
—now, this moment. To every man and woman He declares in tender tones, "I am the vine, ye are the branches." [8]
In Christ, and only in Him, the gap between God and man
is bridged completely, perfectly, and for *always*.

The word *always* is important, since it eliminates the
possibility of confining Christ to a certain period in history. To be sure, Christ chose a definite localized time in
order to become humanity, but we cannot take Him, lock
Him up in this time, and confine Him to it. The original
bridge between God and man is not Christ's incarnation
or death as earthly events; rather, it is man's creation by
God. Jesus came to earth to demonstrate more fully the
creative union of God and man as it was meant to be in a
sinless state. Since man was limited to time, God perforce
must choose to demonstrate His love within some period
of time to show the timelessness of His creative being and
the continuity of His union with humanity.

We cannot confine Christ to a calendar date, for His
personality bridges the before and the hereafter. In April
of 1865, the American Secretary of War, Edwin Stanton,
rose from the bedside where he had been kneeling, pulled
down the blind at the window to shut out the bright April
sunlight, then turning to look at the still form on the bed,
said, "Now he belongs to the ages." Probably this is the
best biography of Abraham Lincoln. It is even a more ac-
curate biography of Christ, for only He belongs to the
ages in the true sense. He is Alpha and Omega. "Who
shall declare his generation?" [9]

In her better moments, the church has kept Christ
at the center of her creed, work, and hope. When she has
spread a veil of heresy between herself and Him, she has

---

[7] Gospel according to John, ch. 1, vs. 14, 12, 16.
[8] *Ibid.*, ch. 15, v. 5.
[9] Book of Acts, ch. 8, v. 33.

no longer prospered. When the church tries to submerge Christ into general God worship, she loses her zest, her greatness. If the church will retain her vitality, she must maintain Christ as the Head—not angels, philosophies, intellectual sophistries, but Christ and all that His name implies. No depth of spiritual life exists without Him. No substitute can take His place. We can plead for better understanding among nations, greater knowledge of world affairs, stronger integrity and morality, but life's essential core is dead without Christ. Life void of Him is not just empty; it is nonexistent. Dr. Joseph Sizoo, an eminent Methodist minister, was thinking of this when he said: "The world is not done with Christ; it is done without Him."

This does not mean that nothing good can be found in non-Christian religions. It is undebatable that some good is found in every religion. But you cannot identify every religion with the truth as it is in Christ. Always we need a Tertullian to insist that Christ as the Head of the church be not squared with or absorbed into some other all-encompassing system. We must increasingly see Christ as towering over man, the church, life itself. Everything we do or try to interpret as having relevance to reality must center in Him.

A Jewish soldier attended a number of services of Christian worship during World War II. He heard, of course, about Jesus the Christ. The Christian minister evidently did a good job, for soon this soldier went to his own chaplain to ask, "What is the difference between the Messiah of the Jew and the Christ?" "One difference," the rabbi replied. "Our Messiah is still to come, while the Messiah of the Christians is already here." A few moments of reflection followed, and then the soldier said, "But, Rabbi, when our Messiah comes, what will he be more than Jesus?"

Commenting on this incident, Robert W. Youngs concluded rightly: "There is only one answer to that. There will be none better than Jesus. In history, leaders who were supposed to surpass Jesus have quickly perished. Utopias and Shangri-las that were expected to exceed the kingdom of Jesus have faded like fancy dreams. So it will be in the future. We cannot even imagine a life better than the life of Jesus, a gospel more challenging. If any one can imagine it, let him tell it to the world, and the world will make him immortal. No man does. No man can. It takes a man, but more than a man to be a Christ. It takes Jesus who by His life, His teaching, and His saving power shows Himself in every age to be full of God." [10]

---

[10] Robert W. Youngs, *What It Means to Be a Christian,* p. 20.

$\mathcal{S}$uffering

$\mathcal{W}$HILE I WAS writing this chapter, a young sophist said: "You know something? Religious writers are phony. They have never gone to bed at night with an empty stomach, not knowing where their next meal will come from; things for them have never been so bad that they genuinely wished for death; yet they think they can reform the world with their noise about inner joy. What a fake!" A deprecative shrug accompanied these remarks.

Trying to harmonize the idea of an omnipotent and benevolent God with what goes on in the world seems to be man's greatest problem. Many treat this problem as a charade. They are in a huddle trying to find clues to explain the parts, but no satisfactory explanation can be found, so the charade remains a mystery.

Cynics say that love is basically selfishness, the home is an artificial restriction prescribed by a narrow culture, morals are rules for weak people, and religion is simply an escape mechanism. The cynic, of course, has his logical arguments. He reasons that the scheme of salvation and eternal joy does not fit into the reality of life as we know it, the reality of existing in a world where leaders with integrity are betrayed by poisonous tongues; where citizens on every social level are tortured by cancer until they finally gasp their last breath; where babies are born with heads too large, stumps for arms, eyes without sight; where the percentage of potentially happy persons is cut down radically by accidental death, financial calamity, catastrophes beyond human control; where innocent people are massacred daily through war and crime; where noble people suffer excruciating mental and physical pains that seemingly have no purpose.

Saint Paul had a different idea. In speaking of God, he said, "Most gladly therefore will I rather glory in my infirmities, that the power of Christ may rest upon me. Therefore I take pleasure in infirmities, in reproaches, in necessities, in persecutions, in distresses for Christ's sake: for when I am weak, then am I strong." [1]

Though the temptation toward cynicism is strong, cynicism is not the answer, nor is it even helpful. What, then, shall we tell those who are ill, suffering physically and mentally? Shall we tell them that God wills life for them to be so tragic? Can God be a god of fury and at the same time be the God of infinite love? Can He be sadistic, yet show immutable good will? I do not believe so. God must either be all evil or all good; no dichotomy can exist, if we are to bring order out of confusion in our understanding of His ways and of His relation to the world He has created.

We hold up Paul as an example of one who knew the joy of conviction that God is good. He was not born to a life of ease. This was a man who, perhaps above all his contemporaries, had reason to be cynical and bitter, for his life was full of bizarre circumstances. He was hampered with physical handicaps, treated harshly by the government, and persecuted by his own countrymen. He was oft

---

[1] Second Epistle to the Corinthians, ch. 12, vs. 9, 10.

in danger from sea travels, robbers, hostile men, the desert. His existence was plagued by many a sleepless night, "in hunger and thirst, in fastings often, in cold and nakedness." [2] In Damascus, royal guards were once posted at all gates to effect Paul's arrest, anticipating his execution, and he escaped the trap only with the help of friendly hands that lowered him in a basket to the outside through an opening in the city wall. The record of the last days of Paul's life is so obscure that little is known of them, but it is assumed he was executed in Rome as a common criminal. Yet at every turn Paul was able to say, "If I must needs glory, I will glory of the things which concern mine infirmities." [3] He was faithful to the end, never doubting that God is good and that for all the vicissitudes of the way, the final outcome would be enthroned high on the pillar of joy.

Let us not become involved in a search for a theoretical answer to the problem of suffering; it does not exist. This lesson Jesus taught His disciples. They were concerned with suffering. One day, as they walked along with the Master, they saw at the side of the road a man blind since his birth. This prompted them to ask Jesus why such blindness existed, from whose sin it resulted—his own or his parents? Jesus answered, "Neither hath this man sinned, nor his parents: but that the works of God should be made manifest in him." [4] In other words, suffering as being caused by God is ruled out. Instead, God's children are to find in it a challenge to do something to alleviate pain, to heal it wherever possible, and in all cases to gain the victory over resentment, frustration, disappointment.

More than any other factor, the injustice and partiality of life discourage man and prompt him to cynicism. The

[2] *Ibid.*, ch. 11, v. 27.
[3] *Ibid.*, v. 30.
[4] Gospel according to John, ch. 9, v. 3.

blows come, irrespective of deserts. The world is dark
with the griefs and graves of men and women who, according to any standard, should have had a better deal. The
good as well as the evil are prone to bear grief. Those
closest to God are not exempt; in fact, many of the most
faithful have no surcease from trials, bearing one after the
other until they lie crushed under the burden. Why? We
cannot hope to provide a satisfactory answer, but there is
an explanation—and a way of escape.

The solidarity of sin in human life is a reality. This
wrongness of our nature, this propensity to "miss the mark,"
conditions our very existence. We are all like "sheep going
astray." [5] The result is the transgression of God's laws. Pain
is the alarm signal that we are at odds with the laws—
physical and moral—God has set for us. Think of it in
this way: When we approach a fire with our hand, pain
warns us and saves us literally from destruction. In this
sense, pain is salutary—a blessing in disguise. And God's
righteousness requires that the same principle apply to
moral laws also. All pain is a warning to us that we are out
of tune with God's law.

Right here I would like to make a statement of deep
truth: We can never feel secure and safe in this world
until we are willing to part with it. Our world has waxed
old like a garment, and knowing that an eternity so much
better than what we presently experience will come, we
can say with conviction, "I can get along without this
world." This is not to say that we shrug off calamity. One
cannot say to a father whose child has just drowned, "Buck
up, old friend, time will cure your sorrow." Christianity
leaves much room for genuine compassion and tears. But
it is comforting to know that the Christian faith centers
in God who in Christ our Saviour took the worst of man's

---

[5] First Epistle of Peter, ch. 2, v. 25.

cruelty, looked even death squarely in the face, and conquered. Like Him, we can take life when it seems most meaningless, so disturbed that no possible sense can be made of it, and we can look it squarely in the face, claiming Christ's victory for ourselves. That victory is shot through with love and eternal goodness. It is Heaven's way of escape. Note that this is not a Pollyanna faith, but simply the practical inner security of one who knows God, depends upon Him, can talk with Him at all times, receiving help, encouragement, and strength, regardless of physical circumstances.

Joy as well as sorrow is a part of man's heritage. Maturity will bring its share of each, to form depth of character and understanding. The same eyes that can sparkle with joy are usually the eyes often bathed with tears. Kahlil Gibran expressed the thought in this manner:

"When you are joyous, look deep into your heart and you will find it is only that which has given you sorrow that is giving you joy. When you are sorrowful, look again in your heart, and you find that in truth you are weeping for that which has been your delight. Some of you say, 'Joy is greater than sorrow,' and others say, 'Nay, sorrow is greater.' But I say unto you, they are inseparable. Together they come, and when one sits alone with you at your board, remember that the other is asleep upon your bed. Verily you are suspended like scales between your sorrow and your joy."

Jesus Himself was no stoic. Often His eyes were clouded with tears. He wept at the grave of His personal friend Lazarus. He wept again during the parade through Jerusalem, at a time when He was being acclaimed and hailed as King of the Jews. Ellen G. White describes with rare sensitivity this moment of Jesus' life:

"Jesus gazes upon the scene, and the vast multitude hush their shouts, spellbound by the sudden vision of beauty. All eyes turn upon the Saviour, expecting to see in His countenance the admiration they themselves feel. But instead of this they behold a cloud of sorrow. They are surprised and disappointed to see His eyes fill with tears, and His body rock to and fro like a tree before the tempest, while a wail of anguish bursts from His quivering lips, as if from the depths of a broken heart. What sight was this for angels to behold! their loved Commander in an agony of tears! . . . Many wept in sympathy with a grief they could not comprehend." [6]

Crowds of Jews came to the Temple yearly to celebrate with pomp and ritual. They gave alms, they knelt at the altar, they offered long prayers, but they did not worship with love; their cult was cold, lacking heart. Yet, when Jesus gave His life in order to show these men and women true love, they crucified Him. Knowing this, Jesus wept profusely.

Another mention of Jesus' tears is a reference to the night in the Garden of Gethsemane. In this instance, Jesus shed tears of loneliness and despair. Feeling completely forsaken, tired and worn from service to mankind without receiving apparent response, He knelt in prayer and poured out His agony. Those who have ever given themselves with dauntless energy to a cause and worked hard only to see it fail can understand these tears of Jesus. Who would not have wept?

Thus we say that the greatest have moments of darkness, when they are shaken to the core. And in fact, we have never been promised blue skies only; but as Christians we have been promised power to withstand any onslaught, even death. This is important. If in the end happiness ensues, then no matter what we suffer on the way it is worth the strain. We do not say that faith offers quick cures

---

[6] Ellen G. White, *The Desire of Ages*, pp. 575, 576.

for suffering or an easy way to happiness. We only say that in God there is new life and new strength to stand up to the circumstances as they are. The joy of the Christian is not that he is swept out of the race, but that he runs with patience, endurance, and courage.

Today, perhaps more than ever, Christians have lost the boldness to dare, to take risks, and to conquer troubles. A survey among college students by *Fortune Magazine* revealed that most young people are more interested in security than in growth. The editors described those whom they polled as "a cautious, subdued generation that will not stick its neck out. It keeps its shirt on . . . its chin up, and its mouth shut!" Apparently the spirit of investing everything into the pursuit of a goal, so dominant in our forebears, has recessed until many of us fear our own shadows. Serenity despite danger has been exchanged for what might be called "the jitters" about staying alive.

The strongest barrier between the present generation and serenity amid danger is that so many of us refuse to live with the mysterious. Because we do not understand much of what happens in the way of suffering, we become frustrated and worried. The why's and wherefore's of life shatter us. To be able to live congenially with life's incomprehensibles is the Christian's great asset. Whereas we must study and develop our innate intellect to the fullest, yet, to make answering every question a primary exercise is debilitating. In part, life is a mystery; death is a mystery; birth is a mystery; love is a mystery; God is a mystery. We need not be under compulsion to dissect any. How much better and less painful it is to accept that the most splendid aspects of life are the incomprehensibles.

Albert Einstein gave help when he said:

"The most beautiful emotion that we can experience is the mystical. It is the sower of all true art and science. He to whom this emotion is a stranger, who can no longer wonder and stand rapt in awe, is as good as dead. To know that what is impenetrable to us really exists, manifesting itself as the highest wisdom and the most radiant beauty, which our full faculties can comprehend only in their most primitive forms—this knowledge, this feeling is at the center of religiousness."

Let us not be deceived into thinking that we can make complete sense out of what happens in the world. We cannot, for instance, rationally explain why fifteen missionaries on furlough should be trapped and killed in a brush fire in California, or why innocent bystanders are beaten to death in a Congolese mob revolt, or why a seven-year-old boy drowns in a swimming pool, or why three innocent women are massacred by a maniac. We do not know why. Nor do we fully understand God. If we could, He would be no greater than we. But we can love God and be loved by Him—this is what counts. It is not so much what we know about God that gives serenity, but simply that we trust in Him as our personal God. Our serenity is the result of our knowledge of God as a Person. This closeness to God allowed Paul to say:

"For which cause we faint not; but though our outward man perish, yet the inward man is renewed day by day. For our light affliction, which is but for a moment, worketh for us a far more exceeding and eternal weight of glory; while we look not at the things which are seen, but at the things which are not seen: for the things which are seen are temporal; but the things which are not seen are eternal." [7]

Complete confidence in God's love and care kept Paul's life from going sour. He could face the worst, because deep down in his being he was familiar with God. He could say, "For we know that if our earthly house of this

---

[7] Second Epistle to the Corinthians, ch. 4, vs. 16-18.

tabernacle were dissolved, we have a building of God, an house not made with hands, eternal in the heavens. . . . For we that are in this tabernacle do groan, being burdened: not for that we would be unclothed, but clothed upon, that mortality might be swallowed up of life." [8]

The future? It belongs to God. He is with us all the way. During the worst days of the Civil War, Stanton, Secretary of War, said to President Lincoln: "I don't see why it is that you are so calm. When everything is going wrong, our generals are losing battles, and we can hear thunder of guns here in Washington, you seem to keep calm and poised. How do you do it?"

"Well, it's like this, Stanton," Mr. Lincoln replied, "when you feel you are only a pipe for Omnipotence to sound through, you do not worry very much."

Summing up, we have not been promised Utopia. We have not been promised explanations for every point in the cycle of human existence. Jesus Himself presented no magic formula relative to the why and the wherefore of suffering. Rather, He incarnated a way of victory in the face of suffering. The secret of His triumph was His identification with the will of the Father in suffering. Likewise, in reconciliation we can identify ourselves with a suffering God, whereby there is a transmutation of sufferings, from pessimism to optimism, from confusion and uncertainty to hope for the banishment of suffering. [9]

In Christ, we have been promised the same thing that was given to Job, Isaiah, Paul, Stephen, Martin Luther, and every other man or woman of God—the will to fight on, the love to overcome evil, the victory to live eternally. We are captives of God. We cannot do otherwise but rest our faith in Him. And this suffices.

---

[8] *Ibid.*, ch. 5, vs. 1-4.
[9] See Book of the Revelation, ch. 21, v. 4; see also Ernest Naville, *Le Probléme du Mal* (Geneva).

CHAPTER 8

Freedom of Choice

ꭰ FEW YEARS ago public curiosity was fo-
cused on Caryl Chessman, convict, and his
spectacular bid for freedom. Should he or should he not
die in the gas chamber? was the topic of heated debate,
private as well as public. With every new stay of execution
people all over the world offered their judgment of this
man.

Beyond the excitable arguments *pro* or *con* capital punishment, we must ask another question: Why did this man
become a criminal? Why was his life a series of evil
deeds, showing deep-rooted hatred of fellow human beings? Was he born this way? Did his environment forge
him into the vicious, devilish man he became? Or did this
man Chessman voluntarily choose stark depravity? Turning from him specifically to human beings as a whole
are we responsible for what we are?

The problem of sin is Christianity's greatest problem.
Other religions have denied this and have created different
oarlocks. Egypt and the mystery religions, for instance,
considered *death* man's greatest problem. The Egyptian
pyramids are a grim memento of their attempt to immor-
talize man. Intricate mummifying processes were a futile
effort to save the human body from death's dread power.

The Grecian era turned from death to *ignorance* with the pronouncement that if man were only willing to learn, he would eventually be delivered from all fears and would find the panacea for his ills. This concept still finds favor in the minds of many who consider education the cure-all for every modern enigma. Another problem, studied and dramatized by certain Oriental cults, is the *pain* from which man cries out to be delivered. Buddhism, probably more than any other religion, has built a system of thought destined to relieve men of this burden. Deliverance has been called Nirvana—a state attained only through the complete extermination of all desire. With the elimination of desire, Buddha felt, would come a lasting freedom from tragedy, frustration, or sorrow. It was a way of escape rather than a solution.

With Christ came a change of emphasis. Though we must not deny that death, ignorance, and pain are evil, yet they are not life's greatest problem. Our overwhelming enemy is *sin;* to its clutches we trace the pathetic circumstance in which the world finds itself. Sin is an item not easily overlooked. We must reckon with it. Too long people have tried to side-step the issue without calling a spade a spade. Were we to believe the sum and total of modern intellectualism, we would submit to the view that man is simply a pawn in a series of alternating changes and chances. A father has a violent temper; his son may unwillingly inherit a disposition favorable to it. People who drink to excess are not doing wrong; they are simply expressing their struggle against feelings of inferiority, inadequacy, or nonacceptance in their group. A thief? Well, he probably came from an unhappy home. And a murderer is one who is seriously ill.

The battle between heredity and environment is waged as heatedly now as when Pelagius first traveled from England to Rome and discovered that the moral degradation of so-called Christians was horrifying. Only 400 years after the Christian church had been founded in purity and truth, men's foulness of purpose and deed was amazing to behold. But when confronted, the Romans made excuses, saying that they could not help their condition, because the grace of God had not chosen to do anything about them.

The scenery may have changed, but the arguments have remained the same. Relentlessly the pendulum swings back and forth. In one corner the theologians accuse, in another the sociologists defend, and yet in another the psychiatrists try to cure. Certainly harmony is absent with respect to man's responsibility in the world. One says the man who kills does wrong; another says he is mentally deranged; the district attorney calls for the death penalty; the jury suggests he be freed because it was justifiable homicide. Who is right?

Through the vagueness of man's subjectivity comes a clear-cut answer. In simplest terms it tells us that *we can help who we are.* We have a moral nature and along with it we have the choice between right and wrong. Any other way is inconceivable. Without the freedom to choose a course there is no knowledge of right and wrong, there can be no moral or spiritual responsibility, and man would be no more than a blob of protoplasm. One of the earliest chapters in the Bible highlights man's awful responsibility: "I call heaven and earth to record this day against you, that I have set before you life and death, blessing and cursing: therefore choose life, that both thou and thy seed may live." [1] Whether Biblically enlightened or not, every human being has the ability to distinguish between right and wrong and to fulfill his obligation to the right. The apostle Paul stresses this skillfully in his address to the church at Rome, maintaining that even the Gentiles "do by nature

---

[1] Book of Deuteronomy, ch. 30, v. 19.

the things contained in the law." Though they did not have codified, organized rules as did the Jews, yet they were "a law unto themselves," because, said Paul, the law is "written in their hearts, their conscience also bearing witness." [2]

Paul's statement is no exaggeration, as was forcefully impressed on my mind when I traveled through Central New Guinea. Here, civilization is catapulted back into the Stone Age. It is as if no social progress had been made for thousands of years. These people, in their primitive state, seem little above the animal. Day in and day out, sometimes as naked as a wild beast, they roam the hills and valleys, stalking game, eating what vegetation and meat is available, and teaching their young to do likewise. But in their moral life they are guided by instinct and the moral code within their hearts. Even these most primitive tribes know the innate meaning of loyalty, honesty, reverence, and gratitude. You might call it a crude development of moral insights. Certainly it does not consist of formal rules; but the groundwork is there just as surely as the apostle stated it—"their conscience bearing witness."

Love can exist between man and God only if it is an act of freedom. God in His freedom chooses us as His children, and we in turn, because of our freedom, may choose God as our Father.

When Patrick Henry cried out, "Give me liberty, or give me death!" he expressed far more than a political ultimatum. Political freedom is to be prized and guarded, but moral freedom is even more essential, for to be politically or socially coerced crushes the spirit, but moral coercion undermines essential manhood.

Jesus took man's freedom seriously. Often He extolled the worth of the human soul, one day saying that it had higher value than every material thing in the world. But

---

[2] Epistle to the Romans, ch. 2, vs. 14, 15.

unless the human soul is free to choose the side to which he will belong, he is dead—a thing, not a living soul. Freedom alone makes it possible to lay a high price on the soul.

Complete respect for man's freedom of will prevented Jesus from imposing Himself upon the masses, though He could easily have done so. He could have overthrown them physically and set up a centralized dictatorship with greater manpower than in the days of any Caesar or Napoleon. He might have persuaded men by the force of His personality, virtually casting a hypnotic spell to fascinate the crowds. Intellectually He could have outshone the best scholars, the craftiest politicians, the smartest businessmen; He could have led men anywhere with brilliance and mental superiority. Or He could have coerced them emotionally, using mass hysteria to press for decisions. However, the Master avoided these means. He forced neither by fear, admiration, nor pity. With divine restraint He waited for quiet, firm decisions. He hoped people would respond, but He did not force. His invitation is recorded in the Revelation: "And the Spirit and the bride say, Come. And let him that heareth say, Come. And let him that is athirst come. And whosoever will, let him take the water of life freely." [3]

Despite the importance of freedom, we must not use it as a goal in itself, for freedom is only the path, not the destination; it is only valuable as a means to move closer to God. The words of W. E. Hocking are valuable in this respect:

"A life lived on the plan of getting along without God, without sense of cosmic demand, is already, whether it knows it or not, sick, off from normal, its values in-

---

[3] Book of the Revelation, ch. 22, v. 17.

en are drawn to the Saviour, not through a code of com-
lsion, but by love—the love of God for His sons.

fested with the dry rot of mortality, intrinsically unhappy because unreal, driven subconsciously by a need which someday it is bound to recognize and define." [4]

Freedom, if made the end product, will lead to pandemonium of the worst kind. No one is more bound than he who thinks himself completely free, dodging hither and yon irrationally without precept or plan. Freedom as an exemption is a dangerous delusion eventually resulting in bondage. Many areas of everyday life serve to illustrate this truth: freedom in music is achieved by the musician only after he has found discipline in exercises and the rules of practice. Wise parents will insist that their children learn this discipline, if they wish them in later years to enjoy the artistry of music. The architect creates freely new styles of symmetry in building, but only after he has conquered the laws of stress and proportion governing architectural design. Every profession requires its hours of study, rehearsal, and concentration. Even sports and games have their definitive rules.

Can we conceive of a God who would create without plan, rules, pattern, discipline? As we see the overwhelming evidence of order in nature, we know that God is a God of discipline.

The Ten Commandments are divine rules which each individual, in freedom, may choose to follow in order to beautify his life and that of his fellow human beings. The Ten Commandments constitute the most succinct formulation of ethics conceivable and are among the most important words in history. Given by God Himself on Mount Sinai, they form the foundation of all law and morals throughout Christendom. They are the most authoritative statement of conscience when interpreted by the mind and spirit of Jesus. Never having been repealed, they are

---

[4] W. E. Hocking, *Science and the Idea of God*, p. 49.

never out of date. As they applied in the day of the ox, so they still apply in the day of the turbine jet. The commandments are phrased simply, easily grasped even by children. They apply at home, in business, on the street, and anywhere else man may be. When God presented His law in written form to man, He encountered man person to person, and it was an awesome moment. Briefly, here are our ten precepts for moral conduct: [5]

I

"Thou shalt have no other gods before me." The first commandment is a summons to worship one personalized God—Him who created the universe.

II

"Thou shalt not make unto thee any graven image." God and His glory cannot be captured in human symbol. Even the most profound intellectual ideas do not express Him. He is beyond being poured into man-made molds.

III

"Thou shalt not take the name of the Lord thy God in vain." This is a condemnation of lip service—admitting God, but having no change or growth take place in one's life to prove that he is God's child. To talk idly about God without bringing His character into daily life is as destructive as denying God.

IV

"Remember the sabbath day, to keep it holy." The sacredness of this specific day lies in that it is a symbol of Creation, making God's creativity irrefutable; therefore no day other than the seventh will do.

---

[5] Book of Exodus, ch. 20, vs. 1-17.

V

"Honour thy father and thy mother." This commandment is the link between divine and human decrees, looking to God as well as man. Our heritage is sacred, for we were created in the image of God. It is not to be pulled into the mud.

VI

"Thou shalt not kill." Killing can be done in many ways: physical murder may be the most obvious; but there is also the slow, torturesome killing with words, unkind thoughts, cruel, cutting action. God's children will build life, not cause death.

VII

"Thou shalt not commit adultery." Moral decay is one of man's worse failures. Human relationships, the family in particular, must be kept intact if man is to enjoy the fruits of peace and joy. Marriage is a sacred estate.

VIII

"Thou shalt not steal." Some political or economic creeds do not recognize the sanctity of personal property; God does. Ownership is part of the good life, and man is admonished to honor another's goods.

IX

"Thou shalt not bear false witness." To love mankind means to be trustworthy in speech as well as action.

X

"Thou shalt not covet." Inordinate greed has no place in the life of those who strive to live by love. Let every human being examine his motives carefully and let him discard feelings of ruthless coveting.

These Ten Commandments are a perfect reflection of God's majesty and man's moral responsibility. The two walk hand in hand to assure true liberty. Though the Ten Commandments are not meant to instill fear or tyrannic obedience, they are a definite requisite to freedom from the bondage of sin. To be truly free means that we have acquired the wisdom to choose a certain path, and to conquer passions, and to grow in learning, foresight, and judgment.

Our freedom to choose is God's greatest gift, and it places before us thrilling possibilities. God's law is there to point the way. In answer to the question posed at the beginning of this chapter, we answer with certainty, Yes, man can help who he is. He can help being the kind of husband he is, the kind of wife, father, mother, businessman, worker, student, son, daughter, or friend he is. Through the right exercise of the will, an entire change may be made in his life. Every human being possessed of reason has power to choose the right.

The moment we choose love over hate, God steps into our life to help us follow through on our choice. Every time we make a choice for kindness, gentleness, peace, patience, joy, or faith, God steps into our life and makes our choice a reality. The first attempt may be shaky and even unsuccessful, but continued effort will eventually bring success. No war or conflict exists between man's freedom and God's grace; one simply supplements the other.

Daniel, Moses, Peter, Paul, and the host of other men who have beautified Christianity were men who made choices for love. They might have been a Judas or a Caryl Chessman had they made a contrary choice.

Our future lies before us, filled to the brim, like a golden chalice, with the opportunity of choosing love and life. God has already chosen us; now let us choose Him.

CHAPTER 9

Eternal Life

DEATH IS a stark reality. The discovery of tremendous sources of power that could obliterate nations and perhaps our entire planet has placed death more than ever in the focus of human consciousness. Men no longer consider it a natural process only, with an indefinite time reference, but as an immediate, valid prospect.

One of the apparent consequences of this fact is the trend toward religion. Churches and synagogues report a higher membership tally than at any other time in recent history. Revivalists preach to capacity audiences in our metropolitan cities. Orthodox Jewish groups are expanding religious facilities, while non-Christian religions are experiencing an unparalleled resurgence.

Naturally the problem of death is an old one. Death has run the whole gamut of interpretation, from the notion that it is merely a natural fact pertaining to man as organic matter, to the idea of death as the goal of life, the distinguishing feature of human existence. From these poles two contrasting thought systems have emerged. On the one hand, there is the stoic or skeptic acceptance of the inevitable, or even the repression of the thought of death by life. On the other hand, there is the idealistic glorification of death. In this concept death is that which gives "meaning" to life, the precondition for the "true" life of man.

It is remarkable to what extent this double notion of death has permeated the thinking of men. The result has been widespread doubt and despair. In both lines of thought the insecurity of life is matched in men's minds by the insecurity of death. Whittier's words express this insecurity so aptly:

> "The life to be
> Is still the unguessed mystery:
> Unscaled, unpierced the cloudy walls remain,
> We beat, with dream and wish, the
> Soundless doors in vain."

The story is one of frustration. The shadow of an inevitable end is thrown backward over the entire human experience. In the midst of life, men are in death. But they find it hard, impossible, to reconcile themselves to the "unguessed mystery." They keep whispering, "Tomorrow, tomorrow, tomorrow," hoping instinctively that something lies beyond the decay of the body. This hope always has been linked with religion, but in itself is a common-sense inference from countless human experiences in which man's hopes live and range at large, laying hold upon a future existence for which man seems to know he was made. This undeniable intrinsic character of our nature is the kind of evidence by which we live in all the most important things of our lives; it leads us to understand and accept a future life that cannot be demonstrated in formulas or laboratory tests.

Think for a moment of the evidences you accept that sunshine exists. In the morning you arise and assume that the sun is shining. But have you actually seen it? Chances are you only caught a glimpse of its rays streaming through the crack between the drawn curtains of your bedroom;

yet it does not dawn on you to doubt for a moment that the sun has sent those rays. Stepping outside your front door, you feel a pleasing warmth. "It's the sun," you notice; but still you haven't actually looked up into the sky.

Or you have observed that wherever light falls, there vegetation grows in special abundance; but where there is no light, growth is limited. Considering all these things, you say that you know the sun is shining. These are the evidences by which we live every day.

You may ask the genuine Christian, "Have you actually seen God?" Even though his answer is No, yet he has seen what God does. He knows that where once darkness prevailed, now there is light. He knows, too, the warmth of Christian fellowship, which cannot be explained apart from God, because, left to their natural tendencies, men do not behave in such fashion. Love, compassion, and life's sweetness grow under the influence of Christ as they do in no other way. Considering all these things, the Christian claims the right to believe in God and His promise of eternal life.

Why should this be so difficult to accept? Certainly eternal life is no greater mystery than life itself. The real mystery is that we have life in the first place. The sublimely baffling moment comes when we contemplate the human beings whom we love, our own joy in achieved aspirations, the thrill of breathing among beauty, intelligence, organization. Having experienced the quality and richness of life as we know it, is it not far more difficult to accept that it should everlastingly end, rather than find extension and perfection in a better world? By the very ache in our hearts, telling us that we are never satisfied with present accomplishments and situations, we long instinctively for perpetuity.

Some of the world's greatest thinkers were convinced of the reality of a life after death. They were not all in agreement with how the transition is made—not in agreement with the Bible or with one another. But the fact of an afterlife was deeply ingrained in their convictions. Henry Vaughan describes it as a "great ring of pure and endless light." Charles Mackay said, "There will come another era when it shall be light and man will awaken from his lofty dreams, and find his dreams all there, and nothing is gone save his sleep." Victor Hugo, France's honored writer, was sure of eternal life. He said: "I feel in myself the future life. . . . The nearer I approach the end, the plainer I hear around me the immortal symphonies of the world, which invite me. It is marvelous, yet simple. It is a fairy tale, and it is history. . . . The tomb is not a blind alley, it is a thoroughfare. It closes on the twilight, opens on the dawn."

Wherever men deny the tugging and pulling of the life beyond the resurrection, blackness spreads across their soul. Compulsively they begin to fill their few numbered days with angry living. Running hither and yon—running, running, they know not where, but hypnotized by the idea that somehow they must crowd as much activity as possible into what little time is left—they bombard life. Restlessly they propel themselves to work, to saloons, to parties. At night they try to sleep, but their eyes stare into the darkness, wide and burning. Schemes and plots are their dreams; their mind is a cyclone at whose center are more wild schemes—schemes for getting rich, famous, powerful. But the next morning brings only an emptiness of spirit, making the burden of life just a little heavier, drearier, and more taxing. The very atmosphere might well cry out, as did the converted Saul of Tarsus: "The things which are seen are temporal; but the things which are not seen are eternal."[1]

---

[1] Second Epistle to the Corinthians, ch. 4, v. 18.

One is safe in saying that most of the misery in our world is due to a lack of perspective in time. Boredom, hypochondria, neurosis, even suicide are the natural results of overlooking life's centrosome, namely, that we are meant for eternity. If we really believe that we are, then all the petty differences between individuals, physical pain, disappointments, losses, and so on would fade into the background of this one brilliant fire—the knowledge that life will come to an end one day and in God's good time will have a perfect beginning once again. Unless we believe in such an eternal beginning, the present has no meaning whatever. Less than that, it becomes a nightmare with a consummation devoutly to be desired. Annihilation would be welcome, if life had no extension. Apart from the lure of eternity, man is like a jungle animal forced into a cage. The smell of the wild is in his nostrils; he wants freedom in the worst way; but the impenetrable iron bars are there holding him back from leaping out and returning to his native domain. All the yelping, whimpering, roaring, will not quiet his restless longing.

The desire to live is deeply entrenched in our innermost being. Would it not be a cruel, diabolic God who would allow us to exist with such a desire just long enough to get a taste of what we would like to accomplish, a whiff of the delicacy of life's loveliness, only to end it all in the bottomless pit of eternal oblivion with one swift downbeat of His divine hand? Just as the artist thinks he could boldly capture on canvas the image before him, he is called away, never to finish his work. A writer spends the best years of his life in writing a work that he hopes will be of some worth to humanity. Just about the time he has an idea, a message that could change people's lives, the curtain falls; he can never finish what he began with enthusiasm.

Life at its best fills us with sadness, because so much

that should have been done, never was; what could have been said, remained unspoken.

The culprit here is sin. The universal sway of sin in mankind condemns men to death save for the gospel of salvation through Christ. "The wages of sin is death," wrote Saint Paul.[2] But this death is not an arbitrary penalty such as that a celestial despot might inflict on transgressors. The root of all sinning is unbelief, which is not an intellectual skepticism but man's refusal to acknowledge God by trusting and obeying Him as Father and Lord. Thus, by its very nature, sin disrupts the relationship in which man stands to God. By his sin man cuts himself off from the Source of life and dooms himself to perish. There is no hope for him apart from the grace of the forgiving God.

This God is the God of the living. He has set out to bring man back to Him—the center of life eternal. He is the same yesterday, today, and forever. Therefore, man's future is assured. God is not bound by the past or present. The future belongs to Him, and by virtue of this the future also belongs to His creation. This future is man's vision splendid.

Prophets, poets, lovers, and dreamers—they all receive their inspiration from the vision of a future; the latter is their driving force, their guiding star. Just so with God's children. The present to them has meaning only as they keep their eyes on tomorrow, knowing that then and only then will they find perfect harmony and fulfillment. Our moral nature demands this future life.

I do not belittle the magnitude of accepting the truth of life eternal with the consequence of a world without end. It is an awe-filled moment when we surrender to such a reality. We might liken it to the experience of a group of children who are telling ghost stories in the dark

---

[2] Epistle to the Romans, ch. 6, v. 23.

when there is a knock at the door. In frozen silence, they draw back. The meeting between the feigned and the real is momentous. In the case of accepting God's gift of eternal life the result is a revolution, but with this revolution also come miracles of beauty and ever-deepening satisfaction. In the words of Ellen G. White:

"When a man is converted [returned] to God, a new moral taste is supplied, a new motive power is given, and he loves the things that God loves; for his life is bound up by the golden chain of the immutable promises to the life of Jesus. Love, joy, peace, and inexpressible gratitude will pervade the soul, and the language of him who is blessed will be, 'Thy gentleness hath made me great' (Ps. 18:35)." [3]

This author notes with great perception also the cause of our hesitation to accept the gift of eternal life. Says she:

"Man through sin has been severed from the life of God. His soul is palsied through the machinations of Satan, the author of sin. Of himself he is incapable of appreciating and appropriating the divine nature. Were it brought within his reach there is nothing in it that his natural heart would desire it. The bewitching power of Satan is upon him. All the ingenious subterfuges the devil can suggest are presented to his mind to prevent every good impulse." [4]

We enter on one final, oft-disputed point on the subject of eternal life: Who is to receive it? The popular view, accepted by many interested in soteriology, is that as long as one is honest and sincere, it makes little difference what he believes; he will be entitled to citizenship in God's kingdom. Surely the earnest seeker after truth cannot accept this premise. While we know that the Lord is

---

[3] Ellen G. White, *Selected Messages*, book 1, p. 36.
[4] *Ibid.*, p. 340.

long-suffering and not willing that any shall go down in nonbeing, He cannot clear the guilty. His own words are:

"Wherefore kick ye at my sacrifice and at mine offering, which I have commanded in my habitation; and honourest thy sons above me, to make yourselves fat with the chiefest of all the offerings of Israel my people? Wherefore the Lord God of Israel saith, I said indeed that thy house, and the house of thy father, should walk before me for ever: but now the Lord saith, Be it far from me; for them that honour me I will honour, and they that despise me shall be lightly esteemed." [5]

The point is that we cannot with safety surrender any seed of vital truth in order to please ourselves or anybody else. Our future life is dependent on our continually feeding on God's truth in order to grow in spiritual stature. Indifference on the subject will lead only to opposition to God.

In a sense we can already dwell in a heavenly home by making God the center of life, trying with all our heart and strength to make this present distorted, confused, corrupted planet into a heaven on earth. Our life here is the beginning of the life hereafter; "what we now are, in character and holy service, is the sure foreshadowing of what we shall be." Even here on earth we can experience a bit of heaven. I shall develop this theme more fully in the chapter "Heaven on Earth."

Jerome Ellison, in his frank biography, tells when the upward lift began for him. Addressing God, he says:

"Then there came the blessed night, the cold and rainy night in November all those years ago, and the meeting at the Y.M.C.A., when You reached down and freed me from the desire to drink. And to the moment I write this, You keep me free!"

---

[5] First Book of Samuel, ch. 2, vs. 29, 30.

No need to waste time convincing such a one that life is a resurrection—that it really begins when a person surrenders to God, to walk forever with Him, until on that day of grand finale—or culmination, if you please—he will cross the bridge of mortality into a land of endless life. In the words of R. W. Raymond, "Life is eternal; and love is immortal; and death is only a horizon, and a horizon is nothing save the limit of our sight."

But what is this "resurrection"? What assurance do we have that we can experience it? When shall be this day of "grand finale," or "culmination"? When shall we cross this bridge of mortality into a land of endless life?

These answers, likewise, we can know—if we will but inquire and accept.

CHAPTER 10

The Resurrection

SIR EDWYN HOSKYNS habitually began
his lectures on the theology and ethics of
the New Testament with the scriptural passages about
Christ's resurrection. Generally the plan is to trace first
the beginnings of the ministry of Jesus, the events of His
life, and the words of His teaching, and then to dwell
climactically upon Calvary. The resurrection is added to
confirm the gospel message. But this is not Biblical.

Without the resurrection the plan of redemption is not
merely a truncated gospel, it is not a gospel at all. Jesus, to
be sure, taught and did great things. The disciples might
have rested in these teachings and in the Master's incom-
parable performance. But had they done so, the dilemma,
doubt, and darkness that assailed them would have remained.
Christ's resurrection threw light backward upon the death
and the ministry that went before; it illuminated the paradoxes and disclosed the unity of His work and message.
Scott Holland states it in these words:

"In the resurrection it was not only the Lord who
was raised from the dead. His life on earth rose with him;
it was lifted up into its real light." [1]

---

[1] Scott Holand, *On Behalf of Belief*, p. 12.

Very evidently the apostles did not build their message upon the words and works of Jesus apart from the climax of Calvary, Easter, and Pentecost. Mighty works had asserted the pre-eminence of the Messiah. The sick were healed; demons were exorcised; the maimed, deaf, dumb, and blind were restored; the hungry were fed; sinners knew the experience of forgiveness—these had their place, but neither teaching nor mighty works had dealt a fatal blow to man's two enemies—sin and death. This mighty blow required the death of the Messiah and His resurrection. Thus, through this resurrection Christians came to know "the exceeding greatness of his [God's] power to us-ward who believe, according to that working of the strength of his might which he wrought in Christ, when he raised him from the dead." [2]

From the start this message of the resurrection was the newest and most startling thing in history. Yet, the first Christians attached the utmost importance to its connection with the Scriptures of the Old Testament. This connection is still affirmed in the Eucharistic Creed, "And the third day he rose again according to the Scriptures"; and it was based on apostolic teaching. Paul wrote to the Christians in Corinth to remind them of what he had originally taught them, hastening to make it clear that his teaching did not originate with himself. He had "received" the form of it from the story of the event, "how that Christ died for our sins according to the scriptures; and that he was buried; and that he hath been raised on the third day according to the scriptures; and that he appeared to Cephas; then to the twelve." [3]

The events of the gospel were to be understood as the fulfillment of the ancient Scriptures. Only thus could they be truly understood. So it was that the resurrection

---

[2] Epistle to the Ephesians, ch. 1, vs. 19, 20, R.V.
[3] First Epistle to the Corinthians, ch. 15, vs. 3-5, R.V.

ent the apostles to the Holy Scriptures. It was there alone
that they could find the significance of this tremendous
vent and its relation to the agelong purposes of God. They
ound there, too, the Old Testament teaching regarding
. literal resurrection of the body of the dead.

In the days of the patriarchs the certainty of a resurrection sustained the hope of God's children. When
Abraham offered up Isaac he was convinced that "God is
ble to raise up, even from the dead; from whence he did
lso in a parable receive him back."[4] In that early period
belief was expressed in a phrase like to "sleep with thy
athers."[5] Sleep presumes an awakening; likewise a burial
mplied a resurrection. The Epistle to the Hebrews speaks
f the women whose dead were raised to life again.[6] Then
he prophet Daniel taught that at the end of the age there
vould be a resurrection of bodies from the dust of the
arth.[7]

Certainly faith in the resurrection of the dead is in
he Old Testament. In an exhaustive study of this subject Edmund Jacobs substantiates fully this view. He summarizes
Old Testament teaching in three points:[8]

1. The God of the Old Testament is the eternal, ever-
living God. 2. Death came as a consequence of sin. 3. If
edemption is to have complete victory over sin and death,
t must ultimately come through the resurrection from
eath. So when Christ rose from death the disciples leaped
o the belief that in this event the Scriptures had been
ulfilled and the doctrine of the resurrection of the dead
onfirmed. The rejoicing apostles proclaimed their belief
ar and near; nor did they so much as falter in this belief.

It should be emphasized here that the theology of the

---

[4] Epistle to the Hebrews, ch. 11, v. 19, R.V.
[5] See Book of Deuteronomy, ch. 31, v. 16; First Book of Kings, ch. 1,
. 21.
[6] Epistle to the Hebrews, ch. 11, v. 35.
[7] Book of Daniel, ch. 12, v. 2.
[8] See Edmund Jacobs, *Theology of the Old Testament*, pp. 308-315.

apostles sprang not from their own theorizing, but from historical events which led them to beliefs far removed many times from their own preconceived notions. The most significant of those events was the resurrection. And clearly the apostles' message rested upon a *resurrection* as distinct from a *survival*. The distinction is essential.

Emphasizing this point, A. M. Ramsey, Archbishop of York, has said:

"The distinction is big and important, between a resurrection and the survival of an immortal soul. In the Platonist doctrine of immortality the body dies, but the soul continues its life. Thus, really and essentially, there is no death for that aspect of man that is deemed to be of eternal importance; the truth is that 'in the sight of the unwise they seem to have died.' Very different is a belief . . . that death is real with no semblance attaching to it, that Resurrection is the raising from out of death."

Thus the central theme of the apostolic teaching is bound up with the belief not that Jesus spiritually survived, but that Jesus was raised. Three essential points can be established:

1. Christ truly died. He experienced the total gamut of death in all its bitterness. He tasted of death for sinners, making Himself vicariously one of them. Jesus took upon Himself the reality of death as the consequence of sin. Were this not so, the basic achievement of the gospel would be void and false.

2. Christ truly lives. Here primary emphasis must be placed upon the act of God in raising Him up. The Christian life is possible only in relation to both this initial act of God and the contemporary presence of Jesus through the Holy Spirit.

3. Christ, by surviving death, does not simply demonstrate that all good men survive. Christ's resurrection is far more than an illustration or example of human survival.

it is a victory uniquely won. This victory makes mankind's participation in Christ's resurrection possible.

The gospel postulates therefore as its basis this miraculous interruption of the hitherto normal workings of the order of human sinfulness. Yet, though Christ's resurrection was a miracle in relation to the law of sin and death, it is in relation to God's new order, natural, lawful, inevitable. Moreover, Christ's resurrection reveals the goal for which human nature was created and to which it will be raised when the law of the spirit of life in Christ Jesus sets men free from the law of sin and death. In a sense, therefore, the miracle of the resurrection can be understood only by those who have experienced the new creation.[9] Nor is it to be just a portent which can be shown to all as an inducement to believe. Westcott's classic words are worth quoting:

"If then the life of the risen Lord had been simply a renovation or a continuance of the former life, subject to the same conditions and necessarily destined to the same inevitable close, then the experience of unbelievers would have been sufficient to test, the witness of unbelievers would have been adequate to establish the reality of the resurrection. But it was a foreshadowing of new powers of human action, of a new mode of human being. Then without a corresponding power of spiritual discernment there could be no testimony to its truth. The world could not see Christ, and Christ could not—there is a divine impossibility—show Himself to the world. To approve by incontestible evidence that Christ rose again as Lazarus rose again, would have been not to confirm our faith but to destroy it irretrievably."[10]

To be sure, the resurrection of Jesus must be spiritually understood by the spiritual-minded child of God. How-

---

[9] See Chapter 14, Regeneration.
[10] B. F. Westcott, *Revelation of the Risen Lord,* pp. 11, 12.

ever, the historical evidence of Christ's resurrection is clear. An apologist could make a mistake by seeking to prove the resurrection and basing his conclusions exclusively on that proof. Historical critics can miss wide the point when they investigate historical documents without due appreciation of the theology with which the resurrection was linked. But let this not imply the need for neglect of what we would call the "direct evidence" involved in the Jerusalem events. Then, let us look next at this direct evidence.

First, it is necessary to note that Christ's resurrection was not expected. The New Testament story suggests that neither the Scriptures nor the words of Jesus had broken through the impenetrable wall of misunderstanding that surrounded the disciples to lead them to a conviction that Jesus would rise again. The predictions by Jesus of His passion seem to have made a point with the disciples. But His predictions of the resurrection caused no clear expectation.[11] Mark records three predictions of the resurrection. After foretelling the passion Jesus added the words "and after three days rise again."[12] In this connection Matthew and Luke use the words "on the third day."[13] Mark depicts the disciples on this occasion "questioning among themselves what the rising again from the dead should mean."[14] There were other allusions to the rising again from the dead. "Howbeit," the Master had said, "after I am raised up, I will go before you to Galilee."[15] Then the sojourn of Jesus in the earth is likened to the sojourn of Jonah for three days and nights in the belly of the whale.[16] There was also the saying recorded in John's Gospel, "De-

---

[11] Gospel according to Mark, ch. 9, v. 31.
[12] *Ibid.*, ch. 8, v. 31; ch. 9, v. 31; ch. 10, v. 34.
[13] Gospel according to Matthew, ch. 16, v. 21; Gospel according to Luke, ch. 9, v. 22.
[14] Gospel according to Mark, ch. 9, v. 10, R.V.
[15] *Ibid.*, ch. 14, v. 28, R.V.
[16] Gospel according to Matthew, ch. 12, v. 40.

stroy this temple, and in three days I will raise it up." [17]
Certainly Jesus had talked with His disciples about this
great event. Yet the implications and the manner of it, and
even the fact, were not grasped. Very evidently the disciples were not anticipating the resurrection. It is possible
to dismiss at the outset, therefore, any view that their belief in it sprang from a projection of their own expecta-
tions.

Second, look at the history of the church following the
catastrophe of Good Friday, when the Master was laid in
Joseph's new tomb. The result of the arraignment and the
crucifixion was a scattered, fearful, dejected group of
men. They barely managed to survive what they considered
to be a total disaster. What happened that could change
the disciples from survivors of a cause that was broken
and crushed, into apostles who could bid the nation to repent and be baptized in the name of Christ and could
proclaim even the crucifixion itself to be a part of God's
good news?

That is a question that no thinking individual can
avoid. Some have advanced the hypothesis that the disciples were led to imagine this event by the projection of
their own hopes and preconceptions. But their hopes were
shattered, and their preconceptions were in the opposite
direction. Belief in the resurrection stretched the disciples
far beyond their own presuppositions, turning them upside down. Had the personality of Jesus so gripped them,
and had His teachings so influenced them that they were
unable to think of Him as dead and gone and were convinced that He lived on? This hypothesis is shattered by
the fact that the personality and teaching of Jesus did not
become the center of the apostolic preaching. This place
was occupied by the cross, the resurrection, and the return

---

[17] Gospel according to John, ch. 2, vs. 18, 19.

to this earth of the ascended Lord. Nor did the teaching and ministry of Jesus provide the disciples with a "message." They had been engrossed in puzzle and paradox until the resurrection gave the master key to the Messiah's work. In fact, Christ's claim to proclaim and to embody the kingdom of God breaks down in deceit or failure if Calvary is the end. Thus, without the resurrection both the problem of Jesus and the problem of the church are unexplainable.

Again, note the impact of the Christian message, after the resurrection and departure of Christ, upon the religious experience of countless Palestinians—among them Saul of Tarsus. In this case the impact began while Saul was persecuting the disciples of the crucified Jesus. The record reveals a complete reversal on the part of this man. His entire relationship to God as well as to Christ was revolutionized. Soon he began to think of himself and of the world in entirely different terms. This revolution he ascribed to an undesired and unexpected act of Christ: "For neither did I receive it from man, nor was I taught it, but it came to me through revelation of Jesus Christ." [18] "I was apprehended by Christ Jesus." [19]

Now this testimony cannot be dismissed, for it is corroborated by the testimony of other apostles and of countless millions of dedicated Christians from that day until this. This revolution was not related to a narrow field of religion or emotion, but to the whole of life. Without the fact of the resurrection, this would be unthinkable. Paul was apprehended by the *risen* Christ. No one else.

Then, of course, there is evidence that Jesus appeared to the disciples. Paul's statements about himself contain this evidence, as do the narratives in the Gospels. The case

---

[18] Epistle to the Galatians, ch. 1, v. 12, R.V.
[19] Epistle to the Philippians, ch. 3, v. 12, R.V.

of Paul is conclusive. The apostle distinguishes the appearance of the risen Jesus to him from "visions and revelations of the Lord." In one of these visions he was caught up into the third heaven.[20] This was an ineffable experience and it was God's way to instruct him. But Paul speaks in a totally different manner about the claim that at the beginning of his discipleship he saw Jesus. It was an appearance of Jesus akin to the appearances to the other disciples. "Am I not an apostle? . . . have I not seen Jesus Christ?"[21] He could not be uncertain about the appearance of Jesus which was the basis of his apostolic mission and authority.

Paul refers also to the appearance of Jesus to the eleven disciples and to others. Recording the primitive tradition he wrote: "[Christ] appeared to Cephas; then to the twelve; then he appeared to above five hundred brethren at once, of whom the greater part remain until now, but some are fallen asleep; then he appeared to James; then to all the apostles; and last of all, as unto one born out of due time, he appeared to me also."[22] Preceding this, the apostle summed up the historical events that were to find their place more fully in the Gospel narrative when he said "that Christ died . . . ; and that he was buried; and that he rose again the third day."[23]

Died, buried, raised—certainly this was apostolic belief. Paul does not mention the empty tomb; but this objection was long ago answered by Lake: "Was there any reason why St. Paul should have supplied these details had he known them? Surely not. He was not trying to convince the Corinthians that the Lord was risen: he was reminding them that he had already convinced them."[24]

[20] Second Epistle to the Corinthians, ch. 12, v. 2.
[21] First Epistle to the Corinthians, ch. 9, v. 1.
[22] *Ibid.*, ch. 15, vs. 5-8, R.V.
[23] *Ibid.*, vs. 3, 4.
[24] Kirsopp Lake, *Historical Evidence for the Resurrection of Jesus Christ*, p. 194.

Such are the main factors in the evidence for the resurrection. And after all, why should it be so hard to believe? To be sure, the resurrection of Jesus establishes all the other doctrinal affirmations of the Christian faith, including those that pertain to our own ultimate destiny. All the Gospel writers make the fact of Christ's resurrection the climax and conclusion of their narratives. In His first postresurrection appearances the full emphasis of Christ's discourse and conduct was the fact that He had risen from the dead. Apostles were chosen because they were witnesses to this resurrection. It was the basic theme of apostolic preaching, as the Book of Acts makes clear. By setting forth proofs of this miracle, the church was able to shake the foundations of the ancient religions then predominant in the Mediterranean world.

In the New Testament Epistles the deity of Christ, the certainty of His coming to judge the world, and the hope of our resurrection are related almost exclusively to the fact of His resurrection. Remove the truth of the resurrection from the New Testament and the whole doctrinal structure collapses—likewise hope vanishes. Thus, once again our hope is in Christ. For every one who identifies his existence with Jesus, death has been forever changed. It is no longer the end of everything, a terrible and adamant finality. It is merely a sleep, or rest—a little nap, as it were, on the road to eternity. The Christian's life is hid with Christ in God, and "when Christ, who is our life, shall appear, then shall ye also appear with him in glory." [25]

Of Christian believers who had died, Paul wrote, "But I would not have you to be ignorant, brethren, concerning them which are asleep, that ye sorrow not, even as others which have no hope." [26] Christians may sorrow but not hopelessly. They have hope that the sleepers will awake.

---

[25] Epistle to the Colossians, ch. 3, v. 4.
[26] First Epistle to the Thessalonians, ch. 4, v. 13.

In sleep, time is unmeasured. Mental activity is suspended for the time being. So it will seem to those who sleep in Christ. They close their eyes in this world, and open them in the glorious morning of Christ's return, the morning of the resurrection. The "resurrection of the dead" is the portal to life eternal.

This resurrection is necessary. It is the only way to eternal life, because of the nature of man. Man is not merely a spirit, but is at least a three-dimensional being: spirit, soul, and body. It was in the beginning, at his creation, that God breathed into man's body the breath of life and he became a "living soul." [27] The time will come when those who have fallen asleep in death will awake to life immortal. "Thy dead men shall live," declared the prophet, "together with my dead body shall they arise. Awake and sing, ye that dwell in dust: for . . . the earth shall cast out the dead." [28] That will be the day of glorious satisfaction. "As for me, I will behold thy face in righteousness," David prophesied: "I shall be satisfied, when I awake, with thy likeness." [29]

Of the condition of those in the sleep of death it is written, "The living know that they shall die: but the dead know not any thing." [30] "In that very day his thoughts perish." [31] Even the holy men of old did not ascend to heaven at death; they are waiting for the resurrection day. We read: "For David is not ascended into the heavens." [32] The fact that his sepulcher was still in Jerusalem, unopened, was offered as proof that he had not yet gone to heaven. [33] "If a man die, shall he live again?" Job wrote. "All the days of my appointed time will I wait, until my change

---

[27] Book of Genesis, ch. 2, v. 7.
[28] Book of Isaiah, ch. 26, v. 19.
[29] Psalm 17, v. 15.
[30] Book of Ecclesiastes, ch. 9, v. 5.
[31] Psalm 146, v. 4.
[32] Book of Acts, ch. 2, v. 34.
[33] *Ibid.*, v. 29.

come." [34] At that day, affirmed Saint Paul, "This corruptible must put on incorruption, and this mortal must put on immortality. . . . Then shall be brought to pass the saying that is written, Death is swallowed up in victory." [35]

Yes, "victory," as the apostle Paul put it, depended upon the resurrection of the dead—that is, on the resurrection of Jesus Christ. But when will the resurrection of the righteous dead take place? Paul made this clear too: "For the Lord himself shall descend from heaven with a shout, with the voice of the archangel, and with the trump of God: and the dead in Christ shall rise first." [36] It is at the second coming of Christ that all the dead in Christ rise glorified "to meet the Lord in the air." Adds the Scripture, "So shall we ever be with the Lord." [37]

It was of this glorious experience which is to come to all God's sleeping saints that the apostle Paul wrote to the Philippians. Speaking of himself, he said, "For I am in a strait betwixt two, having desire to depart, and to be with Christ; which is far better." "For me to live is Christ, and to die is gain." [38] The apostle was inclined to the side of life because, he says, "To abide in the flesh is more needful for you." [39] The good he could do for the Christian cause inclined him to desire to stay and work rather than to depart and to be with Christ. We might ask how would it be better for the apostle to depart, rather than to live on, since he would await in the tomb until the resurrection? The answer is, of course, that no knowledge of lapse of time comes to those who are asleep in Christ, unconscious in death. Though a thousand or two thousand years should elapse before Paul's resurrection, it would seem to him as but the twinkling of an eye. Priestley put it nicely: "The

[34] Book of Job, ch. 14, v. 14.
[35] First Epistle to the Corinthians, ch. 15, vs. 53, 54.
[36] First Epistle to the Thessalonians, ch. 4, v. 16.
[37] *Ibid.*, v. 17.
[38] Epistle to the Philippians, ch. 1, vs. 23, 21.
[39] *Ibid.*, v. 24.

apostle, considering his own situation, would naturally connect the end of this life with the commencement of another and better, as he would have no perception of any interval between them."

H. M. S. Richards told the story on the Voice of Prophecy weekly broadcast how some years ago a man found a Spanish coin in Florida. It bore the date 1796 and the Latin words *Plus Ultra*. There was a time when the legend of the coins of Spain bore one more word: *Ne Plus Ultra*. Why was it changed? In those early days Spain controlled both sides of the Straits of Gibraltar, and the two promontories, one on the African shore and the other on the European shore, were called the Pillars of Hercules. The coins were stamped with a representation of these two great outposts of the Western world, at that time the last known habitable part of the earth toward the west. On the scroll over the Pillars of Hercules appeared the words, *Ne Plus Ultra*—"No More Beyond." But when Columbus sailed into the western horizon and discovered the New World, everything changed. Spain became a mighty empire, with lands beyond the sea. The great New World lay beyond. Then the legend on her coins was changed to *Plus Ultra* —"More Beyond."

Without God's plan of salvation centered in Christ, despair must be written over the graves of men. A fitting epitaph would be, "No more beyond." But God came to us and brought life and immortality to light through the gospel. From Joseph's new tomb, where Christ was buried and from which He rose again, the light shone forth. Now on the memorial of every child of God faith writes, "More beyond."

The old world of hopelessness and despair and night is behind us; the new world of faith and immortality stretches beyond the sea of death. Christ rose; He lives; therefore, we too shall live.

CHAPTER 11

Time

$\mathcal{A}$ LOOK AT history indicates that man has oc cupied this earth for some six thousand years. Is he at the beginning of his lease, or is his occupancy about to draw to an end?

Naturally, in answering such a question, opposing views are entertained and expressed. Some claim that it is impossible to know the future; that the future is en shrouded in mystery. Others, basing their opinion on some interpretation of geology, arrive at the conclusion that humanity will still be here, in more or less the same state, for hundreds of millions of years. Then, too, we have the prophetic forecasts of Holy Scripture. Numerous recorded predictions have come to pass in countless de tails, yet inveterate human bias tends to discount the claims of God's Word.

But, after all, why should there be the slightest preju dice against the study of Bible prophecy? Time is an es sential factor in varied areas of human thought and activ ity; as essential, in fact, as the law of cause and effect. The teachings of God's Word recognize time as well as cause and effect, associating both elements closely in the divine program.

Now, the viewpoint of Holy Scripture is clear: the

present state of the world will come to an end when Jesus Christ appears the second time. To be sure, "the day and the hour" are to remain unknown.[1] This does not mean, however, that nothing concerning the approximate time of Christ's second coming can be known. In the days preceding Christ's coming, the children of God are to be "children of light." This means that they will possess enough special light or knowledge to know when the coming Christ will be "near, even at the doors."[2]

Man's present curiosity about the times in which he lives is not a mere wonderment of the passing hour. Men and women sensitive to divine leadership often have been preoccupied by the march of time. One day Jesus discussed with His disciples His second coming and the end of the world. Very soon this question was asked: "Tell us, when shall these things be? and what shall be the sign?"[3] Jesus answered this question, which proves that He found it legitimate. After His resurrection, the disciples renewed their query in a much more insistent vein: "Lord," they asked of the risen Christ, "wilt thou at this time restore again the kingdom to Israel?"[4] In fact, the attitude of the disciples was well in keeping with good tradition. The apostle Peter tells us that the ancient prophets themselves made inquiry, "searching what, or what manner of time the Spirit of Christ which was in them did signify, when it testified beforehand the sufferings of Christ, and the glory that should follow."[5]

In one of his visions the prophet Daniel recounts that he heard an angel inquire of a celestial companion, "How long shall it be to the end of these wonders?"[6] Then, in

---

[1] Gospel according to Matthew, ch. 25, v. 13.
[2] First Epistle to the Thessalonians, ch. 5, vs. 4, 5; Gospel according to Matthew, ch. 24, v. 33.
[3] Gospel according to Matthew, ch. 24, v. 3.
[4] Book of Acts, ch. 1, v. 6.
[5] First Epistle of Peter, ch. 1, v. 11.
[6] Book of Daniel, ch. 12, v. 6.

another vision Daniel heard this question asked: "How long shall it be to the end of these wonders?"[7] Then, in inquiries, making it clear that God acknowledges a proper desire to understand the sequence of time. In fact, He has answered all these inquiries in four clear, understandable forms:

1. By time prophecies in which literal periods of years express future events in a sequence.

2. By prophetic pictures in which the great events of the future are outlined, including the rise and fall of empires.

3. By long periods of time in which a "day" may be taken to signify a year of time.

4. By descriptive characteristics that are to mark society at the end of history, known throughout the Scriptures as the "signs of the times."

It will suffice here to mention with scriptural reference three illustrations of the first category.

Because of the wickedness of man and the necessity to start again with the human race, God determined to bring upon the world a flood, out of which He was to save one family and the necessary animal and vegetable life to ensure this new deal for man. God revealed His plan to Noah, His servant, and announced to him that the world would endure yet one hundred and twenty years; then God's purpose would find fulfillment.[8] The destruction of the world by flood and the new start came exactly at the time foretold.

To Abraham, God announced that his descendants would descend into Egypt, where they would serve as strangers and would be oppressed for a period of "four hundred years."[9] That forecast, too, was fulfilled literally.

---

[7] Book of Daniel, ch. 8, v. 13.
[8] Book of Genesis, ch. 6, v. 3.
[9] *Ibid.*, ch. 15, v. 13.

The people of Israel marched out of Egypt into the Promised Land, says the record, "the selfsame day" God's plan came to the time of fulfillment.[10] Saint Paul in the book of Galatians (ch. 3:17) speaks of this as a 430-year period, but his calculation was based on an earlier beginning of the period.

Some centuries later, the people of God who had chosen to carry out His purposes fell into apostasy again. God delivered them into the hands of their enemies, marking clearly, however, that the Israelites would "serve the king of Babylon seventy years."[11] This "Babylonian captivity" began with the capture of Jerusalem by the Babylonians in the year 606/605 B.C. and closed seventy years later as predicted, in 537/536 B.C. Under Cyrus, the Israelites were released and led back to Palestine. Such historical events are typical of specific time prophecies of the Bible that have found a literal fulfillment.

Then, illustrative of the second category of predictions are the panoramic views of the future portrayed by the prophet Daniel. In chapter two of his book, the history of the world is represented by a great metal image. The image is in part made of gold, in part of silver, in part of brass, in part of iron, and in part a mixture of iron and clay. The head of gold led the succession of empires and symbolized Babylon, the ruling world power in Daniel's day. Speaking to Nebuchadnezzar, who had seen this great image in a dream, Daniel said, "Thou art this head of gold."[12] But this "head of gold" came to an end and "Darius the Median took the kingdom."[13] Cyrus the Persian led the successful attack in overthrowing Babylon 537/536 years before Christ—more than 50 years after Daniel's prophecy. Medo-Persia, represented by the image's breast and arms of silver,

[10] Book of Exodus, ch. 12, v. 41.
[11] Book of Jeremiah, ch. 25, v. 11.
[12] Book of Daniel, ch. 2, v. 38.
[13] *Ibid.*, ch. 5, v. 31.

then began to rule. Daniel had said to Nebuchadnezzar, "After thee shall arise another kingdom." Medo-Persia was that kingdom.[14]

This second kingdom was in supremacy for some two hundred years. But it also was to give way to another—a "third kingdom of brass, which shall bear rule over all the earth."[15] This third universal kingdom was Greece. How well we remember the maps of these nations as we studied them in history classes! Greece was led to her zenith of power by Alexander the Great, the son of a Macedonian king. He reached the deciding point over the Medo-Persians at the famous battle of Arbela in 331 B.C., more than 200 years after Babylon's fall.

In five short years Alexander swept to victory at the age of twenty-five. Seven years later he was dead. At the age of thirty-two, like a meteor in the night, his light suddenly went out. The decisive battle of Pydna, 168 B.C., is often given as a definite point in Greece's decline. The brass kingdom was finished.

"The fourth kingdom" continued Daniel, "shall be strong as iron: forasmuch as iron breaketh in pieces and subdueth all things: and as iron that breaketh all these, shall it break in pieces and bruise."[16]

Nebuchadnezzar listened in amazement at this thumbnail sketch of world history. And well he could for iron Rome did come upon the scene of action. Hippolytus, who lived from about A.D. 170 to A.D. 236, wrote: "Rejoice, blessed Daniel! thou hast not been in error . . . already the iron rules." He spoke of Rome. Referring to this, Gibbon wrote: "The images of gold, or silver, or brass, that might serve to represent the nations and their kings, were successively broken by the 'iron monarchy of Rome.'"

---

[14] *Ibid.*, ch. 2, v. 39.
[15] *Ibid.*
[16] *Ibid.*, v. 40.

This "iron monarchy" continued, as is well known, under various forms of government and through multiplied vicissitudes, until A.D. 476. Rome was to be divided, and it was, into the ten parts represented by the toes of the image's feet. The modern nations of Europe developed from these divisions. Some were to be strong and some weak.[17] And so they have been. This plurality of states, large and small, was to continue until the God of heaven would set up a kingdom that would never be destroyed. The prophecy stated that "the kingdom shall not be left to other people, but it shall break in pieces and consume all these kingdoms, and it shall stand for ever." [18]

In chapter seven Daniel records a prophecy that covers in general the same ground as the story of the metalic image. The same empires appear on the scene, but in the form of four wild beasts. The Babylonians were represented by a lion, the Medo-Persians by a bear, the Greeks by a leopard, and the Romans by a nondescript beast with teeth of iron and carrying ten horns on his head, marking the division of the empire into ten separate countries.

Here an eleventh power adds its might to the first ten by plucking up and destroying three predecessors. Twenty distinct details indicate that this "little horn," which had eyes like the eyes of man, and a mouth speaking great things," [19] forecasts the great politico-religious power that succeeded Rome in the leadership of Europe. This power, as many commentators for centuries have consistently agreed, could only point to the dominant role assumed by the Vatican.

Daniel's chapter eight unveils another prophetic fresco of the world's empires. This vision dates from the fall of Babylon and deals only with the last three universal

---

[17] *Ibid.*, vs. 41, 42.
[18] *Ibid.*, v. 44.
[19] *Ibid.*, ch. 7, v. 8.

empires. The first symbol is that of a two-horned ram
standing by the banks of a river. The ram represented,
according to the angel's word to the prophet, the empire
of the Medes and Persians. The second symbol was a he
goat that "came from the west," [20] and performed with
such speed that it hardly touched the earth in its fast-moving course. It carried a great horn between its two eyes.
The he-goat cast down and broke the preceding kingdom. "The rough goat is the king of Grecia: and the great
horn that is between his eyes is the first king," said Daniel. [21]

This prophecy is of great simplicity. It summarizes
the history of two world empires—Medo-Persia and
Greece, highlighting the role of Alexander the Great. But
soon the great horn was broken and gave place to four
distinct horns. Thus the Greek power broke into four kingdoms. From one of these horns emerges a "little horn, which
waxed exceeding great, toward the south, and toward the
east, and toward the glorious land." [22] This portrays again
the Roman Empire and its conquests in the West. Again
Western Rome is succeeded by a politico-religious power
that was to lead the nations for centuries on end.

If we look carefully at these prophetic pictures, it is
not difficult to discover that the empires foretold have
come and gone; that the divisions and influences forecast
are still with us, though well on the way to the end of their
course. The major part of these great events have been
fulfilled. According to these same prophecies world history
is fast approaching a grand finale.

God has used another means to instruct us regarding
the times in which we live. These are prophetic periods
that begin at a precise date, continue through events
firmly substantiated in historical fact, and extend on to a

[20] *Ibid.*, ch. 8, v. 5.
[21] *Ibid.*, v. 21.
[22] *Ibid.*, v. 9, R.V.

well-marked conclusion. These time periods are set down in symbolic days, each day having the value of a year. "Each day for a year" [23] was a guide line that had come down from days of old. The prophet Ezekiel understood this principle. The revealing angel instructed him, "I have appointed thee each day for a year." [24]

Let us use this key to unlock the treasure house of predictions that Daniel, a few years younger than Ezekiel (who also lived in Babylonia), has left us in his vision of the four wild animals. Speaking of the "little horn" that had the eyes and mouth of a man, Daniel said his career would last "a time and times and the dividing of time." [25] The significance of this formula is explained in the Revelation, where it is marked as "three days and an half," or "forty and two months." [26] During this period God's faithful would be trodden underfoot. The same chapter eleven of the Revelation explains these two periods of time by a third formula, that of the "thousand two hundred and threescore days" [27] during which the "two witnesses"—the Old Testament and the New Testament—would prophesy "clothed in sackcloth," that is, in obscurity under proscription.

In the Revelation, chapter twelve, this formula of one thousand two hundred sixty days is also used in the story of the Christian church. There God's true people, symbolized by a pure woman, flee to the desert to be hidden for one thousand two hundred sixty days of duress. The same formula returns in chapter thirteen, where a leopard beast, representing the same power, would continue its depredations through "forty-two months," or one thousand two hundred sixty days.

---

[23] Book of Numbers, ch. 14, v. 34.
[24] Book of Ezekiel, ch. 4, v. 6.
[25] Book of Daniel, ch. 7, v. 25.
[26] Book of the Revelation, ch. 11, vs. 11, 2; ch. 13, v. 5.
[27] *Ibid.*, ch. 11, v. 3.

9

PAINTING BY HARRY BAERG

457 B.C.—The 2300 years of Daniel's prophecy began with the decree of Artaxerxes, king of Persia, which restored national government to the Jews.

A.D. 27.—Jesus was anointed by the Holy Spirit at His baptism, at the end of the sixty-nine weeks of the prophecy, and then began His ministry.

A.D. 31.—Three and one-half years later, Jesus the Mes-

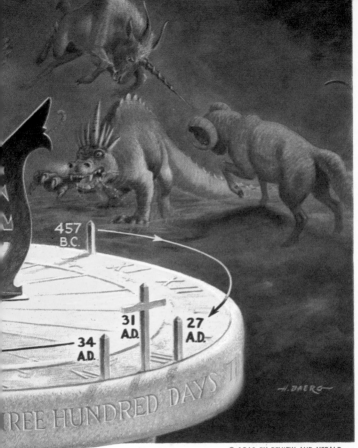

457 B.C.

31 A.D.

27 A.D.

34 A.D.

REE HUNDRED DAYS T

siah was cut off. For three and one-half years more His disciples preached only to the Jews.

A.D. 34.—The stoning of Stephen resulted in the spread of the gospel to the Gentiles, marking the close of the seventy weeks of prophecy.

A.D. 1844.—When the twenty-three hundred years ended, the cleansing of the sanctuary, the judgment of investigation, began in heaven above.

We have three precise periods, therefore, indicated by "three days and an half," "forty and two months," or "a thousand two hundred and threescore days," all meaning one thousand two hundred sixty years.

History tells us that the politico-religious power which succeeded Rome on the Tiber, received authority to "punish heretics" in a decree issued by Emperor Justinian, a decree which went into effect in A.D. 538. From that date forward the oppression of conscience and the molesting of nonconformists continued with varied intensity until the French Revolution. In 1798 the French *Directoire* charged General Berthier to seize Rome. He took the pope captive to France, where the latter died eighteen months later. This catastrophe in the career of the Vatican is characterized by the revelator as the "deadly wound." [28] The wound was to be healed; but the event marked the end of the one thousand two hundred sixty years. The prophetic period thus met literal fulfillment.

Daniel furnishes information on yet another prophetic period—again in chapter eight. Here three symbols represent the Medo-Persian, Greek, and Roman empires. The prophetic outline deals particularly with the third, which was first Pagan Rome, then Christian Rome. The successor to the Roman Empire did two things in particular that were reprehensible. He "magnified himself" and "cast down the truth to the ground." Then the prophet heard a voice inquiring, "'For how long is the vision concerning the continual burnt offering, the transgression that makes desolate, and the giving over of the sanctuary and host to be trampled under foot?'" The reply was direct and introduced a master key to Bible prophecy: "'For two thousand and three hundred evenings and mornings; then the sanctuary shall be restored to its rightful state.'" [29]

28 *Ibid.,* ch. 13, v. 3.
29 Book of Daniel, ch. 8, vs. 13, 14, R.S.V.

This prophetic period of two thousand three hundred days stands, of course, for two thousand three hundred years. The starting point is given in the following chapter in connection with another prophetic period—the 'seventy weeks," or four hundred ninety years, which was the first segment of the total two thousand three hundred years. These first four hundred ninety years were set apart for the Jews, while the remaining period was that of the Gentiles, or nations.[30]

The four hundred ninety years, according to the prophecy, began with the decree that would be given to order the restoration of Jerusalem. The Babylonians had destroyed Jerusalem; the Medo-Persians were to help restore it. This is recounted by Ezra: "They builded, and finished it, according to the commandment of the God of Israel, and according to the commandment of Cyrus, and Darius, and Artaxerxes king of Persia." [31]

It really was God's commandment that counted, and it took the command of three kings before God counted it as the one effective commandment to rebuild. Thus it was in 457 B.C. that the final command to rebuild Jerusalem was given by Artaxerxes in the seventh year of his reign. Incidentally, that date is one of the best established in the history of antiquity. It was corroborated by a series of eclipses, mentioned in the canon of Ptolemy. Of that date there can be no doubt.

This period of 490 years was broken up into a series of events—the first sixty-nine weeks were to reach to "Messiah the Prince," the "anointed one." Jesus was anointed by the Holy Spirit at the time of His baptism, and went forth as the Messiah. This was in the year A.D. 27, or 483 years after the start of the period. The last week (seven years) was allotted to the ministry of Christ. It

---

[30] Book of Daniel, ch. 9.
[31] Book of Ezra, ch. 6, v. 14.

was in the midst of that week that the Messiah would be
cut off by death—and He was, in 31 A.D. At the end of
the next three and a half years, the time allotted to the
Jewish people was to terminate. It did, for in A.D. 34 the
disciples turned to the nations of the world with God's
good news.[32]

The total period of two thousand three hundred years,
starting in 457 B.C., ended in A.D. 1844. Of this terminal
point Daniel said there is a "time appointed" for the end.[33]
The importance of this great date will be further emphasized as we look at what God had in mind when
truth was to be restored and His "sanctuary" shown to be
righteous.

The fourth method in Scripture to instruct on the last
days of history was mentioned definitely by Jesus Himself.
He spoke of the "signs of the times." He outlined these
signs to His disciples as He sat on the Mount of Olives and
expounded the course of the centuries. This is reported
by the disciples who made up the record, particularly
Matthew and Luke.

Jesus proceeded to give His disciples ten great signs.
Some relate to the destruction of Jerusalem, which took
place forty years later, in A.D. 70; some refer to His second
coming; while other signs—most of them, in fact—are applicable to both events. These signs, along with those furnished by the ancient prophets and the apostles (in particular Saint Paul), marked the characteristics by which the
last days could be recognized. A person has traits that
distinguish him—the face, the build, the voice, the walk;
likewise each age or generation reveals specific traits. These
are found in culture, religion, art, science, literature, architecture, war, statesmanship, and many other aspects of
civilization.

---

[32] Book of Acts, ch. 13, v. 46.
[33] Book of Daniel, ch. 8, v. 19.

The signs of the last days can be classified under four main headings:

1. Material preparations for the end—the wild, swift pace of modern life.

2. Political preparations for the end—confusion and fear and turmoil among the nations.

3. Social preparations for the end—moral-structure decay and apostasy.

4. Religious preparations for the end—the final conflict for the soul of man.

We list these signs as "preparations for the end" because that is exactly what the true signs always are. Each condition or event not only is indicative of the approach of the end but also plays some part in preparing mankind for the final consummation. A true sign is also global—not necessarily in extent, but in meaning and implications. It must be understood and appreciated by people of every nation under heaven.

A look in depth at these signs (a look which should be taken by all)[34] will reveal pertinently the time in which we live. We find ourselves on the final frontiers of prophecy. Of all that was predicted by the mighty seers of old, by Jesus Himself, and by the apostles, little remains to be fulfilled. The great highways of prophecy, which have circled the mountains and crossed the valleys of history for more than two millenniums, are about to plunge from time into eternity. The last events are upon us.

These signs must be studied attentively in the light of Bible and fact. Simple curiosity is not enough. We need to give our full attention to these matters in order to know and to be prepared, and not to bring upon us the reproach that Jesus addressed to the people of His time, "Ye can discern the face of the sky; but can ye not discern

---

[34] See H. M. S. Richards, *What Jesus Said*, pp. 159-207; Arthur E. Liçkey, *God Speaks to Modern Man*, pp. 225-265.

the signs of the times?" Jesus accompanied this reproach with the following statement on the reason for the "signs of the times" and other prophetic indications:

"He spake to them a parable; Behold the fig tree, and all the trees; when they now shoot forth, ye see and know of your own selves that summer is now nigh at hand. So likewise ye, when ye see these things come to pass, know ye that the kingdom of God is nigh at hand. Verily I say unto you, This generation shall not pass away, till all be fulfilled. Heaven and earth shall pass away: but my words shall not pass away. And take heed to yourselves, lest at any time your hearts be overcharged with surfeiting, and drunkenness, and cares of this life, and so that day come upon you unawares." [35]

Prophecies of the Old Testament told men that Christ's first coming was near. Likewise, the Old Testament and the New warn men of His second coming. Before Christ's first advent to this earth He had, through His prophets, declared the very year in which He would be baptized and begin His ministry after being anointed by the Holy Spirit. The exact time of His crucifixion was also revealed. Had God's people in these times believed the Holy Scriptures and profited by His divine announcements they would have expected the Messiah and they would have been prepared to receive Him. When John, the cousin of Jesus, began to preach in the wilderness of Judea, he announced with great earnestness: "Repent ye: for the kingdom of heaven is at hand." [36] He knew that the hour had struck for Christ to appear. And when our Saviour Himself was baptized by John in Jordan, He immediately began to preach: "The time is fulfilled . . . : repent ye, and believe the gospel." [37]

---

[35] Gospel according to Luke, ch. 21, vs. 29-34.
[36] Gospel according to Matthew, ch. 3, v. 2.
[37] Gospel according to Mark, ch. 1, v. 15.

At that time a small minority was watching for the fulfillment of the prophecies and was prepared to receive them, but the great masses of people were not watching; they were not waiting, and they did not receive Christ. So it is to be in the latter days, when our Saviour comes the second time. The Scripture declares that this great event will take place as a snare and as a thief in the night. It will be an overwhelming surprise to the nations of the earth. But some will not be surprised; they will be ready, watching for the "signs of the times." Yes, Jesus said, "There shall be signs." When the fig tree and all the trees put forth their leaves in the spring, we know that summer is coming—in fact, is beginning; just so surely, when we see the events take place which Jesus Himself predicted and in which prediction the apostles and prophets joined, we will know that His coming is drawing near, that a wonderful change is coming in the affairs of the earth, that an invasion is about to take place which will change the world for good in all ages to come.

For many years the "signs of the times" have been proclaimed by earnest Christians. In fact, the world-embracing Seventh-day Adventist Church was built on the evidence, revealed in Scripture and matched in present-day events, that the coming of Jesus for the second time is imminent. Have these Christians been mistaken? Not so. They beheld the first phases of an unfolding revelation, the first streaks of light before the dawn, the first muted notes before the grand orchestral music, the first scent of hay before the full rich odor of the harvest field. They saw the bud. Today we who have inherited their spiritual legacy can contemplate the flower. They saw the gleam of distant beacons; we see the full glow of the harbor lights.

Evidences of the coming Christ have been available since the time "appointed for the end." They have been meager in the past, but sufficient. For a hundred years

Seventh-day Adventists have felt that they were on the right track and were moving in the right direction. But today, as signs thicken about us, more numerous, more brilliant, more startling than ever before, we can know for a certainty that the coming of the Lord is nigh, "even at the doors."

The story is told of a minister in Stockton, California. He had just preached an earnest sermon on the second coming of Christ. While he was praying, a woman arose and left the sanctuary hurriedly. After he had finished the service he went to the door to greet the people, and found this woman pacing back and forth in the lobby. The moment the minister appeared, she said: "How did you dare pray as you did—'Come, come, Lord Jesus'? I don't want Him to come. It will break up all my plans. How dare you?" The minister said, "My dear friend, if you love the Lord, you will want Him to come; but He is coming whether you want Him to come or not. If you really know Him and love Him, you too certainly will say in your heart, 'Come, Lord Jesus.'"

This minister spoke well—for you and for me.

CHAPTER 12

Law

RECENTLY A fervent religionist expressed a very shallow view of God in a jubilant outburst to a friend. I happened to be standing nearby when she said triumphantly, "But, Jane, we live under grace. When Christ died, He annulled the law!"

Unthinkingly, many people today believe that Christ's death paled obedience to the Ten Commandments. Of course, they do not come out in favor of those criminal acts forbidden by God's law. They try to make amends for their antinomian attitude by vague allusions to the "commandments of Christ." These, they contend, have replaced the law of God.

A careful examination of the New Testament makes this view untenable. Read the Sermon on the Mount.[1] What does it tell you? In more penetrating words than any other oratory, it republishes what God told His children on Mount Sinai. Christ actually makes the Ten Commandments more binding and more spiritual than does the Old Testament. For instance, to the command "Thou shalt not kill" He adds that even angry words can kill. He pictures the slightest lustful look as committing

---

[1] Gospel according to Matthew, chs. 5-7.

adultery. Of the two, greater condemnation is found in the Sermon on the Mount than in the Ten Commandments.

Those who look for release from obedience to God's law look in vain, for it is not in Christ's teachings. They will find no leniency anywhere among His deeds or thoughts. The grace He offers has nothing to do with "setting aside," "getting by," or "being unbridled." Christ states with absolute authority that "whosoever therefore shall break one of these least commandments, and shall teach men so, he shall be called the least in the kingdom of heaven." [2]

Christ died for sinners, but He did not embrace sin. His death does not introduce the slightest suggestion that God's law might in any way be diminished or shorn of its original jurisdiction. Men have tried to play tricks with the law, but they have not succeeded. Moses smashed the tables of stone upon which the law was carved; Jehoiakim cut up the scroll imprinted with the law and cast it into the fire; church catechisms in variant ways have rearranged and limited certain commandments. Still, the cross stands as a silent reminder that Christ paid the price of His own life rather than change God's law one iota. Christ's broken body, unceremoniously laid away in a tomb, is irrefutable proof that the Lawgiver willingly satisfied the claims of His own unchanging law, lest the whole world perish. He "became obedient unto death, even the death of the cross" so that "he by the grace of God should taste death for every man." [3]

What kind of god could do away with his moral requirements simply because man chose to disobey them? Only a god of compromise, an unjust god, could have a part in such an arrangement. Such a god would not be

---

[2] *Ibid.*, ch. 5, v. 19.
[3] Epistle to the Philippians, ch. 2, v. 8; Epistle to the Hebrews, ch. 2, v. 9.

worthy of our worship. Nor is the requirement for obedience diminished because sin weakened man's ability to comply. God's requirements cannot be lessened without impairing God's own holiness and righteousness.

Hence, our obligation to obey God's law remains based on man's original ability which God gave him in the beginning. Created in the image of God and candidate for the kingdom of heaven, man is to be restored to his original state as a free and law-abiding citizen of God's realm.

The picture would be murky if left at that. It would leave room for little hope or happy expectation, because men have had a long history of pathological disobedience. But the plan does not end here. Something more must be said. Though God did not change His law by one hairbreadth, He did do something else to save a world of sinners. He made provision to change, not the law, but the sinner. We read that "God so loved the world, that he gave his only begotten Son, that whosoever believeth in him should not perish, but have everlasting life."[4] This promise implies a plan. Rise from your melancholy, lift up your woebegone countenance, and listen to what God has set in operation.

Through the grace of God in Christ the sinner's attitude to God and His law can be changed. The sinner need not welter in his own weakness. When he accepts God's love for him in spirit and in truth, this love will create within his heart a fervent desire to obey God's law. Once the sinner experiences true love he no longer envisions obedience merely as a parry to condemnation; he then obeys because God's love fills his heart with a power that is stronger than death. This power will give might to his will—the might it takes to obey.

This will to obey faithfully stems from the sinner's new

---

[4] Gospel according to John, ch. 3, v. 16.

attitude and his new purpose. The love of God creates a new set of objectives in his life. This is the new birth in Christ. The Scriptures describe the experience in these words: "Created in Christ Jesus unto good works." [5]

The divine impulse that converts a lawbreaker into a law keeper is nothing short of a miracle, as anyone will tell you who has experienced the change. Men with brutal passions have become gentle and kind. Women who had lost their virtue have become pure and beautiful in character. One cannot trace the exact steps of how it happens, but it happens when men and women allow God's grace to be operative in their lives. The miracle is aptly described by the apostle John: "By this we know that we love the children of God, when we love God, and keep his commandments. For this is the love of God, that we keep his commandments: and his commandments are not grievous." [6]

As we study God's character we find that it allows for no cleavage between grace and the law. Both grace and law are part of God's nature. In God these two immense qualities are interwoven forever, adding beauty to the stature of a God high and lifted up. But when law and grace are torn asunder, man is left with a god stripped to fickle sentimentality.

The psalmist cried out in rapture, "O how love I thy law! it is my meditation all the day." [7] Is this ecstasy merely the result of a morbid sense of self-punishment? Today many would assent. When they think of the law, they set their jaw, clench their fists, and champ the bit of unpleasant restriction. They scream for freedom; they demand license to burst all chains and to have their own self-

---

[5] Epistle to the Ephesians, ch. 2, v. 10; see our Chapter 13, The Sabbath Day.
[6] First Epistle of John, ch. 5, vs. 2, 3.
[7] Psalm 119, v. 97.

Sermon on the Mount is but the echo of the sermon flared from Mount Sinai fifteen hundred years before.

determined place in the sun. Strangely, however, the more
they rebel against God's law, the more confined, pent up
and shackled they are. True freedom exists only in the
right relationships which law describes. You either live
free within the law, or as a fettered bondman under the
broken law. The only other alternative is to accept the concept of a "flexible law"—in which case man would become
the pawn of a capricious, indiscernible, inscrutable will.

Thus the assurance that God is reliable and depend-
able lies in the truth that He is a God of law. His will
and His law are one. God says that right is right because
it describes the best possible relationships. Therefore God's
law is never arbitrary or subject to whim and fancy. It is
the most stable thing in the universe.

Note this, too—God's law is written in man's own nature. Somewhere, deep inside the being, it has been ingrained and made a part of every human being. The
writing may be dimmed and besmeared, but it is there. Nor
can anyone run away from it. No matter where you may
be, how many arguments against it you may read, or how
bitterly you may deny it, the law is there.

This means that you cannot find harmony or peace
until you are willing to be in harmony with nature upon
which God has impressed His law. Also, that as you stay
in harmony with God's nature, reflected through His law
in your own nature, you are joyful, happy, fulfilled, but
when you break away from this law you become steeped
in misery and can never be at rest.

God's law is part of us—a part of every human being
no matter on what cultural level. Paul makes this eminently
clear in his letter to the church at Rome. Writes he:

"When Gentiles who have not the law do by nature
what the law requires, they are a law to themselves, even
though they do not have the law. They show that what the
law requires is written on their hearts, while their con-

science also bears witness and their conflicting thoughts accuse or perhaps excuse them on that day when, according to my gospel, God judges the secrets of men by Christ Jesus." [8]

All right, granted that you have come to amicable terms with God, His law, and yourself. You realize that true joy comes only within God's law, and you accept the conditions. You may still be in the way of death! Though obeying sincerely what you understand the specifications of God's law to be, you could be slowly dying. How? Saint Paul considered the problem and summed it up in three words: "The letter killeth." [9]

Countless proponents and exponents of religion are religionists of the letter. Theirs is a worship of rules and regulations. Without realizing it, they are slowly suffocating and causing others to do likewise. They go to church week after week. They do not lie. They do not kill. They do not commit adultery. Their life, you might say, is as clean as a white sheet; but they are dying! The reason is that mere slavish obedience to ten directives is not enough. This makes life mechanical—turns a person into a robot, a puppet manipulated by do's and don'ts. Paul had found himself in this very predicament, and he cried out, "O wretched man that I am! who shall deliver me from the body of this death?" [10] But Paul was willing to change. From a legalist he turned into a living Christian, serving God and obeying Him from the depths of his heart. Then Paul became alive to true obedience, proclaiming exultantly, "For the law of the Spirit of life in Christ Jesus hath made me free from the law of sin and death." [11]

On the other hand, a true conception of God's law will not result in idle chatter about love and grace or in breathy

---

[8] Epistle to the Romans, ch. 2, vs. 14-16, R.S.V.
[9] Second Epistle to the Corinthians, ch. 3, v. 6.
[10] Epistle to the Romans, ch. 7, v. 24.
[11] *Ibid.*, ch. 8, v. 2.

expletives about loyalty to tradition. Union with God and His law lies in action, not in empty words, dead creeds, cabalistic signs, or symbols. Jesus said, "Not every one that saith unto me, Lord, Lord, shall enter into the kingdom of heaven; but he that *doeth the will* of my Father which is in heaven." [12]

Obeying God's law means that you are grasped by God Himself so that every act of yours is in pulsation with the Divine Spirit. Any lesser relationship is a form of idolatry. The world is sick of pious talk, hypocritical promises, or any other lip service issuing from pure inertia. *Doers* of the law are invaluable to God's kingdom. To be good is not a trite concept; in fact, it should be your divine concern in life. Halfhearted intentions are not enough. "We should serve in newness of spirit, and not in the oldness of the letter." [13] Your faith in the law must be a leap into action, not a daytime reverie.

Thus we conclude that the eternal law reveals God as unchanging in His demands for holiness, righteousness, and obedience; but we also conclude that the cross of Christ reveals the length to which God went in order to make this righteousness possible in man without abrogating His law.

Do you yearn for God's blessing? You need not torment yourself with your shortcomings; nor should you develop religious hysteria. Simply yield your life to God's holy nature and receive His blessing at once. God's law is reasonable; it poses no absurd demands on any of us. Read it as God wrote it on two tables of stone, for yourself. [14] Observe it. Then you will reason with Paul:

"Do we then make void the law through faith? God forbid: yea, we establish the law." [15]

---

[12] Gospel according to Matthew, ch. 7, v. 21.
[13] Epistle to the Romans, ch. 7, v. 6.
[14] See Book of Exodus, ch. 20, vs. 1-17.
[15] Epistle to the Romans, ch. 3, v. 31.

CHAPTER 13

The Sabbath Day

THE CLATTER and clash of our attempts to gain wisdom through things have all but eclipsed the glory of Creation's crown, the Sabbath. Yet the Sabbath is our precious heritage, the urgent answer to our daily running, screeching to a halt, and running again until we arrive nowhere, out of breath and ready to break. From a purely physical standpoint the Sabbath is an absolute necessity. Six days a week we wrestle with the world and wring our share of profit from it in order to exist. We cannot work continuously and furiously without taking a breath in between. Taking time to stretch and to rest is the natural tendency in an active body. Even athletes collect strength from a breathing spell. One scientific school of thought has suggested that the seven-day cycle with the seventh a day of rest is the natural interruption for the need for rest instilled in the body.

During the French Revolution, lawmakers in Paris tampered with the seven-day week and instituted instead a ten-day cycle. But their arrangement did not fit the needs of man or beast. It seemed even the horses in the streets broke down under this new regime. Neither could the people stand it. One writer was so impressed that he concluded Moses was inspired by some supernatural revelation to adopt the week of seven days. "In fact," he wrote, "it would be as easy to believe that Moses came upon this great principle of six days of labor and one of rest by chance as it would to believe that the *Iliad* was written by a hog scribbling with his snout."

Evidently the attempt in Paris failed conclusively. It struck upon the rock of God's devising. The seventh-day Sabbath is needful to man. Said Jesus, "The sabbath was made for man, and not man for the sabbath."[1] But beyond the physical need for repose, what is the importance of the seventh-day Sabbath?

The Sabbath is the pinnacle of God's creation. On the first six days God created matter, vegetation, and life, which together form a pattern of formidable activity. The combination equals work, worry, competition, and weariness. Then comes the seventh day. What is lacking? Something of tranquillity, serenity, peace, and repose. So God created the Sabbath.

The full difference between Sabbath and the other days of the week cannot be discerned in a physical way. They all are part of time and space. The main difference is a dimension of the spirit. On this day the atmosphere is different from that of the other six days. Even the untutored, unscholarly person, when in tune with God's Spirit, will not fail to sense the beauty and awe of this special creative act. Abraham Heschel has this to say:

"Time is like a wasteland. It has grandeur but no beauty. Its strange, frightful power is always feared but rarely cheered. Then we arrive at the seventh day, and the Sabbath is endowed with a felicity which enraptures the soul, which glides into our thoughts with a healing sympathy. It is a day whose hours do not oust one another. It is a day that can soothe all sadness away."[2]

---

[1] Gospel according to Mark, ch. 2, v. 27.
[2] A. J. Heschel, *The Sabbath*, p. 55.

Seventh-day Adventists have found delight in God's creation and have incorporated into their basic beliefs the observance of the seventh-day Sabbath. This they believe to be a dimension of salvation, for to them it is the highest expression of belief in God as the Creator of heaven and earth. The basis for this point of view was written by God into the Sabbath commandment:

"Remember the sabbath day, to keep it holy. Six days shalt thou labour, and do all thy work: but the seventh day is the sabbath of the Lord thy God: in it thou shalt not do any work, thou, nor thy son, nor thy daughter, thy manservant, nor thy maidservant, nor thy cattle, nor thy stranger that is within thy gates: for in six days the Lord made heaven and earth, the sea, and all that in them is, and rested the seventh day: wherefore the Lord blessed the sabbath day, and hallowed it." [3] Thus every recurring seventh-day Sabbath reminds believers of God's creative power; and they worship on that day in recognition of that power in their lives.

Many try to shrug off this truth by saying that a mere day in the light of eternity is unimportant, that God is too big to worry about whether or not we keep one specific day in His honor; still, if we study the Scriptures we cannot but be impressed with the Sabbath importance as a guarantee for the unity of God with His creation. Again Mr. Heschel expresses the truth with excellence:

"For where shall the likeness of God be found? There is no quality that space has in common with the essence of God. There is not enough freedom on the top of the mountain; there is not enough glory in the silence of the sea. Yet the likeness of God can be found in time, which is eternity in disguise.

"The art of keeping the seventh day is the art of paint-

---

[3] Book of Exodus, ch. 20, vs. 8-11.

ing on the canvas of time the mysterious grandeur of the climax of creation: as He sanctified the seventh day, so shall we. The love of the Sabbath is the love of man for what he and God have in common. Our keeping the Sabbath day is a paraphrase of His sanctification of the seventh day." [4]

We place importance on the Sabbath because it is a sign of allegiance to our Maker, a memorial of His creative power. Every time we keep the Sabbath we disavow the claims of organic evolution; we deny that man started with a germ which as a matter of chance turned into a protozoan, then was divided into two cells, then four, until by fortuitous combination involving higher mathematics the cells developed into an ape and finally into a human being. By keeping the Sabbath we witness that God is all-wisdom, all-power, all-love, and that we are His special creation.

Ellen G. White placed emphasis on this truth in these words:

"The duty to worship God is based upon the fact that He is the Creator, and that to Him all other beings owe their existence. And wherever, in the Bible, His claim to reverence and worship, above the gods of the heathen, is presented, there is cited the evidence of His creative power. . . . 'This great fact can never become obsolete, and must never be forgotten.' " [5]

Through the Sabbath man's sweat and toil are united with his spiritual life. The Sabbath unites the body and the spirit, the physical and the spiritual. A complete life without the Sabbath is inconceivable. We would have gardens, animals, people—physical beauty; but there would be no divine clasp of unity tying all these to God. The great delusion that is presently stifling the minds of men

---

[4] A. J. Heschel, *loc. cit.*
[5] Ellen G. White, *The Great Controversy,* pp. 436-438.

involves the misunderstanding and obscuring of the real meaning of the seventh-day Sabbath.

The Sabbath, when viewed correctly, relieves us from the tyranny of human acts and lifts us into the holy, peaceful atmosphere of heaven. Who can deny that we desperately need this tranquillity of spirit—we of a world that comprehends the atomic bomb, the sun-girdling satellite, and the intercontinental missile? Some will say that this is an eccentric, mystical notion which has no value; but those who have been in tune with God and His Sabbath day know irrevocably of the joy, peace, and serenity that accompany Sabbath-day worship.

We must consider secular labor on the Sabbath day to be inappropriate. The commandment says that we should rest, giving momentary halt to the toil of gaining a livelihood. Worldly pleasure and profit have no place in this special day which is to be devoted to sacred hours of rest, worship, and holy deeds.

Perhaps an illustration of the difference between art and craft will help to point out why it is important that we make a distinction in our way of life between a weekday and the Sabbath. A craft requires the technical coordination of hands and mind; but art, we might say, carries that extra breadth of imagination. To attain excellence in art the artist rises above the paint and canvas into the realm of deep feeling and the soul's searching for an ideal. So it is with the Sabbath. Here the splendor of the day is expressed in special meditation and abstention from secular routines. What better way to express our awe in the presence of divinity than willingly and happily to abstain from noisy acts and from the common, ordinary routine of existing?

I have added the words "willingly" and "happily" because we must not make of God's day mere subjugation to a series of legal codes. In this respect the Jews went astray.

They were no longer absorbed by the wonder and celebration of the Sabbath; rather they made of it a strenuous match to see how fine a line they could draw between deeds acceptable and those not acceptable. They could walk only so far, speak only on certain subjects, eat only certain food, carry only certain burdens, in an endless list of legal "don'ts" that combined to make the day miserable and to blind God's children to the Sabbath's true value.

Certain types of work are completely in order on the Sabbath. Nature, after all, though created by God, does not halt its course. The sun shines on Sabbath, the breezes blow, vegetation continues, man himself breathes and lives. God does not for a moment withdraw, or man would perish. Thus man also has a work to perform on this day. The necessities of life must be attended to, the sick must be cared for, the wants of the needy must be supplied. How could God's child be held guiltless should he neglect to relieve suffering on the Sabbath? God's holy rest day was made for man; acts of mercy are in perfect harmony with its intent.

In answer to the suggestion that any day can be chosen as the holy Sabbath day, we say that this is impossible. The Sabbath is a specific creation in time and space. "All things were made by him; and without him was not any thing made that was made." [6] John is referring to the Word—God made flesh to dwell among men. Thus God made the Sabbath. He "rested on the seventh day," and "blessed" and "sanctified it: because that in it he had rested from all his work which God created and made." [7] To change the day of Sabbath would be to erase creation. The God Creator ordained but one rest day, and it was established in His completed work of creation.

It is significant that Christ Himself, when on earth,

---

[6] Gospel according to John, ch. 1, v. 3.
[7] Book of Genesis, ch. 2, vs. 2, 3.

observed the seventh-day Sabbath. This is confirmed in Luke's story, "And he came to Nazareth, where he had been brought up: and, as his custom was, he went into the synagogue on the sabbath day, and stood up for to read." [8] The disciples of Jesus followed Christ's example. Paul "reasoned in the synagogue every sabbath, and persuaded the Jews and the Greeks." [9] Luke adds that Paul stayed in one place to preach the gospel for seventy-eight Sabbaths. Throughout New Testament times Christians observed the seventh day of the week as the Sabbath. In view of the great importance the Jews attached to the Sabbath, and in the light of the opposition aroused by the Christian neglect of ritual observances [10] any deviation from the Sabbath commandment, by Paul or others, would inevitably have aroused a storm of protest. Contention over the observance of the Sabbath, had there been any, would have found mention in the apostolic records. But there is only profound silence. The simple fact is that from first to last the Holy Scriptures know of no other day than the seventh-day Sabbath.

The suggestion, then, that any day in the week could be kept holy is invalid. Only a being with creative power could establish such a day. And there is only one Creator. Certainly no human being can take it on himself to usurp God's creative power. And if God were to acknowledge another Sabbath besides the seventh-day which He originally set aside and blessed, He would have to negate His own creation, destroy part of Himself; and this God cannot do and still remain God. To change His creation would make God subject to change, and then all stability in the universe would be gone. This is an impossible view for anyone who believes in God's perfection.

---

[8] Gospel according to Luke, ch. 4, v. 16.
[9] Book of Acts, ch. 18, v. 4.
[10] See Book of Acts, ch. 15; Epistle to the Galatians, ch. 2, v. 3.

Nevertheless, the Scriptures did prophesy that an attempt would be made to broach another day: "And he shall speak great words against the most High, and shall wear out the saints of the most High, and think to change times and laws." [11] The only part of the Decalogue that deals with time is the fourth commandment regarding the Sabbath. And indeed, the first civil Sunday law establishing the first day of the week as a day of rest came in A.D. 321, during the reign of Emperor Constantine. Nowhere in either the Old or the New Testament do we find a hint that such a change would be in order.

Furthermore, Jesus was deeply concerned about the Sabbath. In looking to the imminent destruction of Jerusalem, He said to His disciples, "But pray ye that your flight be not in the winter, neither on the sabbath day." [12] These words were spoken after His ascension, so we see that Jesus had no intent of changing His creation. He gave His life on Friday, rested in the tomb on the Sabbath, and arose on the first day of the week to start anew His work. Since then no time has been lost. In 1582 a change was made from the Julian to the Gregorian calendar, but the weekly cycle was not affected by this. We can sincerely say that promoting the sanctification of any day except the seventh-day Sabbath is an attempt to usurp God's power; it is blasphemy. Those of us who believe in God's sovereignty will not wish to let such blasphemy go by default. We will oppose the appropriation of God's livery for false use.

God asks us simply to keep His commandments if we love Him. He also asks that we love our fellow men—"Thou shalt love thy neighbour as thyself." [13] We would not, therefore, condemn religious persuasions that do not

---

[11] Book of Daniel, ch. 7, v. 25.
[12] Gospel according to Matthew, ch. 24, v. 20.
[13] *Ibid.*, ch. 19, v. 19.

accept the seventh-day Sabbath. Ours is not to judge and condemn; ours is only to love God and keep His commandments. We are, however, duty bound to point to the importance of Sabbathkeeping. Our passion for God and His expressed will constrains us to do so.

Sabbathkeeping presupposes church membership.[14] Tragically, society as a whole has become increasingly neglectful of this high privilege, thinking that it is nice but not necessary, something that only the weak in heart and faint of spirit actually need. To them we must say that church fellowship is a component of salvation. Christ "is the head of the body, the church." [15] It is incogitable that we could find salvation without belonging to the body of which Christ is the head.

Scripturally, Christ is the bridegroom and the church is the bride. When we become official members of the church we are following the Biblical precept: "For this cause shall a man leave his father and mother, and shall be joined unto his wife, and they two shall be one flesh. This is a great mystery: but I speak concerning Christ and the church." [16] By belonging to Christ's church we enter into the closest relationship possible with God—a relationship pictured in human language as a marriage so that we can understand the mystery of divinity reaching to humanity. Those who say this is not important deny the wholeness of true worship.

Worship of God through the vehicle of the church is infused with magnificent strength to help us achieve the Christian ideal. This process is well illustrated in the organization called Alcoholics Anonymous. As far as the individual member is concerned, he has nothing of which to be proud. Probably humanity's lowest, most wretched form

---

[14] See Chapter 17, The Church.
[15] Epistle to the Colossians, ch. 1, v. 18.
[16] Epistle to the Ephesians, ch. 5, vs. 31, 32.

is represented here. But in terms of what is accomplished in the individual life of the alcoholic through the organization, the results are wondrous. By the power of banding together to fight their moral degradation, those in earnest can overcome their weakness and gain victory over drink.

Similarly, as we band together with other church members—all of us weak, frail, and failures in terms of perfection—we gain power from this fellowship to strive on and to overcome sin.

From time to time individuals have expressed to me their opposition to the idea of belonging to the church, saying, "Too much hypocrisy, too much inconsistency, too many high-pressure drives for money and too much emphasis on statistical goals pervade this institution. I don't want to have any part in this." To hold this view is once again to misunderstand the function of the church. No one would be so foolhardy or prideful as to assume that the church is spotless. It cannot be as long as defective human beings make up its membership. The church, however, is still the "communion of the saints" because Christ is its head and is working through its imperfect members for the purification and sanctification of the individual.

Errors and mistakes have been made by the church as an institution, a corporate organization; but we must never confuse this as representative of the total church. That the church as an institution is imperfect was recognized by Saint Paul when he said, "We have this treasure in earthen vessels." [17] The physical church plant, the business it conducts, even perhaps its leadership, are imperfect; but this is not the church. This is only what might be called the ecclesiastical shell—an earthen vessel. God's redemptive community embraces God, the "treasure" and the "earthen vessel," the worship and the worshipers. In

---

[17] Second Epistle to the Corinthians, ch. 4, v. 7.

togetherness this community reaches toward a closer relationship with God. Thus every member of the church, regardless of rank or hierarchical position, becomes the bride of Christ, part of the treasure. The congregation can meet in a dingy cellar, an old attic, out under the blue sky, but the worshipers are still Christ's bride—and they hallow His Sabbath. In this act they identify themselves with God's power to create and to re-create in His likeness.

In summing up, the Sabbath is a bridge between the temporal and the eternal. Created from the foundation of the earth, it will remain throughout eternity. "And it shall come to pass, that from one new moon to another, and from one sabbath to another, shall all flesh come to worship before me, saith the Lord." [18] Once having bridged that nameless gap between the now and the then, the here and the there, we shall continue to rest on and rejoice in the Sabbath.

On God's holy Sabbath day it is our joy to share in what is eternal, to advance beyond the results of creation to the mystery of creation, from the world of creation to the creation of a new world. Little wonder, then, that the God of the Sabbath promises:

"If thou turn away thy foot from the sabbath, from doing thy pleasure on my holy day; and call the sabbath a delight, the holy of the Lord, honourable; and shalt honour him, not doing thine own ways, nor finding thine own pleasure, nor speaking thine own words: then shalt thou delight thyself in the Lord; and I will cause thee to ride upon the high places of the earth, and feed thee with the heritage of Jacob thy father: for the mouth of the Lord hath spoken it." [19]

---

[18] Book of Isaiah, ch. 66, v. 23.
[19] *Ibid.*, ch. 58, vs. 13, 14.

CHAPTER 14

Regeneration

*C*LARENCE DARROW, eminent criminal lawyer, cleared many a defendant by convinc-
ing the jury that his client acted the way he did because of
his environmental history.

He would face the jury with earnest eyes and say, "If
any of you had been reared in circumstances like that of
the accused, or if you had had his parents, you would now
be standing in the dock."

We repeat the question asked in our chapter on "Freedom of Choice": Was Clarence Darrow right? Is the criminal responsible for his actions, or is he not? In an article
entitled, "What Means This Freedom?" John Hospers writes:

"Let us take as an example a criminal who, let us say,
strangled several persons and is himself now condemned
to die in the electric chair. Jury and public alike hold him
fully responsible (at least they utter the words, 'he is
responsible'), for the murders were planned down to the
minutest detail, and the defendant tells the jury exactly
how he planned them. But now we find out how it all
came about; we learn of parents who rejected him from
babyhood, of the childhood spent in one foster home after
another, where it was always plain to him that he was not
wanted; of the constantly frustrated early desire for affec-

158

tion, the hard shell of nonchalance and bitterness that he assumed to cover the painful and humiliating fact of being unwanted, and his subsequent attempts to heal these wounds to his shattered ego through defensive aggression." [1]

When we look at sin in this way we begin to wonder if the good life, the holy life, is possible for anyone, because all men are to some extent the product of a definite environment. None of us has issued from a perfect heritage. At best, the world is a mixture of good and evil, of stardust and mud. On the one hand, every cloud has a silver lining; on the other hand, every rose contains a canker in its bosom. Accordingly, do we have the right to be optimistic?

We can cite a number of famous witnesses who found no possible reason for optimism. Sophocles said, "Not to be born is past all prizing best; easily the next best is to return as soon as possible whence we came." Homer believed that "no more piteous breed than man creeps or breathes on earth." Gibbon stated, "History is a record of the crimes, follies and misfortunes of mankind." And there is the testimony of John Stuart Mill: "The mass of the human race live a life of drudgery and imprisonment." And that of George Gissing: "History is the lurid record of woes unutterable."

Frankly, we find no difficulty in collecting support for the idea that people are hopelessly degraded. A few philosophies have tried to save mankind. Marxism pointed out that the root of all evil was poverty and that if we could once establish a classless society we would be all set. But Marxism forgot that it had no answer for man's arrogance, his pride, his lust for vulgarity, luxury, and power to dominate others.

---

[1] John Hospers, *Determinism and Freedom,* p. 120.

Along came psychology offering cures for the mind. Sin was described as nothing more than a thwarted libido or an inferiority complex or a lack of integration on the part of the total personality. But take a look at the people who supposedly have the know-how of human nature and how it can be improved. Take a look at those who have undergone the best in psychoanalysis. Are they notably better, or even appreciably different from other people? Have they been rid of their irritations, their hostilities, their unhappy moments? I do not believe that they themselves would give an affirmative answer. Most probably they, like other men, look back on their past with many regrets and with the recollection of relatively few truly happy moments. Some of them are like the legendary Caliphate of Cordova who, preparing his last will and testament, wrote as follows:

"I have now reigned more than fifty years, always victorious, always fortunate: cherished by my subjects, feared by their enemies, and surrounded by general reverence. All that men desire has been lavished on me by Heaven; glory, science, honours, treasure, riches, pleasures, and love; I have enjoyed all, I have exhausted all! And now, on the threshold of Death, recalling to remembrance all the past hours in this long period of seeming felicity, I have counted the days in which I have been truly happy: I have been able to find only eleven! Mortals, appraise by my example the exact value of life on earth!"

The world's latest pretender to optimism is science. For a while the world was breathless with anticipation. By means of eugenics socially desirable types were to be bred and undesirable ones were to be eliminated. Perfect machines were to come to the aid of imperfect human beings. Drudgery and beastly toil were to be eliminated. At last man was to be free to enjoy life at his leisure.

What a prophetic fiasco!

Never have people been busier. Though science has helped to diminish disease, it has also made the threat of complete annihilation a reality. In short, as we observe what goes on about us, we find it difficult to believe that science has made us better off now than we have ever been before in terms of final optimism.

Now, think about life. Assuming that our moments of happiness were few, whence came what little happiness we have gleaned from life? Is not happiness most prevalent when we feel the satisfaction of having done something morally right? When we have sacrificed unselfishly for another, or created an object of beauty, or bridled our angry tongue, or forgiven instead of seeking revenge? These, I believe, are the moments of man's deepest joy. He finds satisfaction in doing right and dissatisfaction in doing wrong. Even tribes without modern culture have the inborn longing to pursue what is in harmony with moral law.

So, once again, in another important facet of human life, namely, in the realm of joy and peace, we find that we can make no headway, no progress, without God. Negating God, we are doomed to a paltry few years of labor and disappointment.

But not so for those whose hopes are in God. Habakkuk, a godly man, was able to say with conviction: "Although the fig tree shall not blossom, neither shall fruit be in the vines; the labour of the olive shall fail, and the fields shall yield no meat; the flock shall be cut off from the fold, and there shall be no herd in the stalls: yet I will rejoice in the Lord, I will joy in the God of my salvation. The Lord God is my strength, and he will make my feet like hinds' feet, and he will make me to walk upon mine high places." [2]

---

[2] Book of Habakkuk, ch. 3, vs. 17-19.

The greatest organizational transaction a businessman can undertake is to enter into partnership with Christ.

Habakkuk's kind of joy, however, is conditioned upon *regeneration.* In other words, if we seek the kind of joy that is completely unrelated to outward or material circumstances, we must experience a complete inner revolution. The apostle Paul used the expression "to be born again." He wrote to the Christian church at Ephesus, saying: "That ye put off concerning the former conversation the old man, which is corrupt according to the deceitful lusts; and be renewed in the spirit of your mind." [3] To the Corinthians he wrote: "If any man be in Christ, he is a new creature: old things are passed away; behold, all things are become new." [4]

The Biblical outlook is certainly far more optimistic than anything politics, psychology, or science has provided. We must simply be born again in order to acquire the joy that righteousness alone can supply. But this new birth or regeneration is often misunderstood. The Manichaeans, in the days of the sixteenth-century Reformation, taught that the regeneration was an actual change in the substance of human nature. But this is false. In the new birth no new physical seed or germ is implanted in man, neither does human flesh cease to be human flesh.

Other religious thinkers have said that regeneration was simply the illuminating of the mind. But this, too, is false, because it disregards the heart of man. Nor is regeneration the complete or perfect change of the whole nature of man so that it is no more capable of sin, as was taught by the extreme Anabaptists.

Regeneration as explained in the New Testament consists in the implanting of the principle of new spiritual life in man. Under the influence of the Holy Spirit a radical change takes place in man's direction, and this change gives birth to a life that moves Godward.

---

[3] Epistle to the Ephesians, ch. 4, vs. 22, 23.
[4] Second Epistle to the Corinthians, ch. 5, v. 17.

This change affects the whole of man. It affects the *intellect* first. "The eyes of your understanding being enlightened; that ye may know what is the hope of his calling, and what the riches of the glory of his inheritance in the saints." [5] Next it affects the *will*. "For it is God which worketh in you both to will and to do of his good pleasure." [6] And finally, it affects the *feelings,* or *emotions.* "Whom having not seen, ye love; in whom, though now ye see him not, yet believing, ye rejoice with joy unspeakable and full of glory." [7]

Note well that this new-birth experience is not sanctification. The new birth is an instantaneous change of man's goals, whereas sanctification is perfection, the work of a lifetime. In other words, when you accept God's righteousness in Christ Jesus, you are instantly born again. You are alive as opposed to being dead; and there is no intermediary stage between life and death. Once man is born again, a change takes place in his life. The full scope of this change may not be perceived at once. Some of it even may be on the subconscious level. The important thing is that it is an inscrutable work of God in the human life.

Louis Berkhof defines regeneration in this wise: "Regeneration is that act of God by which the principle of the new life is implanted in man, and the governing disposition of the soul is made holy and the first holy exercise of this new disposition is secured." [8] In other words, the act of regeneration takes place at one leap. From that time forward man no longer has an appetite for wrong. This does not mean that he will make no more mistakes. He may make many mistakes, but his life's trend will be upward toward the goal. This is sanctification.

The regenerated individual stands before God as Adam

---

[5] Epistle to the Ephesians, ch. 1, v. 18.
[6] Epistle to the Philippians, ch. 2, v. 13.
[7] First Epistle of Peter, ch. 1, v. 8.
[8] Louis Berkhof, *Systematic Theology*, p. 469.

stood before God prior to his fall. This implies much more than pardon. The Lord said to Joshua, the high priest who, as the representative of Israel, stood with filthy garments before the Lord: "Behold, I have caused thine iniquity to pass from thee, and I will clothe thee with rich apparel." [9] On the road to Damascus, Jesus made it clear to Saul of Tarsus that by faith we obtain "remission of sins and an inheritance among them that are sanctified." [10] This is what is meant by "justification."

Once man has made the decision to be God's child at all costs, he is then accepted by God at the very stage at which he made this decision. At that particular point he may be a drunkard, a pathological criminal, or some other type of moral deviate. Regardless of his status, God counts him among His righteous children. He is adopted and initiated into the kingdom. When a sinner is thus adopted, he becomes an heir to God's kingdom, having all the rights this legacy entails, just as a legally adopted child becomes heir to his adopted parents' fortune. This means that one who was formerly a sinner with no rights in terms of the eternal, now may not only lay claim to the blessings of the Spirit on this earth but to the blessings of the future life.

This brings us right back to our opening problem, Can a criminal be regenerated?

God's Word certainly leaps up with an affirmative answer. Nobody, regardless of where he was born or under what circumstances he was reared, needs to lose his chance of eternal life. Ample provision has been made for even the worst to make a recovery. The drunkard can crawl out of the gutter; the homicide can throw away his gun; the sex maniac can become as gentle as a lamb. Every human being with a properly functioning mind can be born

---

[9] Book of Zechariah, ch. 3, v. 4, R.V.
[10] Book of Acts, ch. 26, v. 18, R.V.

again, because this new birth requires really only one thing, and that is complete surrender to God. This surrender implies the sinner's complete trust that God is able to impute Christ's righteousness to him as promised in the Word of God. Paul delineates the divine promise clearly:

"Even the righteousness of God which is by faith of Jesus Christ unto all and upon all them that believe: for there is no difference; for all have sinned, and come short of the glory of God; being justified freely by his grace through the redemption that is in Christ Jesus: whom God hath set forth to be a propitiation through faith in his blood, to declare his righteousness for the remission of sins that are past, through the forbearance of God." [11]

The story goes something like this: Satan, the worst possible tyrant, challenged God with his declaration that man, left on his own, would choose Satan rather than God. God accepted the challenge and implemented His plan of love. Thus God in Christ came to this earth, took on human form, and was completely open to the attacks of the tyrant. He joined Himself to sinners of His own accord. Satan charted his course too. He used every ruse possible. His tactics were ruthless and clever. He cajoled, he tempted, he mocked; but he was powerless to overcome Christ.

Innocent though He remained, Christ willingly bore punishment for the sins of humanity. Vicariously Christ endured all the heartache and pain that comes with a sinful life. He exposed Himself to all the penalties of the sinful life. Satan was sure he could destroy Christ, like all other men, in death. But love is stronger than death. Seeking to vanquish Christ, the tyrant of the world was himself vanquished forever. Of this encounter Martin Luther said: "It was a wonderful combat, when the Law, which is a creature, assaulted its Creator, who might easily

---

[11] Epistle to the Romans, ch. 3, vs. 22-25.

have abolished it by an act of sheer power from on high, but who chose instead the way of humiliation and suffering because of His inestimable love for men."

Let us never underrate what God did. The fact is that if love had failed, God would have abdicated His Godhead and left His creatures to perish forever. But, you see, divine love proved invincible, and God is still God, even where He is denied.

No Pulitzer Prize novel could be more thrilling than the drama of Christ's victory on the cross and over the tomb. There He vanquished sin, death, world, hell, devil, and all evil. In dying and rising again, He won the decisive cosmic battle between God and the forces of evil. Although the conflict still rages today, the final issue of the war is certain. The end is still to come, but there can be only one end.

What makes this story so splendid is that it is so appropriate. It has relevancy to every moment of each of our days, for every believer can share in Christ's triumph. Because Christ died and rose again, after having lived a sinless life, He is now able to make up for the deficiencies in the life of every sinner on earth who is willing to let Christ be his life. No more lambs are needed, no more burnt offerings. Christ is all in all. This whole process of righteousness by faith has been described in a nutshell: "When it is in the heart to obey God, when efforts are put forth to this end, Jesus accepts this disposition and effort as man's best service, and He makes up for the deficiency with His own divine merit." [12]

Of course, as long as we are in the world we shall feel the constant tension between the moral world and the material world. On one side is the downward pull toward the lower level of a life in which God plays a minimal

---

[12] Ellen G. White, *My Life Today,* p. 250.

role; on the other side is the upward tug that demands exclusive devotion to God. Dietrich Bonhoeffer, a Christian martyr to Nazi tyranny, was aware of this inescapable tension, and he said: "When Christ calls a man, He bids him come and die. The Christian is committed to a daily warfare against the world, the flesh and the devil. At the very moment of their call, men find that they have already broken with all natural ties of life. Between father and son, husband and wife, the individual and the community, stands Christ the Mediator."

In loving sinners enough to die for them, God never for a moment condones their sin, nor compromises with evil, but seeks actively to overcome it. You see, believers do not stand by, twiddling their thumbs. Effort is required. The drunkard must try. So must the criminal, and so must every Christian, no matter where he stands in relation to the goal of perfection. Every day the regenerated person stretches out his antennae for more light and more truth. The process is one of growth.

The quest means being a better husband, a better wife, a better parent, a better friend. The regenerated person sets out on the most fascinating adventure known. His business is not dull, because to emulate Christ is enthralling. Regeneration means growth in every phase of Christianity—in our sense of mission, in our service to others, our patience, our kindness, our gentleness, and in our love for God and man.

The best part is that it is not too late to begin now. We can start wherever we are. It is not the distance from the goal, but the fact that we are moving toward the goal that is counted as righteousness through the perfection of Christ. Don't look with a sickness unto despair at the person ahead of you, nor with a sneer of superiority at the person behind. Just look to Christ and keep growing, saying as did Paul:

"Not that I have already obtained this or am already perfect; but I press on to make it my own, because Christ Jesus has made me his own. Brethren, I do not consider that I have made it my own; but one thing I do, forgetting what lies behind and straining forward to what lies ahead, I press on toward the goal for the prize of the upward call of God in Christ Jesus." [13]

---

[13] Epistle to the Philippians, ch. 3, vs. 12-14, R.S.V.

CHAPTER 15

Freedom From Guilt

*W*E FIND ourselves in a grotesque predicament. The picture of society in periscope is grim, so grim that the only relief some human beings find is by running away from it all through drug addiction, drink, or sometimes suicide. The specter of people driven by shame and guilt to the edge of insanity is a vivid testimonial to how we look down deep on the inside.

Those born today will inherit as their legacy an era in which crime has soared as on wings. The view is of a gray, chilly landscape. Juvenile Hall is crammed with angry children who, because of their bewilderment and confusion, prowl the streets at night, courting mischief, taunting the law. Some legal courts hand out divorce papers as though they were common traffic tickets. The earth's map is sprinkled with spots where men of heated temperament gather their straggling platoons to march against tyranny and dictatorship. Mobs with an urge for power or driven by racial hatred make law and order well-nigh impossible in some countries.

The horns clamor on, the brakes shriek, and our civilization seems impersonal and all-inclusive. But could we see behind the mask, we would catch an agonizing glance of individual heartbreak and despair. We would see

171

eyes whose tears have long since dried but which still burn
in their sockets with the pain of problems too deep to
solve. Mothers weep because their children turn against
them. Wives weep because their husbands are brutal. Husbands weep because their wives are devious. Church members weep because they have been cut with the sharp criticism of religious people who never really met Christ.

If you sit in judgment on these scenes you show only
that you have misunderstood the human dilemma, for all
of us partake in some measure of the disruption and corruption around us. Without exception, each of us has
added a streak of ugliness to the whole tainted picture. If
you search your heart honestly, you may find motives toward wrong that you really cannot explain. Perhaps you too
have dreamed dreams of hate and assassination.

Yet, if someone were to ask, "What sort of a person
should you be?" I believe we could give the correct answers. Even little children know what kind of persons
they ought to be. The problem is not knowing *what* to do,
but *how* to do it. This problem is best expressed in the
words of the apostle Paul. He said, "To will is present
with me; but how to perform that which is good I find
not."[1]

The tremendous gap between what we know we should
be and what we are is our lament of defeat. The outcome
is that we are filled with guilt. Every night we go to sleep
with the creeping sensation that we have not measured up
to our own standard. Time after time we admit, "I know
better. I should have; but [and the pause is awkward] I
didn't." We know what we are supposed to do, but we
don't do it. We know what we are supposed to feel, but
we don't feel it. We know what we are supposed to say,
but we don't say it. We know what we are supposed to

---

[1] Epistle to the Romans, ch. 7, v. 18.

think, but we don't think it. We sense our failure and
are tortured with guilt. As long as no crisis hits us, we
manage to keep our sense of balance, but when we are in
trouble, the whole problem explodes like a bomb.

Into this distressing human situation, I would like to
bring the words of King David:

Blessed is he whose transgression is forgiven,
whose sin is covered.
Blessed is the man unto whom the Lord
imputeth not iniquity,
and in whose spirit there is no guile.
When I kept silence, my bones waxed old
through my roaring all the day long.

For day and night thy hand was heavy upon me:
my moisture is turned into the drought of summer.
I acknowledged my sin unto thee,
and mine iniquity have I not hid.
I said, I will confess my transgressions unto the Lord;
and thou forgavest the iniquity of my sin.

For this shall every one that is godly pray unto thee
in a time when thou mayest be found:
surely in the floods of great waters
they shall not come nigh unto him.
Thou art my hiding place;
thou shalt preserve me from trouble;
thou shalt compass me about with songs of deliverance.

I will instruct thee and teach thee
in the way which thou shalt go:
I will guide thee with mine eye.
Be ye not as the horse, or as the mule,
which have no understanding:
whose mouth must be held in with bit and bridle,
lest they come near unto thee.

Many sorrows shall be to the wicked:
but he that trusteth in the Lord,
mercy shall compass him about.

Be glad in the Lord, and rejoice, ye righteous:
and shout for joy, all ye that are upright in heart.[2]

These words are the heart history of a man who sinned,
for a time refused to confess, endured the torture of guilt,
finally acknowledged and confessed, and gained forgiveness. This psalm unites the personal penitence of one
man with instruction to all men. It shows that blessedness
of forgiveness and the wonder of freedom from guilt that
results. It was composed after David committed his grievous
sin against Uriah and Bathsheba. In spirit, the words
written by David belong to us as well. We may claim
them for such a time as we descend to the blackness of
guilt.

This psalm became a favorite with Saint Augustine.
Lying on his deathbed, he asked that it be written on the
wall before him so that he might drink deeply of its in-
spiration during the last moments of his life. Martin
Luther called it "the Paulinian psalm," for it describes
Paul's solution to the problem of guilt in life.

More than anything else—more than material security,
physical health, or intellectual prosperity—we need to
know that all wrong is righted; that we have been fully
reconciled. Without this joy we are doomed to self-rejec-
tion and hate. Psychiatrists tell us that the problems of people beyond thirty-five years of age are uniform in their requirement for a pertinent solution. They list approximately
twelve solutions. Very high on this list is the need of a
return to a living faith in God as a release from what
they call the "guilt complex." I can think of no place

---

[2] Psalm 32.

where this release is outlined more clearly step by step than in David's psalm.

The first two verses introduce the four ugly facets of guilt. They are: transgression, sin, iniquity, and guile. The Hebrew rendering of these four words is highly significant.

The first word used is "transgression." The Hebrew word is *pesha,* meaning "rebellion." This is man's revolt against his God, involving the will. Transgression means to set your will against the will of God.

This cause of guilt began at an early point in human history. In the Garden of Eden, where our first parents dwelt, the seed of *pesha* was sown; and it grew until it engulfed Adam and Eve. They began to set their wills against the will of God. This spirit of rebellion characterized man's first withdrawal and estrangement from God.

Human willfulness saturates the history of mankind. Wherever we find human beings, there we find men and women who deliberately place themselves in opposition to divine instruction. They are like impudent children who dare to pretend that they are able to change the stars in their course.

In the days of Noah men rebelled against God's law by indulging lustful appetites and by holding to debauched standards. Corruption followed until its stench filled the universe with repulsion. The rebellion placed this world in such a precarious position that God had to destroy it.

However, soon after the Flood, murder, bloodshed, and widespread corruption once again became the symbol of strength and success. Even God's chosen people preferred their foul ways to God's way. Hatred took the place of love. Good was misused. Love was turned into lust. Purity became filth. Confidence was blasted by suspicion. Fullness was replaced by emptiness. In short, men deliberately set themselves at cross purposes with the nature of God as revealed in His Ten Commandments.

We need not think that we would have done better than our forebears. Our rebellion is just as conspicuous as theirs. How difficult we find it to give up our ideas, our pet theories, our deluded way of operating! We too have run away from God. We have said No when we should have said Yes.

The second word used is "sin." *Chata'ah* is the regular Hebrew word. In *chata'ah* sin is defined as "missing the mark." Like an arrow shot through the air, then falling down without having hit its goal, sin means that either we did too much, or not enough; we aimed too high or too low; we went too far or not far enough; we veered too much to the right or too much to the left. We missed God's mark.

Defective sight is the reason for *chata'ah*. Our obliquity of vision causes us to stray from the mark. Many people have the idea that misdirection is lack of information. They say that we could solve our problem if only we had the right knowledge. They claim, for instance, that if we teach our children to do right, then they will do right. As long as people are informed, they will go straight.

This is not always so, for the simple reason that instruction can be misshapen, twisted, and given a wrong slant by those whose motivation is not functioning for God. People today have much knowledge. Many times they have been trained by conscientious parents, taught by good teachers. Boundless sources of information are at hand. But have we hit the mark? If we are honest, we will admit that we have strayed often and far.

The third word used is "iniquity," translated from *'awon*, signifying "moral crookedness," "lawlessness."

More than any other facet this inward crookedness, this twisted and warped mold of man, produces anguished guilt. Paul suffered immensely in trying to understand why it was that man was filled with such a strange infatuation for the obvious wrong. Over and over again he asked himself why, when he wanted so badly to do what was noble, he remained hypnotized by evil.

We ask this same question. Why are we so mean when we should be honorable? Something is distorted and wrong at the very core of our desires. Our reason is misdirected. Our mind is cloven. Our whole being is sick unto death. We are in need of the Great Physician.

The fourth word used is "guile," from the Hebrew *remiyyah,* meaning "deceit." The implication is self-deceit, falseness within.

No falseness is quite so destructive as lying to one's self. Those who allow this dishonesty to develop in them are fools. The wise man said, "The way of a fool is right in his own eyes." [3] One who has seduced himself to the point where he no longer knows what is moral and what is not is on shaky ground. His bias makes everything he does seem right. Nothing is offensive. "Know thyself" was the essence of Greek wisdom. "Fool thyself" is plain stupidity.

According to Saint John, self-deceit was to be a mark of Christians in the latter days. The revelator describes thus their condition: "For you say, I am rich, I have prospered, and I need nothing; not knowing that you are wretched, pitiable, poor, blind, and naked. Therefore I counsel you to buy from me gold refined by fire, that you may be rich, and white garments to clothe you and to keep the shame of your nakedness from being seen, and salve to anoint your eyes, that you may see." [4]

We have sketched in brief the four facets of sin. They are familiar to us. Because men have allowed themselves to become embroiled in these four snares, they are restless, dissatisfied, driven by guilt. Now, how is this four-dimen-

---

[3] Book of Proverbs, ch. 12, v. 15, R.S.V.
[4] Book of the Revelation, ch. 3, vs. 17, 18, R.S.V.

sional guilt effaced? In our day the urgency of this question has taken on gigantic proportions.

The most calamitous thing we can do is to conceal our guilt. Yet this is exactly what we are prone to do. David did it. For a whole year after stealing Uriah's wife, Bathsheba, he refused to confess his guilt—even to himself. He could not face the sight of his true self, though he continued to rule Israel, apparently secure. But his heart was smarting with pain as his ugly deed ate away at him, not leaving him peace day or night.

At last David cried to God in agony: "Be gracious to me, O Lord, for I am languishing; O Lord, heal me, for my bones are troubled. My soul also is sorely troubled." [5] Until David had the courage to face his condition, he was a miserable man. His own words portray most graphically how he felt: "When I declared not my sin, my body wasted away through my groaning all day long. For day and night thy hand was heavy upon me; my strength was dried up as by the heat of summer." [6]

Finally David found the only way to restore unity to his dismembered spirit. He says, "I acknowledged my sin unto thee, and mine iniquity have I not hid. I said, I will confess my transgressions unto the Lord; and thou forgavest the iniquity of my sin." [7]

David chose the way of wisdom. The peace that resulted from his choice prompted him to counsel all of us, "Be ye not as the horse, or as the mule, which have no understanding." [8] He strikes straight at our stubborn pride, our stupidity for not freeing ourselves from the horror of sin. We do well to follow David's counsel. If we allow wrong to churn in our hearts, it will soon form a putrefied mass, an ugly abscess that will drain into our life and poi-

[5] Psalm 6, v. 2, R.S.V.
[6] *Ibid.*, 32, vs. 3, 4, R.S.V.
[7] *Ibid.*, v. 5.
[8] *Ibid.*, v. 9.

son it. The only way we can be healed is through repentance, confession, and forgiveness.[9]

Many here confuse the process of repentance and confession, claiming forgiveness on the grounds of acknowledgment of guilt alone. However, God is interested in the practical aspects of the case. Besides sorrow for sin and the confession of it, repentance includes the expulsion of sin from the life. This expulsion is an act of the soul itself, energized by power from above. Ellen G. White makes this point clear:

"True, we have no power to free ourselves from Satan's control; but when we desire to be set free from sin, and in our great need cry out for a power out of and above ourselves, the powers of the soul are imbued with the divine energy of the Holy Spirit, and they obey the dictates of the will in fulfilling the will of God."[10]

Wonderful! God can forgive all manner of sin that is driven from the life. He can cleanse such a life from guilt. The tragedy is that some Christians seem more concerned about obtaining forgiveness than about ridding their soul of known sin. They keep their confession list up to date—a noble objective; but this has merit only if the confession has in each case been accompanied by an expulsion of sin. The righteousness of Christ—our only hope—will not cover one cherished sin. A body can never be clean as long as it is clothed in filthy garments; so forgiveness is real forgiveness only when we cooperate with God and sincerely lay aside the tattered garments of inherited and cultivated wrongdoing.

David obtained forgiveness, and his excruciating guilt vanished when he came to loathe the sin of which he had been guilty. In its true perspective, it became unbearable.

Four further points need to be considered:

---

[9] See Book of Isaiah, ch. 1, vs. 5, 6, 18, 19.
[10] Ellen G. White, *The Desire of Ages*, p. 466.

1. The fear of consequences sometimes drives the sinner to seek pardon. Such was the case with Judas. Or material advantage lures him, as it did Esau. But if Judas had thought that he could betray his Lord without suffering punishment, he would have continued his life of subterfuge. If the birthright had been restored to Esau, he too would have pursued his sinful course. God is not found in fear or clever manipulation.

2. If we continue to do wrong, knowing that it is wrong, we may reach the place where we no longer want to do right. God never turns a deaf ear to sincere pleading for pardon, but habitual pursuit of sin makes us insensitive to the Spirit's guidance. After a while there is no longer a desire to be cleansed of defilement. This condition is described in the Scriptures: "If we sin wilfully . . . there remaineth no more sacrifice for sins." [11]

3. Many feel that they can indulge in sin, for a time at least, without serious consequences to themselves or others. How often I have heard someone say, "I'm going to go out and 'live' for a while, then I'll come back to the church." He believes that at a convenient moment he will give up everything contrary to God's will and will obtain forgiveness.

This risk is a great hazard, because the tragedy of wrongness is that, like a viper, it coils around the heart, fastens itself securely upon the soul, becoming an integral part of the life pattern, so that there is no desire later to give it up. A person may speak up lightly and romantically for the good life. He may claim superficially to want to do what is right; but genuine repentance goes hand in hand with the effort of walking in the light. Without this, the search for salvation is vain.

4. The acknowledgment of sin—its confession and

---

[11] Epistle to the Hebrews, ch. 10, v. 26.

also riddance—must be specific, without mitigation. It must offer no excuse. To invoke extenuating circumstances by comparing our difficult situation with that of someone who seems to have a much less difficult time is a form of self-deception.

In this respect the self-styled reformer and professional critic is possibly the greatest guilt concealer of all. One who is forever finding fault with his neighbor or declaring the shortcomings of the church in general, is usually a creature driven by his own guilt to judge and criticize. He thinks that by framing the guilt of his neighbors, he lessens the glare of his own poor performance. The Scripture has words for him too: "Thou art inexcusable, O man, whosoever thou art that judgest: for wherein thou judgest another, thou condemnest thyself; for thou that judgest doest the same things." [12]

David found the true answer to sin. His story is fascinating. How he was able to rise from a feeling of complete worthlessness to the sublime joy of inward manhood is a drama that leaves us breathless.

The story is delightful; but it is not so much the plot that strikes the chords of our hearts as it is the feeling we have in reading David's life that we have been over this territory before. It is familiar to us. Have we not also felt guilt, hating ourselves for missing the mark? When we look at David we breathe a sigh of relief. If this ecstasy of full acceptance to God could happen to him, then there must be hope for us too.

One thing we must understand. No condition of purity on our part earns us God's forgiveness and acceptance. None of us is worthy of forgiveness. If forgiveness were extended on the basis of our sanctity, not a one of us would deserve to be forgiven; we would not have a chance. The

---

[12] Epistle to the Romans, ch. 2, v. 1.

marvel is that we receive forgiveness without deserving it
on the basis of full confidence in God and the desire to be
His child.

Freedom from guilt can be ours regardless of the
depravity of our past. "Whatever may have been your past
experience, however discouraging your present circumstances, if you will come to Jesus just as you are, weak,
helpless, and despairing, our compassionate Saviour will
meet you a great way off, and will throw about you His
arms of love and His robe of righteousness. He presents
us to the Father clothed in the white raiment of His own
character. He pleads before God in our behalf, saying: I
have taken the sinner's place. Look not upon this wayward
child, but look on Me." [13]

God not only forgives sin but He also accepts the
truly repentant one as if he had never sinned. Every sin
that oppressed him is lifted away. Resting in this security
of full acceptance by God, we will resist despair. Nothing
can overpower us. Evil forces will be as feathers assailing
an iron bulwark. The enemy's darts will splinter into a
million fragments before our eyes. We shall be uncon-
querable. Life will not defeat us, nor will death shake us.
Our hope and courage will remain high as we pledge to
walk hand in hand with God.

Circumstances may for a time be difficult, confusing,
and weighted with sorrow; but this is only temporary, since
God is helping us to find the answer. It will not always be
dark. Our future is not a long dark corridor along which
we crawl in fear, driven by shame and guilt. Nothing in
the whole world can crush us when we know that God has
granted forgiveness. The light in our eyes glows steadily.
We have come home to the heart of the Father. We have
found freedom from guilt.

---

[13] Ellen G. White, *Thoughts From the Mount of Blessing*, p. 9.

CHAPTER 16

Worship

*M*ODERN MAN IN SEARCH OF A SOUL is a book by Carl G. Jung, one of the founders of modern psychiatry. The title awakens our imagination. We picture a hollow-eyed, animallike being, frightened and alone, roaming the earth looking for that foggy something which will make him complete. Man without a soul is not man. In the closing chapter of his book, Dr. Jung makes a powerful observation. He says:

"During the past thirty years, people from all the civilized countries of the earth have consulted me. . . . Among all my patients . . . there has not been one whose problem in the last resort was not that of finding a religious outlook on life. It is safe to say that every one of them fell ill because he had lost that which the living religions of every age have given to their followers, and none of them has been really healed who did not regain his religious outlook." [1]

Spiritual illness is the modern plague. In a faint way the world knows this, or at least senses that something is wrong; but, with the boom in technology, people are embarrassed to admit that the problems of the spirit are some-

---

[1] Carl G. Jung, *Modern Man in Search of a Soul,* p. 229.

thing they cannot control through the laboratory. They cling to sexuality separate from love; they read up on facts, remaining aloof from faith. The result is that they are disillusioned by life.

With all man has, he has failed to read the meaning of his own existence. Poor creature! He struggles on without recognizing humanity's four highest achievements: faith, hope, love, and insight. Dr. Jung suggests that the psychotherapist and the clergyman join efforts. Perhaps the suggestion is important, but I am convinced that it is less important than the reason behind it.

Society has become complicated, involved, and intricate. Our affluence has purchased all, except a proper perspective. Every step forward materially has made us slide two steps backward spiritually. But we are not completely obtuse. We are convinced that we need deliverance from something, but we know not what; by someone, but we cannot define whom.

Modern man never has been surpassed in his intellectual successes, either. He has become a competitor of the stars. But in a soul sense, he has been the greatest possible disappointment. He has taken full credit for his special success and has gradually withdrawn from One greater than he, from the One who made it possible for him to conquer the skies in the first place. What man needs is to realize that he is no superman; that, indeed, he is nothing so long as he ignores the Supreme Being to whom he owes final allegiance in all matters of mind, spirit, and body.

Man needs to look up, saying with the psalmist, "Whom have I in heaven but thee? and there is none upon earth that I desire beside thee. My flesh and my heart faileth: but God is the strength of my heart, and my portion for ever." [2] The human soul needs above all a reconcilia-

---

[2] Psalm 73, vs. 25, 26.

tion with God, acknowledging that in the universe there is One of higher rank than he. In short, man needs to return to genuine worship.

What is worship? Is it something approaching an occult science? Is it a mystical stage where man becomes suspended between dream and fantasy? Is it simply repetitive quiet introspection? I believe worship is an attitude of mind and heart in which man is able to love God with his whole heart, his whole mind, and all his strength. We recall that Christ said this was the fulfillment of the first commandment.[3] Thomas Aquinas once said that man reaches relative perfection on this earth when there remain no obstacles to prevent him from loving God with all his being. In other words, worship is basically the wholehearted response of the creature to the Creator. Worship points to man's profound sense of dependence upon the spiritual side of the unknown.

The first thing we do when we take this matter of worship seriously is to indicate that we believe. We believe it is possible to discern spiritually those things that otherwise leave us baffled. For man to worship is a natural instinct. And if this instinct is not a deception, then it must be the recognition of a metaphysical reality that stands above and beyond all physical realities.

The most primitive human turns his glance toward this reality above physical realities. His silent, wide-eyed puzzlement as he stands outside his grass-roofed hut and looks into the sun is of the same essence as that of the most cultured saintly prayer. Man's urge for worship may be crude, it may be imperfect, it may find expression

---

[3] See Gospel according to Mark, ch. 12, vs. 28-30.

Worship is basically the wholehearted response of the creature to the Creator in adoration and communion.

in mistaken form, but it is always there. Wherever there is man, there is striving upward. Eternity makes its impact on the jungle heart as well as upon the worshipers in cathedrals.

Worship, then, points first and foremost to God. However thick the veil that separates Him from the worshiper, and however grotesque the ritual through which worship tries to find expression, the act of worship itself always gives God priority. No other action demands of man more acknowledgment of his limitation than this.

Now, worship itself contains three separate and distinct acts which fuse into one to make up the total act of worship.

First, worship means *adoration.* No symbol is more classically appropriate for this part than the hymn:

"Holy, holy, holy! Lord God Almighty!
Early in the morning our song shall rise to Thee;
Holy, holy, holy! merciful and mighty!
God over all who rules eternity!"

We fling ourselves at God's feet in order to praise His splendor. We do this because we have become aware of the awful perfection of God in comparison with our total imperfection. This, by the way, clinches our conviction regarding our sinful nature. Look at the King of kings. He is sublimely perfect. In contrast, our frailties and defects become glaringly obvious. We cannot but kneel at our Lord's feet in appreciation of His divinity.

Second, worship entails an *offering.* After man has understood, as best he is capable of understanding, God's immense sacrifice in giving Himself to save the world, then he feels a compulsion to give something in return. In a sense we might say that this urge is pitiful, for what can we, way down here, offer to God, way up there? Nevertheless, we awaken to the realization that a sense of awe for

God is not enough. We wish to offer something to this Power that is unseen yet so closely felt.

In the primitive man, this sense of offering will be the result of fear. He wants to do something in order to mollify what otherwise might destroy him. He feels guilty about the hidden aspects of his life and he wants very badly to atone for this feeling. But when man comes to a fuller understanding of worship, his urge to produce an offering becomes a more positive act. Realizing that the heart of religion is the willingness to share, as God so splendidly shared, he places an offering before God.

The little girl who wanted to place her Raggedy-Ann doll in the church offering plate understood the principle of offering in worship. Parents ought to encourage their children early in life to experience the blessing of this ritual. Without it, worship can easily degenerate into mere emotional outbursts. The offering itself may be something small, but it must always symbolize a greater thing; namely, the fully consecrated life.

Abraham of old offered Isaac, his son. The widow offered her mite. Both offerings indicated that the one presenting the offering loved God unconditionally. In terms of material value, no matter what we might give would be a speck in God's sight. There isn't gold enough or treasure enough in the world to impress the heavenly hosts. But when what we give unveils the deep movements of the Spirit, it becomes a crown to human worship. God is pleased.

De la Taille describes the basis for an offering in worship, saying: "Because man is not a pure spirit, he feels the need to translate this interior gift of himself into an outward rite which symbolizes it. For this reason, he presents to God the homage of some material gift." [4]

---

[4] De la Taille, *The Mystery of Faith*, p. 6.

In other words, we make a "covenant with sacrifice" much as a little child brings from the fields a bouquet of wildflowers to his mother. The flowers are not artfully arranged, some of the stems are broken, the whole thing really is not worth giving, but the point is that it is the best the child can do. The parent is pleased.

In Christian history the building of the Temple at Jerusalem was an act of offering on the part of the children of Israel. Into it they had placed all their skills, their love for beauty, their time and labor. In a sense every church we build is that same kind of offering. It is, or should be, the result of our desire to give of our best to God.

On several occasions we find that the prophets of the Bible were very heartless in their denunciation of the rituals of sacrifice. The prophet Amos, speaking for God, says:

"I hate, I despise your feasts, and I will take no delight in your solemn assemblies. Yea, though ye offer me your burnt offerings and meal offerings, I will not accept them: neither will I regard the peace offerings of your fat beasts." [5]

Are you surprised to hear this harsh scolding? Why did God not want sacrifices? On closer investigation, we find that this tongue-lashing is not directed against offerings to God at all, but against the degradation of such offerings. God was warning His people that He could not tolerate an ugly caricature of true offering. He could not appreciate empty tokens void of meaning. He could not accept a routine giving without the giver's being aware of the implications of his gift. In other words, unless the offering symbolized a greater surrender to God it was absolutely nothing—a hypocritical farce.

Third, worship is *communion.* A popular attitude among busy Christians is that they can worship without

---

[5] Book of Amos, ch. 5, vs. 21, 22, R.V.

going to church. They feel that lying on the beach contemplating the sky is worship. Since they see people so much during their business week, they contend that it is better for them if they worship God alone among the trees in their garden, or in a mountain cabin, or by listening to a religious broadcast on radio.

I shall not dispute nor would I detract from the beauty of solitary devotion. We are in desperate need of this; but let us not confuse personal oblations with communion in worship, for this is something entirely different. Communion in the fullest sense means a gathering of saints; not of perfect beings, but of men and women with their families who have felt the challenge of God's perfection and who desire to join together, responding to the pressure of holiness and striving ceaselessly toward purity and perfection. Communion means steadfast devotion to what is good and noble. Sanctification of life is the goal toward which the communion of saints marches. They do it together because they know that in numbers, perhaps only two or three but at least more than one, there is encouragement and a generosity of spirit.

Christian worship has never been a one-man affair. From its beginning it has been social in nature. The worshiper comes before God as a member of a great family. The first word in the Lord's Prayer reminds us that we do not worship alone. God is *our* Father.

Christian worship is based on a grand tradition of spiritual culture. For thousands of years God's church has gathered in regular communion. Through wars, plagues, persecution, and individual crises, the church has carried on as the center of worship for those who have longed for salvation. The tradition cannot be ignored, because it is God-ordained and divinely blessed. Individual worship cannot be any richer than the riches we bring to the common store of worship.

Excuses are cheap and readily given. We can say that we have been more mystically refreshed by a personal experience with God when we are all by ourselves. Personal experience is wonderful; but nothing can replace the utter completeness of worshiping God as part of a congregation ordained by and dedicated to God. Personal devotions are needed. Spiritual progress depends on it; but neglecting communal worship for private worship ushers in barrenness.

Such, we believe, is a unified picture of worship. Man needs this worship. As Ernest, in Hawthorne's tale, came to resemble the Great Stone Face by living close to it and worshiping it, the Christian comes to the likeness of God through worship.

Shall we not henceforth worship more fully—in the full splendor of holiness?

"He who neglects worship neglects that which separates man from the birds, the animals, the insects, and the fishes.

"The unworshipful man is an anthropoid with a highly developed brain. He may be a paragon of morality, but so are bees and ants, with a highly developed brain. He may be keenly intelligent, but so are wolves, foxes. He may provide for his family, but so do hyenas and orangutans. He may be successful in his affairs, but so are beavers, muskrats. He may be artistic, but so are spiders and butterflies.

"Worship is the chief concern of highly developed human beings. The human being must be graded according to his capacity for worship."—DWIGHT BRADLEY.

CHAPTER 17

The Church

RECENTLY I became acquainted with a young graduate, fresh out of law school, who had high political aspirations. We talked. As a youngster he had gone to church regularly, but later—he could not remember exactly when—he had decided that church took too much of his time which should be devoted to studies, so he quit religion and the church. Apparently, this person had funneled his energies into one aim, making a name for himself. He did say this: "Pretty soon I'll need to pick out a church and join up again, because nowadays you can't get anywhere in politics unless you belong to a church."

Is this a valid reason for church membership? Is church membership simply a tag to label you as a decent citizen? Does the Biblical concept of the church lend support to such rationalizing?

In the original context the Christian church was represented by the Greek word *Ecclesia.* Literally translated the word meant "an association or congregation of people called out by God." This Greek word forms an undeniable bridge between the church in the Old Testament and the church in the New Testament. In the third century before Christ, when the Greek language became dominant in the Mediterranean world, the Hebrew Bible was translated into

13

Greek, because Hebrew had become an almost forgotten
language among the dispersed Jews. When Paul and the
early missionaries began their journeys to announce the
news that Jesus of Nazareth was indeed the Messiah, they
went to synagogues in which the Greek Old Testament was
used. Moreover, in the New Testament most of the quota-
tions from the Old Testament use the terminology of the
Septuagint. Thus the term *Ecclesia* of the New Testament
takes its name and primary idea from the *Ecclesia* of the
Old Testament. The *Ecclesia* of the apostles is a continuing
reality, without dissolution or interruption.

The actual word *Ecclesia* is confined in the Gospels to
two passages in Matthew.[1] In the first passage the Master
speaks about the building of Messiah's *Ecclesia.* In a sense,
this was a rebuilding of God's temple, as suggested by the
prophet Amos: "In that day will I raise up the tabernacle
of David that is fallen, and close up the breaches thereof;
and I will raise up his ruins, and I will build it as in the
days of old."[2] Thus the "called out ones" of the Old Testament period find perfect fellowship with the saints of the
New Testament. They unite in faith, hope, and love, so that
God might work out in them His eternal purpose.

One must recognize the centrality of the church in the
message and mission of Jesus. Apart from Jesus' intention
to form a community, the events recorded in the Acts are
unintelligible. The importance of that implication lies in
the knowledge that God's revealing and saving action in
Israel has been decisively sealed and extended universally
through the work of Jesus Christ and the reconstituting of
the church by Him.

In the New Testament numerous figures of speech are
used to characterize the nature of the church. Christ is the
Vine, the church members are the branches. He is the

---

[1] See Gospel according to Matthew, ch. 16, vs. 17, 18; ch. 18, v. 27.
[2] Book of Amos, ch. 9, vs. 11, 12; Book of Acts, ch. 15, v. 16.

Shepherd, they the sheep. He is the Head of His body, the church, of which believers are organic members. But these figures of corporate unity and solidarity with the living Christ have also active reference to the mission and extension of the church. The whole vine grows. There are other sheep who must be brought in. The body increases in growth and is inwardly built up until the fullness of Christ is attained in the time of the consummation of God's kingdom.

The apostle Paul in particular described the assembly of God's people as the "body of Christ." Writing to the Corinthians he began: "For as the body is one, and hath many members, and all the members of that one body, being many, are one body: so also is Christ." His concluding statement was, "Now ye are the body of Christ, and members in particular." [3] Whether or not this body concept is interpreted literally, spiritually, or metaphorically is still an argument among New Testament scholars; the principal implication, no doubt, is that God's church is Christ's presence in the world through the indwelling Spirit.

The *Ecclesia* of the Old Testament was the dwelling place of God among men. "Let them make me a sanctuary; that I may dwell among them," [4] was Jehovah's call. Then, according to promise, God was made flesh and dwelt among men—at which time men knew the will of God by the words Jesus spoke, the deeds of love He performed, the life He lived when He walked among them. As the time approached for this earthly ministry to end, Jesus gathered about Him a group of disciples. These came to be known as the *Ecclesia*, or congregation, of Jesus. To this group, following the crucifixion and resurrection, was given the Holy Spirit to carry on the ministry which Jesus had begun in His body. As the church grew in numbers,

---

[3] First Epistle to the Corinthians, ch. 12, vs. 12-27.
[4] Book of Exodus, ch. 25, v. 8.

it became necessary to systematize further the life of the
community. Through the centuries the record has been
stained repeatedly with impurities, but the *Ecclesia* of the
Old and the New Testament has carried on. Actuated by
the Spirit, the organs of this body perform many functions
in accomplishing God's work.

In the beginning the "called out ones" of the Christian
church were not separated from their race or their citizenship or their occupation. They simply witnessed wherever
they could during the day's ordinary activities. Soon the
complexity of the task required, however, that men be set
apart for the ministry of the Word, according to their
personal gifts.[5] In his letter to the Ephesians Paul men-
tions the resulting facets of that ministry. Some were ordained to travel into other countries. At Antioch, Barnabas
and Saul were separated for the work to which the Holy
Spirit had called them.[6] The church was perfectly sure that
God meant for these men to set out for lands afar. But the
church went with them. At home and abroad the appointed
ministry led the faithful to the ends of the known world.

Young and old, all went under the pressure of the
divine Hand. They felt compelled to go. Something had
happened to them that demanded obedience to the Master's summons to evangelize. As a result, the world was
turned upside down. There is no hidden secret to this
apostolic achievement. God did a quick work upon the
earth. He could do a quick work because the "called according to his purpose" accepted His program and did His
bidding—all of them in united action. Nor has this apostolic pattern been changed. "Every soul whom Christ has
rescued is called to work in His name for the saving of the
lost."[7] Every associate in the *Ecclesia* is to carry the flam-

---

[5] See Epistle to the Ephesians, ch. 4, vs. 11, 12.
[6] See Book of Acts, ch. 13, v. 2.
[7] Ellen G. White, *Christ's Object Lessons*, p. 191.

ing torch of evangelism, beginning with the man next door and encircling the earth with God's good news.

So the total church serves as the body of Christ in a worldwide ministry. Evidently, then, this body must not only sustain itself; it must also minister to all men, even as did Christ's own body when He walked among men. Christ commissioned His followers to go into the world teaching and preaching, winning and baptizing "every creature." [8] The church exists, therefore, not for itself alone, but for those outside of it too. It must reach relentlessly beyond itself until the God of heaven will "set up a kingdom, which shall never be destroyed." [9] Said Jesus, "The field is the world." [10]

Christ set the stage for a positive, a militant church. He repeatedly urged His disciples not to be apathetic and insipid, but instead to season society like a savory salt. The history of Christianity reveals the vital importance of a militant spirit in the church. Never has the church been effective when its people have been acquiescent, lackadaisical, spineless, spiritless, and indifferent. Wherever the church is destined to be a dimension in salvation, men and women work together, shoulder to shoulder, dauntless, determined, and eager in Heaven's righteous cause. They march with the everlasting gospel into every nation, and tribe, and tongue, and people. [11]

Tendency exists today in Christian lands to encourage the kind of religion in which each goes alone to pray before a candle, or a statue, or an altar. Little chapels are erected where people can conveniently slip into them off busy streets. This may in some respects encourage religious practices; however, such individual worship is far removed from what is most valuable in the Christian

---

[8] Gospel according to Mark, ch. 16, v. 15.
[9] Book of Daniel, ch. 2, v. 44.
[10] Gospel according to Matthew, ch. 13, v. 38.
[11] See Book of the Revelation, ch. 14, v. 6.

church. Individual worship has no need of outward para-
phernalia. Bowing before a shrine for a brief moment is
really a throwback to a heathen concept, with emphasis
upon the physical setting. Christ's idea of a redemptive
community, which came from the Old Testament and
brought together the "newborn," the "elect," the "saints,"
in a church "service," was something very different.

The church will, according to Scripture, prevail against
the gates of hell, until the redemptive purposes of God
have been achieved and the restoration of all things has
been brought to pass.[12] The church endures while earthly
institutions collapse. Standing upon the ruins of Mycenae,
on a Greek mountainside, Will Durant examined the
work of archeologists excavating a distant past. His eyes
went to a modest little church in the valley, and he wrote:
"Civilizations come and go, they conquer the earth and
crumble into dust, but faith survives every desolation."
Arnold Toynbee has referred to fourteen civilizations that
the church has already outlived. Some have thought to destroy the church; cynics have tried to disfigure it; dema-
gogues have belittled it; yet the church moves forward,
unshaken. Theodore Beza reportedly said to Henry of Na-
varre, "Sire, it belongs in truth to the church of God, in the
name of which I speak, to receive blows and never to give
them, but it will please your majesty to remember that the
church is an anvil that has worn out many a hammer."

The church is to be God's community and witness until
His purposes are fulfilled and the Christian hope has become a reality throughout the universe. Those who center
their life in God will have a high consideration for the
church. To think they march with God, even though they
are not active in His church, is to forget that in the New

---

[12] Cf. Gospel according to Luke, ch. 1, vs. 16, 17; Gospel according to
Matthew, ch. 17, v. 11; Book of Acts, ch. 3, vs. 19-21; Book of Malachi,
ch. 3, vs. 1-4.

Testament the child of God does not stand apart from church fellowship. None in ancient Antioch could have believed fervently enough or lived abundantly enough to have been recognized as a Christian had he held himself aloof from the *Ecclesia,* the blessed community. Indeed, worship together helps make men true children of God.

But the church must measure up to the community ideal. The apostolic church was a fellowship united by the Holy Spirit. The "called out ones" "devoted themselves to the apostles' teaching and fellowship, to the breaking of bread and the prayers." [13] Christ had said, "Where two or three are gathered together in my name, there am I in the midst of them." [14] The early Christians believed this, and when they were together in prayer and study and communion, Christ seemed more real to them than when they were separated. This church was held together more by fellowship than by good organization.

Nor is this church fellowship just a casual friendship, similar to that enjoyed in any association set up to share like interests and achieve common goals. Here all peoples become members of a new humanity—God's universal family. Here, said the Master, "You are all brethren." [15] Here, then, brother cares for brother when he is sick, shares with him when he is destitute, labors with him when he is mistaken, strengthens him when he is tempted, abandons him not in besetting peril.

The spirit of Kaj Munk dramatized the reality of church fellowship during the World War II invasion of Denmark. That great Danish writer was ordered not to pray for the persecuted Christians of Norway. He refused and the result was death. Why did he not obey the Nazi order? Here is the answer:

---

13 Book of Acts, ch. 2, v. 42, R.S.V.
14 Gospel according to Matthew, ch. 18, v. 20.
15 *Ibid.,* ch. 23, v. 8, R.S.V.

"I feel bound to my Norwegian brothers because they are brothers in the faith. They fight for ideals that I, too, have sworn to fight for. If, for fear of men, I should sit as a passive onlooker, I should be a traitor to my Christian faith, to my Danish mind, and to my clergyman's oath."

This was the spirit of the Christian fellowship when the church was young. Such a spirit has characterized the true church in all ages. It will actuate the church today, when God's men and women stand together for truth.

The prophetic picture convinces us that just before the appearing of our Lord, great issues will challenge both the church and the world. Circumstances will so shape themselves that every earthly inhabitant will be tested in his loyalty to God. In this last crisis, too, God will have His community. This church of the remnant[16] will gather into the great Shepherd's fold a multitude of earnest, sincere believers. Finally, the remnant (the last segment) will include all God's children in one great fellowship. Here is a thrilling view of the triumphant church:

"Among earth's inhabitants, scattered in every land, there are those who have not bowed the knee to Baal. Like the stars of heaven, which appear only at night, these faithful ones will shine forth when darkness covers the earth and gross darkness the people. In heathen Africa, in the Catholic lands of Europe and of South America, in China, in India, in the islands of the sea, and in all the dark corners of the earth, God has in reserve a firmament of chosen ones that will yet shine forth amidst the darkness, revealing clearly to an apostate world the transforming power of obedience to His law."[17]

So will the church be God's community and witness until His purposes have been fulfilled and the Christian hope has become at last a reality throughout God's domain.

---

[16] See Book of the Revelation, ch. 12, vs. 12-17; ch. 14, v. 12.
[17] Ellen G. White, *Prophets and Kings*, pp. 188, 189.

CHAPTER 18

Guidance

*W*HAT DOES God want of us? In our childlike, dependent way we wish for a detailed answer, preferably in the form of a two-column list, one for the do's and one for the don'ts. We are evermore searching for the specific command, for God's personal guidance.

Many things make it hard to believe in the guidance of God. When the astronomer turns from his telescope to tell us that the star nearest to the earth is probably twenty-five billion miles away, and that the total number of stars in the universe is something like the total number of grains of sand on all the seashores of the world, our minds are terrified, and confidence in God's personal care seems unbelievable and unrealistic. As we peer into the vastness of space, it seems pitifully naive to ask, Is God interested in *my* doings? Will He direct me in the details of *my* life?

Yet we cannot ignore the evidence of God's personal care for us. Rich experience witnesses to God's guidance. Neither the vastness of space nor of time excludes it. Besides, who made vastness a standard of value? A baby is more than a mountain. A man is more than a star. Though astronomy and geology conspire to prove the utter insignificance of man, man is still the astronomer and the geologist. He can be a child of God.

To those who disclaim the guidance of God we can say that their idea of God is too closely built on a human model. Convinced that managing directors of earthly enterprises leave details to subordinates, they are quietly scornful of the idea that God's care envisions details. But we accept God's personal care, not in spite of His greatness, but because of it. Though God is far above our thoughts, we dare believe that He stoops to ask the love of our poor hearts. Though whirling worlds move at His word, we dare believe that He says, "I will guide thee." "Be still, and know that I am God." [1]

The soul making its first venture into the spiritual life is like a radio operator on his first tune-in. At the mercy of myriad electrical whispers, the novice at the receiver does not know what to think. The noises seem pointless, but they are curiously insistent. They seem to be only tuneless splashings—echoes perhaps of the singing of the spheres, the electrical turmoil of stars beyond the reach of the telescope. Something is there, but it is yet unintelligible in pattern or meaning.

E. Herman recounts the experience of a novice radio operator who almost missed his message in this splash and wail of interstellar sound, and concludes:

"So the soul that waits in silence must learn to disentangle the voice of God from the net of other voices—the ghostly whisperings of the subconscious self, the ruling voices of the world, the hindering voices of misguided friendship, the clamor of personal ambition and vanity, the murmur of self-will, the song of unbridled imagination, the thrilling note of religious romance. To learn to keep one's ear true in so subtle a labyrinth of spiritual sound is indeed at once a great adventure and a liberal education. One hour of such listening may give us a

---

[1] Psalms 32, v. 8; 46, v. 10.

deeper insight into the mysteries of human nature, and a surer instinct for divine guidance, than a year's hard study or external intercourse with men." [2]

The immature disciple must be warned against too positive an assertion that he knows the voice of God. One person insists that he found the answer to an anguish-producing problem by opening his Bible at random and pointing his finger anywhere on the page. Another person invents a scheme into which God is to fit His divine will. He says to himself, "If I receive a telephone call from John Smith, that will be the sign determining my action." The desire is to be an obedient disciple, yet in each of the above circumstances God's providence is restricted and coerced.

A study of God's dealings with men shows how dangerous it is to trifle with magic or chance when seeking His will. Chance and magic have never been the means by which God has guided His children. As a matter of fact, they are dangerous threads to weave into our devotional life, for they so easily turn into a broken cobweb, leading only to spiritual destruction. What, then, is true guidance?

The principles of divine guidance are founded on Scripture and are tied in with intelligent behavior—always. God does not expect any human being to use irrational methods to discern His will.

Be sure that knowledge of God's will comes first of all by *daily dedication* to Him. Paul beseeches us: "Present your bodies a living sacrifice, holy, acceptable unto God, which is your *reasonable* service. And be not conformed to this world: but be ye transformed by the renewing of your mind, that ye may prove what is that good, and acceptable, and perfect, will of God." [3] The picture is quite clear: we are to keep presenting ourselves to God, refusing to succumb to the pressure exerted by the evil age to which

---

[2] E. Herman, *Creative Prayer*, p. 70.
[3] Epistle to the Romans, ch. 12, vs. 1-3.

we belong. By our inner experience, by our spiritual intuition, we shall then be able to discern God's will for us. Saint Paul is a witness to this. When he looked to God, asking, "What wilt thou have me to do?" he had experienced an inner conversion. His mind became linked with the divine will and his ear, tuned to the Infinite voice, was able to receive clear messages from God concerning his work as an apostle of Jesus Christ.[4]

We must not presume to know God's will until we are ready in mind, body, and soul to receive it. We cannot receive guidance from God while we deliberately court sin. Let us not think for a moment that God's will is in our lives as long as we cling to our secret scandals, our silent atrocities, all knowingly performed. Central to the requisite of guidance is cleansing the heart from wrong.

This often is quite unpalatable to us. We find sin thrilling and full of excitement, and we equate virtue with boredom or at least with dullness. We think that cleansing the heart means giving up vitality, vigor, enthusiasm. We could not be more mistaken. Joy in its most jubilant aspect is the joy of sanctity. To become so close to God that we experience the effervescent delight of doing what is morally right is life's highest satisfaction. Being linked by purity of heart and action to eternity is a pleasant lot indeed.

We would suggest, therefore, a quiet time in the early morning when the mind is rested and fresh and the day is still ahead. "Make conscience of beginning the day with Him," said Bunyan. And one of the best ways of beginning the day well is to begin it the night before. Early rising may require early retiring. Wesley is said to have left the company of Dr. Johnson because it was near his bedtime. He had an appointment with God at 4:00 A.M.

---

[4] See Book of Acts, ch. 26, vs. 1-23.

and he would not risk the peril of oversleeping, not even for the greatest literate of the age.

A brief time of prayer at night can round out the day and help to check the cleansing and guidance with which the day began. It is of special value that our last thoughts of each day be thoughts of trust and peace, that while we sleep the intricate thought processes of our subconscious mind should be occupied with higher things. But this must not be a substitute for the morning watch. Theory and experience combine to stress the importance of the morning hour.

To make use of the word *guidance* with no such background of daily cleansing and communion is to misapply a precious yet awesome term, and to bring it into disrepute. God does not treat us as dictaphones. His guidance is given on condition. He has guided men and women in every age, but with all the variations of circumstances they had this in common—they gave God time. In daily communion and obedience the child of God will come to discern his God's voice. The apostle John wrote, "And the sheep hear his voice; and he calleth his own sheep by name, and leadeth them out. . . . And the sheep follow him: for they know his voice." [5]

Men and women who have long made a practice of listening to God claim that they can distinguish between their own imagination and the impress of God's will. They do not claim that this gift fell upon them suddenly; it is the product of long practice in the art of listening. And they commend such constant practice to all who would qualify for the gift. In Franz's *Book of Discipline* we read: "Our power to perceive the light of God is, of all our powers, the one which we need most cultivate and develop. As exercise strengthens the body and education enlarges

---

[5] Gospel according to John, ch. 10, vs. 3, 4.

the mind, so the spiritual faculty within us grows as we use it in *seeing* and *doing* God's will." [6]

While God has sometimes spoken clearly to men who had no rich background of devotional life, the rules do hold that those who would cultivate the power to know His voice set a time aside specifically to commune with God and set it aside consistently.

Granted, now, that we have asked for guidance in the right light and have put forth every human effort to co-operate with God's Spirit and to live according to the example of Christ, have we, then, the right to expect that God will favor us with special signs or particular revelations of His will? Did not Gideon expect such a sign and did he not receive it? True, God did choose to reach the children of Israel through supernatural signs, but this does not mean that we can expect Him to do the same for us today. We must remember that we are not in the same circumstances as were the Israelites. When Jesus departed from this earth, He left us His special representative, the Holy Spirit, to guide us and to illuminate our reasoning. Guidance in the sense of a spectacular miracle should not be necessary to people who have the enormous advantages of centuries of culture and Christianity. God's guidance for them will be chiefly through directing their will and intelligence from experience and counsel.

Of course, we do not rule out the possibility of God's voice speaking directly to men. But we must be careful from whom we accept such a claim. Mentally ill people often have hallucinations, thinking that they hear voices and that God has singled them out to become spiritual leaders in the eyes of the world. Their "voices" will command them to commit distasteful, improper acts. A man claimed that God's voice told him to witness for Him by

---

[6] *Christian Life, Faith and Thought,* p. 83.

kneeling down and praying out loud on the pavement of a busy London street. Another person, a woman, declared that she heard God's voice telling her to drown herself in the Thames. Another once placed an advertisement in the newspaper declaring that God had told him that on a certain date He would return to earth. These instances are apparent conditions of mental illness rather than communication between a human being and God. God does speak directly to human beings as He spoke to His prophets of old; but we can be sure that whatever God would choose to communicate would be in complete harmony with His Word as recorded in the Holy Scriptures.

Ellen G. White wrote: "The Lord works in no haphazard way. Seek Him most earnestly in prayer. He will impress the mind, and will give tongue and utterance. The people of God are to be educated not to trust in human inventions and uncertain tests as a means of learning God's will concerning them. Satan and his agencies are always ready to step into any opening to be found that will lead souls away from the pure principles of the Word of God. The people who are led and taught of God will give no place to devisings for which there is not a 'Thus saith the Lord.' " [7]

The point is that Satan can produce signs and miracles that will confuse those who are not strong in their study of truth. Man's safety is to count on receiving illuminations from God's law and His Word.

Guidance does not imply continual success. I know of businessmen who think God has led them in their financial transactions because they have been so successful. God is the Source of all our blessings; that is true. But God is always more concerned with our spiritual success than with our material prosperity. The holy life is by no means a

---

[7] Ellen G. White, *Selected Messages,* book 2, p. 326.

sinecure—a spiritual merry-go-round. Behind us lie thousands of years of sorrow, sickness, sordidness, and sin. Our environment, if we are at all concerned with it, will give us moments of deep grief. Our Lord warned us that in the world we shall have tribulation. As Christians we must not expect exemption from immersion in pain, which is the common lot of humanity.

Let us recall that when Christ was baptized and filled with the Spirit, "immediately the spirit driveth him into the wilderness. And he was there in the wilderness forty days, tempted of Satan; and was with the wild beasts." [8] Had Christ been misled? No; but God often leads along the roughest roads in order to teach some of life's most valuable lessons—the kind that could never be learned on a couch of ease. The promise is that if we sincerely seek God's guidance and if we follow what our conscience in tune with God suggests, being willing to follow the insight and understanding received, then we shall not be misled.

If we have a decision to make and are convinced that according to every Christian measure the decision is right, we need not fear the consequences; nor need we blame ourselves if our course of action leads to unexpected difficulties. Human as we are, we may make mistakes even though we have laid ourselves open to God's guidance and have invoked it earnestly. Errors committed in good faith may teach us to avoid greater errors in the future.

Guidance may not always involve action, either. In fact, it may lead to *refrain* from action. The devoted Christian is a thoughtful person. He chooses to view his problems thoroughly. Some decisions have eternal consequences. They ought not to be made in momentary ecstasy or passion. Guidance entails thinking, using all men-

---

[8] Gospel according to Mark, ch. 1, vs. 12, 13.

tal faculties in an effort to reach the best conclusion. Very rarely does haste become the primary consideration. More often than not "haste maketh waste." Those who act with precipitancy usually do so because they want to get rid of the uncomfortable feeling indecision provokes. At times, one might even gain through standing by as doors open and close. Life has a way of proving that what one would have done on first impulse would have been disastrous. The prophet spoke wisely when he said, "In quietness and confidence shall be your strength." [9]

What I say next may seem paradoxical; nevertheless it is an important part of guidance. Divine guidance may come from the counsel of fellow human beings. Godly men whose experience in life qualifies them to give advice are intermediaries God expects us to use. Often such a one can interpret our circumstances far more coherently than we can, because we may be swayed more by emotion than knowledge. However, a counselor should be chosen with care. Meddling gossips and foolish friends are not fit to give counsel. They may be eager to direct lives, but the chances are their motives are self-centered and their judgment unbalanced. Both he who seeks and he who gives advice have a responsibility to truth uncolored by personal preference.

God's guidance ofttimes appears in what seems to be a trivial circumstance. But great events often turn on apparent trivialities. Heavy doors, we are reminded, swing on small hinges. True, and divine providence often emerges in some apparently inconsequential twist of life. The case of Albert Schweitzer is instructive:

In the Whitsuntide holidays of 1896 young Schweitzer made up his mind he would devote himself to art and science until he was 30, and afterward to the direct service

---

[9] Book of Isaiah, ch. 30, v. 15.

of humanity. But the quest for a sphere of service did not prove easy. He thought first of caring for and educating abandoned children. His efforts to find such work proved unsuccessful. He thought next of discharged prisoners, and for a while he assisted in work among these men. But no real sense of mission came with any of these tasks. Then finally the light came. In the autumn of 1904 he found one of the green-covered magazines of the Paris Missionary Society on his desk at the college where he taught. In the very act of putting it aside to get on with his work, he opened it mechanically to an article entitled "The Need for the Congo Mission." Here is Schweitzer's account:

"It was by Alfred Boegner, president of the Paris Missionary Society, an Alsatian, and contained a complaint that the Mission had not enough workers to carry on its work in the Gabon, the northern province of the Congo Colony. The writer expressed his hope that the appeal would bring some of those 'on whom the Master's eyes already rested' to a decision to offer themselves for this urgent work. The conclusion ran: 'Men and women who can reply simply to the Master's call, "Lord, I am coming," these are the people whom the church needs.' The article finished, I quietly began my work. My search was over." [10]

So all the glorious work at Lambarene turned on so trivial a thing as a green-covered magazine and its mechanical opening. Certainly this was nothing short of guidance. The child of God will recognize such providence as a true privilege and a fruit of salvation.

Think of the wonder of it, the peace of it, and the security of it. In a way, all Christian achievement is the fruit of God's guidance. The sincere Christian will appro-

---

[10] Albert Schweitzer, *My Life and Thought*, p. 107.

Albert Schweitzer's dedicated life testifies to the wisdom accepting God's guidance in our lives.

priate this dimension of salvation. In each of our lives God's voice speaks quietly, one syllable at a time, trying to tell us the answers that we eagerly seek yet so often willfully reject. All we need to do is to listen. We shall be surprised, yes, shocked by the force and clarity with which the voice can speak to our heart. But if calamity knocks at the door, and God's way seems obscure, he who has learned to obey with confidence will steer right onward under Heaven's banner. The way that opens may be man's second best, yet eternity will reveal that it was God's first choice, and man's ultimate best.

CHAPTER 19

Prayer

IN TRYGVE GULBRANSSEN'S book *The Wind from the Mountains* one character is unforgettable—old Dag. Dag's life is a painful trek, but he progresses toward the light amid his sorrows and troubles. One day, opening the bishop's Bible he sees these lines on the flyleaf:

"Our human thoughts and works are not so mighty
That they can cut a path to God, unbless'd,
And so from Him the gift of prayer is sent us
To hallow both our labor and our quest.
Over life, and death, and starlit spaces
The high road runs that at His word was laid,
And reaches Him across the desert places;
By prayer it is our pilgrimage is made."

That day Dag found new support in his struggle.

Indeed, prayer is the highway to God. In this fast-moving age men are highway conscious. Fascinated with space exploration, they concentrate on finding interplanetary paths through the skies; nonetheless, through life and death and the starlit spaces themselves, prayer is man's essential highroad.

We need to understand more about prayer than we do. True, prayer is one of our common religious practices.

213

That is not all. We recognize that it is a privilege; but privileges are easily taken for granted. Prayer probably is one of the most often contorted and misapplied facets of salvation—so used by people who would be shocked to hear that they have never discovered the real intent of prayer. Thus, prayer can be dangerous—dangerous because it is the way into God's presence, and woe to him who comes before the God of the cosmos glibly, ignorantly, and without a sense of sublime embarrassment. Better to be like the illiterate beggar who stutters and mutters his plea but does so with artless sincerity and out of a sense of overwhelming inner need, than to mistake and misuse the power of prayer.

One thing is certain: prayer is unmistakably a factor in the God-centered life. In the Old Testament, communion between God and His people was personal and intimate. Petitionary prayer was common, as were also adoration, praise, and thanksgiving. Then, in the New Testament, Jesus reaffirmed the role of prayer. He taught that true prayer is spiritual, not formal. Spontaneity, therefore, was to characterize prayer. Prayer was to be the outgoing of the heart toward the heavenly Father in unclouded faith. In fact, the Lord's Prayer is a fitting summary of Jesus' teaching on the subject. His address to God the Father captures in six immortal sentences the function and purpose of prayer:

"Our Father which art in heaven, Hallowed be thy name. Thy kingdom come. Thy will be done in earth, as it is in heaven. Give us this day our daily bread. And forgive us our debts, as we forgive our debtors. And lead us not into temptation, but deliver us from evil: For thine is the kingdom, and the power, and the glory, for ever. Amen." [1]

God who dwells in heaven receives His children's

---

[1] Gospel according to Matthew, ch. 6, vs. 9-13.

adoration. The aim of this prayer is not the imposition of man's will upon God, but the hallowing of His sacred name, the extension of His kingdom, the submission to His will. Only after the proper setting is created does Christ direct us to petition the Father. The prayer ends not with our needs or desires but with God, with whom it began— with His kingdom, His power, His glory. Augustine said, "When we pray rightly and properly, we ask for nothing else than what is contained in the Lord's prayer."

Saint Paul's Epistles obviously were written by a man of prayer. The apostle is constantly breaking forth in thanksgiving, adoration, petition, doxology. Paul dealt with the varied aspects of prayer, individual and corporate; he instructed the churches in a proper understanding of the objectives and results of prayer. He made this astonishing point: Under an inner compulsion, God's children may intercede without understanding the petition. They may simply sigh out inarticulate desires. These unspoken aspirations, Paul teaches, are engendered by the Spirit, who is able to present them to the Father as intercessions. And when Paul received something different from his request, it only deepened his communion with God.[2]

While there is much in prayer that we must understand and explore, on this we can rest assured: In His way and time God answers prayer. His answers ofttimes are miraculous and breathtaking. When perhaps for the first time, men find themselves faced with desperate danger, how wonderful it is to understand the exercise of prayer. During World War II, millions turned to God for help, and though inexperienced in praying, they found Him a wonder-working friend. Unforgettable, for example, is the story of Lieutenant Whittaker and his companions, who on a life raft in the Pacific, prayed for water and saw a rain cloud

---

[2] See Second Epistle to the Corinthians, ch. 12, v. 7.

come to them against the wind; or the story of Maj. Allen Lindberg who, in a similar tragic plight, prayed for deliverance and was providentially found by heathen tribesmen; or the well-known rescue of John Kennedy by Methodist and Seventh-day Adventist natives on the Solomon Islands. Writing for the *American* magazine about these many trials and triumphs, Chaplain William C. Taggart says:

"I know of men lost and starving in the deserts of Australia who were found and brought to safety after asking God for help. Of men in bombers shot to pieces by enemy gunfire who, quite literally, prayed their way back to base. I know, too, that many times appeals uttered by mothers, wives, and sweethearts in the United States stretched a protective mantle half around the globe to shield us in the South Pacific. One high-ranking general told me that he owes his life, in part, to the petitions voiced by his closest friend and former business partner. I, myself, am living on borrowed time because my parents prayed for me in a situation of great danger."

All this is thrilling, but poses a basic question too: Does God change His purpose or His plans because men pray? Is anything at all changed because men desire to have it changed?

Prayer does not change God. Prayer is not intended to change God. His purpose is not changed. There are times, however, when God may have alternate ways of working or He may permit a certain choice of procedure. Such was the case with David, who was given a choice of three kinds of punishment because of his transgression: seven years of famine, three months of defeat in battle, or three days of pestilence.[3] God's purpose was not changed. The king was simply granted a choice of punishment.

---

[3] See Second Book of Samuel, ch. 24, vs. 12-14.

Prayer is not primarily to get from God what man wants, but rather to change man and to bring him into harmony with God's will. Prayer brings man to understand and accept God's mind. Prayer is not an effort to outline some plan of action for God to follow, but to ascertain what God's plan is so that man may follow it. Through prayer man does not ask that God's will be changed, but that God's will be *done*. The chief aim of prayer is for the supplicant to come so completely into harmony with God that God's will becomes his. And what is accomplished by this identification?

1. The man is now a partner with God and ready to cooperate with Him in whatever God wants.

2. Man's mind is taken from what he prayed for to something better. He forgets what he was so intent upon getting and is now occupied with what God wants him to do. He accepts what Paul did when he said, "I have learned, in whatsoever state I am, therewith to be content." [4] Before, he fretted; now he is content. He knows that he is in God's hands, that God is working on His plan with him, that all things will work together for good.

3. Man has learned to trust God fully, having discovered that answer to prayer is no longer a problem. He knows that all his prayers are answered according to the promise, "What things soever ye desire, when ye pray, believe that ye receive them, and ye shall have them." [5] A true Christian will ask of God only that which God wants him to have. His will is God's will, and he asks that God's will be done. Hence, whatever he asks, he will get.

Prayer is that simple—and just that wonderful. Could we only understand fully what the prayer life can do for us personally and for our influence on others! There is nothing that prayer cannot accomplish. However, this high-

---

[4] Epistle to the Philippians, ch. 4, v. 11.
[5] Gospel according to Mark, ch. 11, v. 24.

road does have its pitfalls. How well we know! Then, to better understand these pitfalls let us ask ourselves three very significant questions:

1. *Do we pray because we were taught to do so?*

At mother's knee, in school, in church, we were introduced to the mechanics of uttering prayer. In this respect we hasten to say that it would be a blessing if everyone had received this training. Those of us who have had it are fortunate; but so many make crooked paths for their feet. They offer prayer in a loose, haphazard manner, trusting in a virtue rather than in a relationship to God.

So often the efficiency of prayer is but feebly understood. The proof of this lies in how easily we are frustrated when our prayers seem to reach no higher than the ceiling of the room in which they are offered. It appears also in the fact that our lives are inconsistent with our prayers. We pray for forgiveness, but remain laden with guilt. We pray for joy, but our faces portray anguish. We pray for power, while we are monuments to weakness.

It is actually possible, you know, to pray without believing in God. Irrational? Not when we consider that believing *in* God is different from believing *about* God. We are deft at arguing *pro* God's existence. We do not hesitate to take immediate exception with the atheist who tries to prove that God is nonexistent. We know there is a God, yes; but do we know Him personally? Do we feel ourselves enveloped by His holy presence as we talk to Him in friendship?

For so many of us, I fear, prayer becomes merely a conditioned reflex, a conventional speech pattern, a long-continued practice. Rarely do we pray because we know God as our dearest friend and because He is our life, the fiber of our existence and the center of our aspirations. When we discuss our business affairs, our cheeks burn with excitement. We talk of our friends with a light in our eyes. But what is it that allows us to mumble a prayer without change in expression? We have far greater reason to be moved in spirit and heart when we talk with God than with any other person. It should be the most natural thing in the world to talk with Him and to glow with excitement, joy, and love.

At some time we were told that we should pray in Jesus' name. Do we comply perfunctorily by making mention of this at the end of our prayer? To pray in the name of Jesus does not mean simply to prefix or suffix our petition with His name. It means to pray in the mind and spirit of Jesus —to pray with the same attitude and purpose as He prayed when He was on earth. Prayer is empowered and real; it never is to be used lightly, thoughtlessly, or irreverently.

2. *Do we pray simply because we want something?*

If the answer is Yes, it is so because we do not stop to think beyond our immediate longing for this certain object. God enters the picture as a magician who is expected to grant that twice two be not four. We pray, "God, cure my pain." "Keep me safe from harm and danger." "Save my marriage." "Don't let the diagnosis be cancer." How easy it is for us to pray when we are in a pinch! This kind of prayer arises out of fear; in fact, some would never dream of taking a prolonged trip without first praying for a safe journey. They hang a prayer, so to speak, around their neck as a charm against possible disaster. But in such petitions one may not in any way hallow the name of God —and prayer may be a travesty.

Actually, such misconception of prayer is tragic. For example, here is a person who prayed regularly for years. Morning and evening he offered his oblations to God with the idea that surely such regular praying would keep him from harm and danger. But one day he is faced with the medical verdict of terminal cancer. In a frenzy he cries to God, "Save me. Don't let me die!" Alas, he finds himself in the same state as did King Claudius in Shakespeare's Hamlet:

> "My words fly up, my thoughts
>   remain below:
> Words without thoughts never to
>   heaven go."

Now he finds neither peace nor hope in prayer. His world crashes around his feet, because he had never really walked with God. For all his praying, God was a stranger to him. So this man, ostensibly religious, turns against God with bitterness, believing that God has forsaken him. With numbed fingers he flounders desperately to catch a safety rope; but nothing happens. After a lifetime use of prayer as a mechanical thing, a charm against evil, he finds that when he is faced with ultimate reality, his whole structure crumbles.

Through the years he had prayed for matters to go his way; now something happens against his will and he thinks God has forsaken him. But he never had prayed to God, really. Rather, he had attempted to turn God into his private bellboy, expecting Him to appear, ready for service, whenever he pressed the button.

On the other hand, it is possible to be so intent, so single-minded in our prayer that we actually force an answer to our petition by our own God-given energy. In such desperation we may even answer our own prayer—in conformity with *our* will instead of God's. Individuals may band together and by sheer psychological force apparently turn events in their direction. But this, too, is perilous. True prayer is not so. In true prayer, when we do not receive the things we asked for, we still believe that God hears and that He has answered our prayer. In our shortsightedness we often ask for things that would in the end be a curse. Thus God may, in love, answer our prayers by giving us not what we asked for, but what in the long run is most blessed. Again Shakespeare spoke with wisdom:

"We, ignorant of ourselves,
  Beg often our own harms, which the wise powers
  Deny us for our good; so find we profit
  By losing of our prayers."

Let this not be misconstrued. God does want us to keep our desires, joys, sorrows, and cares before Him. We cannot burden or weary Him. He has numbered the hairs of our head and is certainly not indifferent to our wants. His heart of love is touched by our grief. We are encouraged to "take to Him everything that perplexes the mind. Nothing is too great for Him to bear, for He holds up worlds, He rules over all the affairs of the universe. Nothing that in any way concerns our peace is too small for Him to notice. There is no chapter in our experience too dark for Him to read; there is no perplexity too difficult for Him to unravel. No calamity can befall the least of His children, no anxiety harass the soul, no joy cheer, no sincere prayer escape the lips, of which our heavenly Father is unobservant, or in which He takes no immediate interest. . . . The relations between God and each soul are as distinct and full as though there were not another soul upon the earth to share His watchcare, not another soul for whom He gave His beloved Son." [6]

Christ's promise remains true: "I have chosen you . . . that whatsoever ye shall ask of the Father in my name, he may give it you." [7] But to interpret God's promise as meaning that prayer must always be answered in just the way we want it to be is presumption. God is wiser than we are and His ways are above human ways. He does not err, but we do. So, before everything else—before sorrow grips us

---

[6] Ellen G. White, *Steps to Christ*, p. 100.
[7] Gospel according to John, ch. 15, v. 16.

and before heartache tears us to pieces or bitterness infests our minds—let us walk in step with the divine will and pray according to God's limitless grace, not according to our selfish insistence.

3. *Do we pray because we fear?*

The world seems to be gathering speed in the treadmill of ominous peril. Country after country is involved in political disaster. Revolutions and counterrevolutions take place, followed by threats of complete world destruction through methods of warfare aimed at destroying with finality. In the face of nuclear destruction, many persons pray because this seems to be the only salvation from extinction. They regard God as a vague spirit of universal good will. They have heard it said that the world is His and all that is in it, so He appears to be the most likely solution to their terrible fear. His philanthropic humanitarianism might do some good, so they pray. Today the newspapers carry earnest admonitions to "visit the church of your choice" and to pray for world conditions. However, unless to us God is a Person of supreme reality, and our relationship to Him is one of obedience, such prayer is not effective. Unless we are united with Him in spirit, in truth, in deep love for Him, what good is such a prayer? How can we find light if we are headed in the direction of shadow? Impossible. God must not be a vague state of mind when He ought to be the most vital part of our lives. We pray, "Hallowed be thy name," but often we have not the slightest idea what it is to hallow God's name, for to hallow His name is to discover that God and we are one; that His will is our will.

Another prayer of fear is offered by people who pray because they think that by their so doing God will keep things as they were a hundred years ago. Specifically, they

yer is opening the heart to God as to a friend. It ngs finite man into the audience chamber of Heaven.

pray because they think prayer will exterminate what they consider to be evil.

In true prayer God must be our complete reality, the highest attainment of good. He must be the means and the end of our living, whether we live for many more years or only one more day. Beside God all else must seem fleeting, shadowy, ephemeral, and of no consequence. In prayer our frail humanity, with all its errors, mistakes, prejudices, and pettiness is caught up and exchanged for God's omnipotence and great love. To pray to God is to be involved with Him and to feel our heartbeats in tune with the divine heartbeat. This kind of prayer, when so prayed, leaves no doubt that it is heard. One who has learned to pray aright knows the power of prayer; his life shows a poise and serenity that are the result of having been lifted to God.

Frequently someone expresses the opinion that God speaks to man through nature, revelation, His providence, and by the influence of His Spirit, so that prayer is superfluous. But this is not true. We need desperately to pour out our heart to God. Life and energy come only as the result of a two-way communion with Heaven. Our minds may gravitate toward God; we may know instinctively that He is near; but this is not in the fullest sense communing with Him. In order to commune, we must *share with God* the vital issues of our life.

Prayer thus understood and practiced will support and enhearten us in every trial. Trials there will be; make no mistake in this respect. All who inherit God's kingdom will experience days of darkness and deep perplexity— even in the prayer life. Trusting God when all is sweetness and light and His smile is apparently upon us is far easier than trusting Him when we grope along in the dark, when our life's experience requires unqualified trust and confidence. Yet, as we pray and agonize in times of darkness, we can really see God as He is. The veil is drawn aside and we behold Him who loved us and gave Himself for us. Then we can see at the center of the universe not an impersonal God, not an "absentee landlord," but a loving Father—One who is touched with the feelings of our infirmities, and whose great heart of love answers prayer.

> "Lord, what a change within us one short hour
> Spent in Thy presence will prevail to make!
> What heavy burdens from our bosoms take,
> What parched grounds refresh as with a shower!
> We kneel, and all around us seems to lower;
> We rise, and all, the distant and the near,
> Stands forth in sunny outline brave and clear;
> We kneel, how weak! we rise, how full of power!
> Why, therefore, should we do ourselves this wrong,
> Or others, that we are not always strong,
> That we are ever overborne with care,
> That we should ever weak or heartless be,
> Anxious or troubled, when with us is prayer,
> And joy and strength and courage are with Thee!"

RICHARD CHENEVIX TRENCH, 1807-1886

CHAPTER 20

Judgment

CHARLES G. FINNEY, a young law student, was sitting in a village law office in Upper New York State. It was early morning, and he was alone. He had studied law for four years, and now—it seemed to him—was spending his life selfishly. In fact, life's prospect depressed him.

Suddenly it was as though a voice spoke within his heart, "Finney, what are you going to do when you finish your law course?"

His immediate answer followed a well-beaten routine in his thinking: "Why, put out my shingle and practice law, of course."

"Then what?"

"Make some money—be successful; get rich."

"Then what?"

"Build a beautiful home, have a family, and be respected by everyone."

"Then what?"

"Well, finally I'll get old and retire."

"Then what?"

"Well, men must die, and so will I."

"Then what?"

Those words kept driving into Finney's mind. "Then what?" "Then what?" Suddenly from the storehouse of memory, words of Holy Scripture heard in childhood flashed across his mind: "It is appointed unto men once to die, but after this the judgment." [1]

The young lawyer leaped to his feet and to a new realization of life's true purpose. He saw himself at the judgment bar of God. Henceforth this realization gave a sense of accountability to his existence. Daniel Webster had said, "Gentlemen, the most serious question which has ever engaged my thoughts is my personal accountability to God." Finney joined Webster in this conviction; and from that day Finney's life was dedicated to the high purpose of the Christian ministry. He became known not as a lawyer, but as a great preacher and evangelist. During a ministry of more than fifty years he brought many thousands to a God-centered life.

No one can escape God's judgment. This is one of the most certain teachings of Scripture. "We must all appear before the judgment seat of Christ," wrote Saint Paul to the Corinthians.[2] Some may say, "The judgment is such an old-fashioned subject." Yes, it is old-fashioned—old-fashioned like God's Word, the sun, the stars; like God. Old-fashioned like the law of cause and effect. Saint Paul understood this well, too, as is gleaned from what he wrote to the Galatians: "Be not deceived; God is not mocked: for whatsoever a man soweth, that shall he also reap." [3] The Old Testament preacher recognized this law; then proclaimed: "Know thou, that for all these things [the ways of life] God will bring thee into judgment." [4] Underlying the Old Testament ideas of temporal judgment was increasing emphasis on the truth that ultimately there must come a *final judgment.* Time was to the Hebrews like a line with beginning and end—the linear concept of history

---

[1] Epistle to the Hebrews, ch. 9, v. 27.
[2] Second Epistle to the Corinthians, ch. 5, v. 10.
[3] Epistle to the Galatians, ch. 6, v. 7.
[4] Book of Ecclesiastes, ch. 11, v. 9.

as opposed to the pagan cyclical concept. Ultimately all men must appear before God. The outstanding characters of the Old Testament voiced their consciousness of a certain universal divine judgment. The preacher spoke perhaps most clearly when he said: "God will judge the righteous and the wicked, for he has appointed a time for every matter, and for every work." [5]

The great preachers of the New Testament were certain of a final judgment. After asserting that all must appear before the judgment seat of Christ, Paul continued: "That every one may receive the things done in his body, according to that he hath done, whether it be good or bad." [6] Peter also understood the judgment truth. In connection with his visit to Cornelius and the start of the gospel message in the midst of a non-Jewish population, he said: "[Christ] commanded us to preach to the people, and to testify that he is the one ordained by God to be judge of the living and the dead." [7]

The apostle John associates the judgment with heavenly records preserved in scrolls or books, one of these being the book of life. "I saw," he said, "the dead, small and great, stand before God; and the books were opened: . . . and the dead were judged out of those things which were written in the books, according to their works." [8] John gave special prominence to the idea of judgment in his Gospel story where the noun *judgment* and the verb *to judge* are found at least thirty-one times.

The idea of a judgment ought not to come as a surprise to anyone who is familiar with Scripture, for the religion of the Bible is ethical, emphasizing a distinction between loyalty and disloyalty, between good and evil. The reward of the righteous man and the destiny of the

---

[5] *Ibid.*, ch. 3, v. 17, R.S.V.
[6] Second Epistle to the Corinthians, ch. 5, v. 10.
[7] Book of Acts, ch. 10, v. 42, R.S.V.
[8] Book of the Revelation, ch. 20, v. 12.

wicked are set forth clearly. The distinction between these two destinies involves judgment—a process of investigation, verdict, and execution. The course of this judgment hinges on man's acceptance or rejection of Jesus Christ.

To be sure, the apostles did not have to rely exclusively on the Old Testament teaching. They had the words of Jesus too. In His early statements Jesus made clear the role He was to play in judgment. "God sent not his Son into the world to condemn [charge] the world; but that the world through him might be saved." [9] Jesus also said, "I judge no man"; and "I came not to judge the world, but to save the world." [10] Christ's primary function during the Incarnation was to save, not to judge or condemn. However, the record indicates that His future role includes judgment. Jesus said: "The Father judgeth no man, but hath committed all judgment unto the Son." [11] Here the Greek noun for "judgment" is *krisis* and has, in this context, the meaning of judicial authority. Jesus added that the Father had given Him "authority to execute judgment." [12] Thus we are to recognize that when a man is brought face to face with Jesus Christ, he must perforce decide whether he will accept Him now as Redeemer, or hereafter as the executor of final judgment. This decision is the real crisis that faces every man in this life.

Jesus made it clear also that judgment would come upon every man. Answering pharisaical charges of devil possession, He made this comment upon the scope and inevitability of future judgment: "I say unto you, That every idle word that men shall speak, they shall give account thereof in the day of judgment." [13]

Jesus taught a number of other vital truths in connec-

---

[9] Gospel according to John, ch. 3, v. 17.
[10] *Ibid.*, ch. 12, v. 47.
[11] *Ibid.*, ch. 5, v. 22.
[12] *Ibid.*, v. 27.
[13] Gospel according to Matthew, ch. 12, v. 36.

tion with the judgment. He makes the following points:

1. The day of judgment was still future in our Saviour's time, because Jesus made the statement that "it shall be more tolerable for . . . Sodom";[14] "it shall be more tolerable for Tyre and Sidon at the day of judgment."[15] In other words, the day of judgment had not yet come for the cities mentioned. Sodom, Tyre, and Sidon had been destroyed many centuries before the time of our Lord, yet the day of judgment had not yet come to them, that is, to the people living in those cities.

2. Men are responsible for the light of truth which comes to them—for acceptance or rejection of that light. Christ's reasoning was that if men rejected Him, it would be more tolerable for Sodom, Tyre, and Sidon than for them in the day of judgment, because those to whom He had preached in person had received more light. This shows unmistakably that in God's judgment men are judged according to the light they have.

3. Christ emphasized the importance of hearing and accepting His words. God committed all judgment to His Son. "For the Father judgeth no man, but hath committed all judgment unto the Son: that all men should honour the Son, even as they honour the Father."[16] The point is, we are to stand before God in judgment on the basis of whether or not we accept the Son and honor Him as we honor God. "Verily, verily, I say unto you," are Christ's words, "He that heareth my word, and believeth on him that sent me, hath everlasting life, and shall not come into condemnation; but is passed from death unto life."[17] The only way to avoid the condemnation and execution of judgment is to believe on Christ.

4. Not only those living on earth today, but all the

---

[14] *Ibid.*, ch. 11, v. 24.
[15] *Ibid.*, v. 22.
[16] Gospel according to John, ch. 5, vs. 22, 23.
[17] *Ibid.*, v. 24.

dead of past ages must stand before God in judgment. This, too, Jesus affirmed when He said: "The dead shall hear the voice of the Son of God: and they that hear shall live. For as the Father hath life in himself; so hath he given to the Son to have life in himself; and hath given him authority to execute judgment also, because he is the Son of man." Jesus continued: "Marvel not at this: for the hour is coming, in the which all that are in the graves shall hear his voice, and shall come forth; they that have done good, unto the resurrection of life; and they that have done evil, unto the resurrection of damnation." [18]

Only two classes will be in the judgment—not the rich and the poor, not the wise and the simple, not the cultured and the ignorant, but the righteous and the wicked. In Christ's teaching, this division is likened to a shepherd separating his sheep from the goats. Jesus made it clear, however, that it is He, not man, who makes this division.

"When the Son of man shall come in his glory, and all the holy angels with him, then shall he sit upon the throne of his glory: and before him shall be gathered all nations: and he shall separate them one from another, as a shepherd divideth his sheep from the goats: and he shall set the sheep on his right hand, but the goats on the left. Then shall the King say unto them on his right hand, Come, ye blessed of my Father, inherit the kingdom prepared for you from the foundation of the world." "Then shall he say also unto them on the left hand, Depart from me, ye cursed, into everlasting fire, prepared for the devil and his angels." "And these shall go away into everlasting punishment: but the righteous into life eternal." [19]

Naturally the teachings of Christ and the apostles concerning the judgment had a special meaning for the Christians of that day. Most of them had a Jewish, scriptural

---

[18] *Ibid.*, vs. 25-29.
[19] Gospel according to Matthew, ch. 25, vs. 31-34, 41, 46.

background; and the Jewish concept of divine judgment centered in the sanctuary service. The Scriptures reveal two sanctuaries: the one built by Moses in the desert, where was enacted the ancient passion play; another, the great original in heaven. The sanctuary in the desert had long been nonexistent. It had portrayed on earth the program of salvation as conceived in heaven and executed in behalf of men. The first Christians understood this, though two new factors had become standard belief. First, the priests no longer were to offer sacrifices for sin "often" and "every year." By one transcendent event Christ had "appeared once for all at the end of the age to put away sin by the sacrifice of himself." [20] Second, at a fixed point in time Christ would return for a final settlement of the problem of Satan, sin, and sinners, and for the complete redemption of His saints. What had been a dim outline now became a glorious hope. The first coming and the ascension of our Lord assured a second coming and the resurrection of the saints. "I will come again," He promised. [21] The first advent, the resurrection, and the ascension thus established the certainty of universal judgment to come.

Now, we pointed out that Christ and the apostles taught the day of judgment was to be in the future. Carrying through on this, John the revelator set down vital "messages" that would be proclaimed to the world at the "time of the end." These messages were introduced by these words: "And I saw another angel fly in the midst of heaven, having the everlasting gospel to preach unto them that dwell on the earth, and to every nation, and kindred, and tongue, and people." [22] The message was to be "gospel," that is, "good news." At this particular juncture in history, however, the gospel would be proclaimed in the setting of

---

[20] Epistle to the Hebrews, ch. 9, v. 26, R.S.V.
[21] Gospel according to John, ch. 14, v. 3.
[22] Book of the Revelation, ch. 14, v. 6.

God's judgment hour, for these words follow: "Fear God, and give glory to him; for the hour of his judgment is come." [23]

Here is an announcement that the judgment "is come." The judgment, at that point, no longer is in the future. Evidently the judgment, or at least one phase of it, will already be in session when men hear this message. This can only be that God's judgment—the deciding part—will be carried on in heaven during the closing period of earth's history. Thus, those who preach the everlasting gospel in the last days would be able to know exactly when the judgment began; for how could they announce the judgment hour *had* begun if they did not know *when* it began?

Mind you, we are not speaking about the second coming of Christ. We have pointed out elsewhere that the Scriptures emphatically withhold the specific time of Christ's actual return. In all the 260 New Testament references to that supreme, climactic event, nowhere is given any hint of the actual year, day, or hour. However, God did not withhold knowledge as to the time of His judgment.

Turning once again to God's revelations in the area of time, we recall the short, crisp prediction made by the prophet Daniel many centuries ago. It reads: "Unto two thousand and three hundred days; then shall the sanctuary be cleansed." [24]

In our previous discussion of this prophecy [25] we came to understand the accepted principle of prophetic interpretation, to the effect that a day in symbolic prophecy represents a literal year. The period of time with which we are dealing, then, is one extending two thousand three hundred years into the future from the starting point. The starting point, as we learned, was the autumn of 457 B.C.

---

[23] *Ibid.*, v. 7.
[24] Book of Daniel, ch. 8, v. 14.
[25] See page 129.

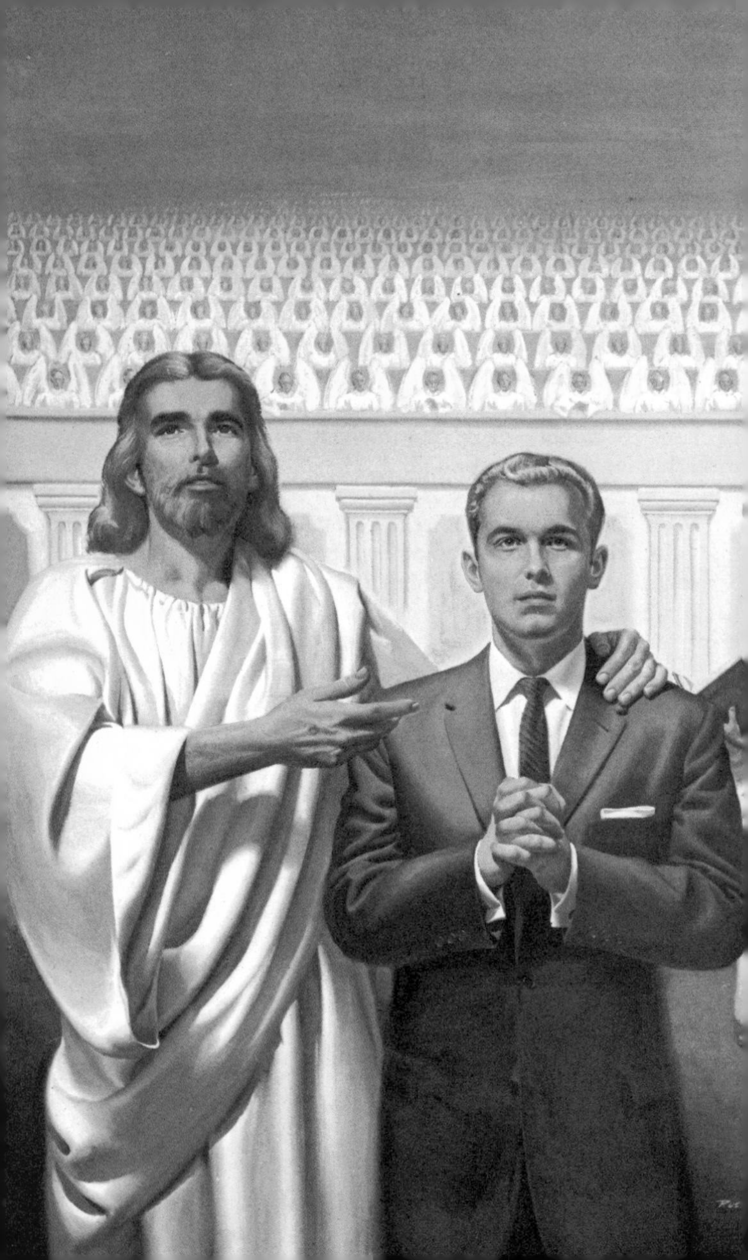

Simple arithmetic takes us down across the centuries to the fall of the year 1844, at which time the sanctuary was to be cleansed. But what was this cleansing of the sanctuary? What does this have to do with the judgment? Let me explain that it has much to do with the judgment.

Writing to the Hebrews, the apostle taught that the ancient desert sanctuary and its services were "figures of the true." [26] Is it not reasonable, therefore, that we should find in the ancient service a clear type, an illustration of what was to take place in the heavenly sanctuary in 1844?

The Book of Leviticus describes the most interesting and important service of the Hebrew sanctuary, the yearly Day of Atonement. Of this day we read that it was to take place "because of the uncleanness of the children of Israel." [27] This day, then, was the day of "cleansing."

Now note the significance of this day. The Jews called it *Yoma,* "the day." It was the keystone of the sacrificial system. Whoever did not on that day afflict his soul was cut off from Israel. [28] The Day of Atonement occurred on the tenth day of the seventh month, about the latter part of our October. The special preparation for this day began ten days earlier. Of this the *Jewish Encyclopedia* says:

"The first ten days of Tishri grew to be the Ten Penitential Days of the year, intended to bring about a perfect change of heart, and to make Israel like new-born creatures, the culmination being reached on the Day of Atonement, when religion's greatest gift, God's condoning mercy, was to be offered to man." "The idea developed also in Jewish circles that on the first of Tishri, the sacred New-Year's Day and the anniversary of Creation, man's doings

---

[26] Epistle to the Hebrews, ch. 9, v. 24.
[27] Book of Leviticus, ch. 16, v. 16.
[28] *Ibid.,* ch. 23, v. 29.

e must all appear before the universal judgment seat heaven, but we can choose Jesus Christ as our advocate.

were judged and his destiny was decided; and that on the tenth of Tishri the decree of heaven was sealed." [29]

The Jewish conception of what took place on the Day of Atonement is emphasized further in a statement ascribed to Rabbi Amnon of Mayence: "God, seated on His throne to judge the world, at the same time Judge, Pleader, Expert, and Witness, openeth the Book of Records; it is read, every man's signature being found therein. The great trumpet is sounded; a still, small voice is heard; the angels shudder, saying, this is the day of judgment." [30]

How was this service a cleansing? How was it a judgment? Through the year the people, when they sinned, had brought their offerings. These pointed forward to the Lamb of God who would one day give His life. The children of Israel might delay to confess their sins, but they dared not delay beyond the Day of Atonement. The climax of the year's round of service was the day of judgment, a deadline beyond which they could not go without being cut off from among God's people. At that time, the sanctuary was "cleansed" from the sins of Israel that through the year had been transferred to it in type by the offering of sacrifices. It was an illustration of how God will finally deal with sin.

Thus, the sanctuary in heaven must also be cleansed from the record of man's sin—not with the blood of animals, but with the blood of Christ "once and for all." That cleansing must involve the work of judgment, an investigation of the records of men. For remember, the judgment is not primarily set up to determine what God will do about man's estrangement, but what men have done about it. Have they, or have they not, accepted the blood of Christ to cover their sins and to "cleanse" from "all unrighteousness"? [31] It all narrows down to this: Are our

[29] *Jewish Encyclopedia,* vol. 2, p. 281.
[30] *Ibid.,* p. 286.
[31] First Epistle of John, ch. 1, v. 9.

sins forgiven? Or are they not? Man decides his own eternal destiny.

Our decision to accept Christ at conversion actually does not seal our destiny. The life record after conversion is also important. A man may go back on his repentance, or by careless inattention let slip the very life he has espoused. Nor can it be said that a man's record is closed when he comes to the end of his days. He is responsible for his influence during life, and is just as surely responsible for his influence after he is dead. To quote the words of the poet, "The evil that men do lives after them," leaving a trail of sin to be charged to their account. In order to be just, God takes all this into account in the judgment. This fact is proof, moreover, that judgment cannot come at death. It must come when God has resolved to put an end to sin's course in the universe.

But you say, Does not God know the end from the beginning? Is He not well acquainted with the records of every individual?

Were God alone concerned, there would be no need of an investigation of the life records of men in this judgment. Even before the creation of the world, He knew man would sin and that he would need a Saviour. Moreover, a sovereign God, He knows just who will accept and who will reject His great salvation. If God alone were concerned, there would certainly be no need of records. But in order that the inhabitants of the entire universe, the good and evil angels, and all who have lived on this earth, might understand His love and His justice, the life history of every individual has been recorded. In the judgment these records will be disclosed. Just what these records are like, we do not know. That has not been revealed. But the Scriptures make it plain that whatever their nature, they play a vital role in the judgment scene, clearing only those who have overcome sin.

It is clear in Bible teaching that prior to the Second Advent the Lord has settled who among the dead and the living are His saints. It has been determined who are "the dead in Christ" and who are the living saints to be "caught up together with them in the clouds" [32] for when He comes His reward is with Him "to give every man according as his work shall be." [33] The sheep and the goats have been predetermined and separated in the divine councils. The church has been judged and accounted worthy through faith in Christ. The closing acts of intercession and the great work of cleansing coincides with the judgment of investigation. The subjects of the kingdom are made up. This phase of judgment determines who of the myriads sleeping in the dust of the earth are worthy of a part in the first resurrection; and who of the living multitudes are worthy of translation.

So this work of judgment began in 1844. We need to reflect upon the nature of the event and what it means to men today. Let us first make clear, however, the various phases of God's judgment. They are three, and are exemplified in a trial in our civil courts. There is the trial proper, or as is sometimes called, the investigation. Then there is the decision, or verdict. Finally there is the executive phase—the execution of the decree of the judge. All these might be called the judgment. The Scriptures reveal that it is the first phase—the investigation—that began in 1844 and is now in progress. The verdict and the execution will come in due course.

Now let us look at the scriptural picture of heaven's tribunal—God's court session. Notice these details:

"I beheld till the thrones were cast down, and the Ancient of days did sit, whose garment was white as snow,

---

[32] First Epistle to the Thessalonians, ch. 4, vs. 16, 17.
[33] Book of the Revelation, ch. 22, v. 12.

and the hair of his head like the pure wool: his throne was like the fiery flame, and his wheels as burning fire." [34]

How awesome is the scene! This is heaven's supreme tribunal. The angels are there arrayed in thoughtful attention. The interceding Christ stands before the throne as man's Advocate. There stands your Saviour and mine to plead for the sinner. Yes, the scene has everything in it we find in trials today—except what? God the Father is there; the angels are there as the witnesses to every act. There stands, too, the One who will intercede. But men are not there. They are judged on the record.

John gives the panorama of this judgment procedure and how the decisions are reached. "And another book was opened, which is the book of life: and the dead were judged out of those things which were written in the books, according to their works." [35] The dead, you see, are judged by their records. The moment is big with destiny for the living too. Through the years since 1844 the tribunal makes progress. Beginning no doubt with Adam, Abel, Noah, Abraham, Joseph, David, the work of investigation proceeds. For those who accept God's plan of salvation Jesus immediately steps forward, and standing between the broken law and God the Father He holds out His hands saying, "My blood, Father, my blood!" For those who do not accept the plan there is no word of intercession. Jesus can say nothing. Their names cannot appear in the book of life.

And so on down through the years. Then, in a time just before the end, the judgment turns to the living. Just when that takes place we do not know. And how long it will take to judge the living, we cannot tell. We do know that all will proceed in God's time and order. Finally the last soul is sealed for eternity. Probation closes. Then Jesus

---

[34] Book of Daniel, ch. 7, v. 9.
[35] Book of the Revelation, ch. 20, v. 12.

will take off His priestly robes and prepare to return to
this earth as King of kings and Lord of lords. At that
moment He will stand and send forth throughout the universe this decree: "He that is unjust, let him be unjust still:
and he which is filthy, let him be filthy still: and he that
is righteous, let him be righteous still: and he that is holy,
let him be holy still." [36]

Happily, God's court is still in session. We can still
be represented there in the person of God our Redeemer.
What a day! What an hour!

A cultured woman, a child of the age in which she lives,
did not wish to hear about the judgment or about moral
responsibility. She wanted to live as she chose to live. Near
her house was pitched one day a big white tent. Passing
by a few nights later she heard beautiful music and a pleasing voice speaking. Stepping inside she heard the minister
speak about "the judgment." The message went straight
to her heart like an arrow.

But she did not wish to hear about it. In fact, she would
not hear about it. She arose and left in the middle of the
service. Approaching her home a few blocks away, she
heard a newsboy selling his papers on the corner. She got
a glimpse of the headlines and heard him cry, "Judgment
is rendered; judgment is rendered!" There it was again—
"the judgment." She entered her house and went to her
room. There she shut the door, and tried to forget in
sleep. But the great hall clock, inherited from past generations, seemed to be repeating, "The judgment! the judgment!"

The judgment! There is only one thing we can do
about it, and that is to surrender to God in acceptance of
His provisions for salvation. Then, and then only, are we
prepared for judgment and for eternity.

---

[36] *Ibid.,* ch. 22, v. 11.

$\mathcal{A}$tonement

ONCE UPON a time a young man asked a wise man for the definition of love. "My son," said the wise man, "what will you do with the definition?" "Do?" answered the young man. "Why, I shall then understand love." The wise man shook his head in silence, then gazed into the young man's eyes and spoke: "I cannot give you a definition. You must discover love for yourself. Watch for it in the eyes of a mother nursing her child. See it in the heart of a father searching for his lost son. You must find it as it is lived and you must weave it into your own experience; for, my son, only as you love and are loved can you begin to understand love."

This, in a way, is the problem we face when we speak of atonement. Like "love," "atonement" is a word whose meaning we can never fully exhaust with definitions. We can only understand it as we observe it in a dynamic relationship—indeed, as we experience it in our own life. Meanwhile, in theological circles the term has assumed a variety of technical meanings. Generally, it is used to describe the redeeming effect of Christ's incarnation, suffering, and death. A survey of the theories which have proliferated across the centuries will show that the Biblical data have been hammered into many conflicting shapes, often

241

in forgetfulness of what the Word of God itself teaches. What is regarded as man's fundamental need? Is it deliverance from ignorance? or misery? or sin? The answer conditions the theological view of atonement. From a more general viewpoint, three dominant interpretations are set forth. The first is the "dramatic" or classic theory, which sees in atonement man's liberation from the tyranny of sin, law, death, wrath, and the devil. This view was advocated by the early Church Fathers, and can be called the Greek or "patristic" view. The second holds that Christ's death was a sacrifice by which God's honor was satisfied and His holy judgment vindicated. This was the so-called Latin view. There is the third, a "subjective moral concept" which considers the cross to be primarily a moving demonstration of forgiving love, eliciting in return man's love for God's self-sacrifice.

The result of these centuries-old debates has been ponderous theories and lengthy manuscripts. In our view, these theories are partial and incomplete. First, they restrict and limit God's work of salvation. Then, they tend to consider the atonement in at least partial isolation from the person, life, ministry, resurrection, and eschatological teaching of Christ. Such views are centered exclusively in the cross, where the once-for-all, the all-sufficient, atoning sacrifice of Christ was offered for man's salvation. Certainly, we must agree that "we are sanctified through the offering of the body of Jesus Christ once for all." [1] But atonement cannot be restricted to what Christ accomplished on the cross. A Biblical view must include the application of the benefits of the sacrifice on the cross to the individual sinner and the actualization of these benefits in his life. Moreover, we believe Biblical atonement has a yet wider connotation, encompassing God's complete

---

[1] Epistle to the Hebrews, ch. 10, v. 10.

work of salvation and restoration of His creation to its original state. In this larger total sense, atonement involves in broad outline the issues and events in the great controversy between Christ and Satan.

Now let us look at the Biblical terms of reference. The New Testament uses a Greek word that in various forms means "to reconcile," "reconciling," "reconciliation." The King James Version, in one case,[2] translated the word into English as "atonement," though the Revised Standard Version more precisely renders this passage with the word *reconciliation.* Thus, in the New Testament the word *atonement* appears only once and there should be rendered as it is in most other languages, "reconciliation." The word *atonement* is much more frequent in the Old Testament. There the Hebrew word means "to cover," and often is translated as "to atone or make atonement." In its various forms and contexts atonement connotes "making amends," "making matters right," "to take the place of the people," "to make adequate compensation for wrong," or "to serve as mediator." A study of certain Old Testament experiences illustrates these various meanings.[3]

Now, looking at atonement in broad outline, let us consider the great controversy between Christ and Satan. It was in the course of this agonizing struggle that Christ died on the cross. Whatever meaning the word *atonement* conveys, it certainly must be understood in this context. But first, why was atonement necessary? What problem was there that required atonement? This question leads us back through the corridors of time to before the creation of the world. Indeed, to before the creation of persons. The great truth of atonement comes into clear focus only as it stands out against the truth of

---

[2] See Epistle to the Romans, ch. 5, v. 11.
[3] See Book of Exodus, ch. 32; Second Book of Samuel, ch. 21; Book of Numbers, chs. 16; 25.

creation, and the basic truth of creation was love. In fact, love is the foundation of divine government. God created because He loved, and when He created persons His love led Him to grant the sacred gift of freedom—freedom to fulfill the purpose in creation. God desires a spontaneous love from His creatures—a love built upon the appreciation of divine character. Love cannot be coerced. It cannot be required. It can only flow from a heart free to fellowship or to refrain from fellowship. Free choice entails thus two minimum essentials—understanding and alternatives, without which personhood does not exist. A person must not only be able to say Yes, but he must also be able to say No. God wanted freedom and love in the universe. Thus at the risk of losing creation, He made it possible for a person to say No as well as Yes to God.

Lucifer, the son of the morning, said No. With this answer something new and mysterious entered the universe. We call it evil. Why did Lucifer say No to God and presume to rebel against his Creator? To find the cause for evil or an excuse for its being, could be to lay the blame at the feet of God. Thus, the advent of sin and rebellion in the universe raised some speculative issues. Had God withheld freedom from His created beings? Was it really possible to act in harmony with His law? Was it right to let the innocent suffer in a great experiment? Was not God as author of creation at once the author of evil?

Such perplexities were the risk God took in creating the subjects of His dominion free. He foresaw the tragic course of rebellion with its endless train of suffering and violence. But He knew also that if freedom were ever to mean anything at all—and it is an essential to love— Lucifer's freedom to demonstrate his point of view had to be guaranteed. God's love sought to protect Lucifer and his followers from the headlong plunge into darkness, loneliness, and the overwhelming horror of existence that would and did result in separation from the Source of life. His heart longed after Lucifer upon whom, as a loving Creator, He had bestowed honor and glory. But the mighty prince would not turn aside from his evil course. Then, lest all heaven become diseased with this strange infatuation, God in sorrow drove Lucifer from the courts of heaven. Bonds of love and friendship were strained and broken on that tragic day when Lucifer, with one third of the angels, left the home of their communion with God.

Many times we picture Satan only as the antagonist of God, forgetting the love that once crowned the governing cherub in the days when he worshiped in adoration and filled heaven with praise to his Creator. Yet, Lucifer chose his own destiny. In *Paradise Lost,* Milton portrays thus his departure from heaven:

> "Farewel happy Fields
> Where Joy for ever dwells: Hail horrours, hail
> Infernal world, and thou profoundest Hell
> Receive thy new Possessor."

Eventually the earth became a hell for men and evil angels. Adam and Eve, created in the image of God, endowed with intelligence and every good thing, soon were seduced by the fallen angel. They joined the rebellion with Satan and were estranged from their Maker. But God, who had yearned to redeem Lucifer in heaven, sought to redeem the fallen race on earth. By now questions were raised in the minds of all created intelligences. Could it be possible that Lucifer had a point? Perhaps God was unjust in driving man from his home of innocence. Maybe some modification in the divine government would be good after all. Why should death be the consequence of rebellion? If God really gave freedom to His subjects, why should they die as a consequence of using this gift? These we call "questions of estrangement." Not that by the mere raising of the questions a person would be in a state of rebellion; but unless the questions were answered they might well be the seeds of corruption that would alienate the whole creation from its Creator.

Now unfolds the marvelous plan to overcome the estrangement of God's beloved creation. God would win back the love of His creation. More than risking His creation, He would risk Himself to save sinners. Perhaps it would have been safer to have blotted out creation and to have begun again with an untainted universe. In a moment creation could have vanished and God could have created a fresh universe. But this is not the nature of our Creator. He loved His creation. He loved the persons He had created. He would risk all to reveal His heart of love. Satan must be unmasked and his charges must be proved false. To make this universe safe against rebellion, sin, and death, God chose to enter the stream of creaturely existence and there to reveal Himself. He would overcome the estrangement of rebellion, but He would do it in such a way as to overcome also the estrangement the questions implied.

As man multiplied and covered the earth, few looked for deliverance from sin. Corruption was added to corruption. Murder and bloodshed were extolled as evidence of strength. Values were perverted, and the race was depraved. Freedom to serve the living God became precarious. It looked as though Satan was winning the battle for the human race. Then came the universal Flood. The earth's surface was destroyed, and man and beast perished in the raging storm. No doubt more questions were raised by the sons of God. Lucifer could point to this destruction, accusing God of destroying freedom along with His creatures. He could charge God with making freedom an empty word.

Time marched on. From the ark of safety, man once again multiplied over the face of the earth. Once again the race chose rebellion rather than fellowship. The ugliness of sin was seen by heavenly intelligences. The stench from earth filled the universe with nausea. Still, Satan persisted in his claim that God was responsible for it all. And curiously enough, he masked his intentions and work so artfully that he had sympathizers among the heavenly hosts.

Though the knowledge of God was dim in the minds of men, God continued to restore their freedom by offering them the option of fellowship with their Creator. In the type and symbol of the sanctuary service He taught them the hideousness of sin and that its consequences result in death. The sanctuary service also foretold the final triumph over this death by God Himself.

Thus into the need of human history God became the Son of man. He came to reveal divine love and to ensure man's freedom. As man was experiencing the anxiety of estranged existence, Jesus came to offer the opportunity for fellowship with God. In Christ the image of God was restored. God and man became one. God bridged the estrangement in the person of Jesus. With amazement heavenly beings and the forces of evil witnessed the Creator-God walking among men, sharing their lot, and depending upon God for sustaining power. Now the questions began to be answered. God had completely identified Himself with His creation. His life was a rebuke to Satan.

Then came the final crisis—the cross. In the Garden of Gethsemane the future of creation hung precariously in the balance. The Son of God became one with the guilty race to the degree that He assumed the results of their sins. To His suffering soul came the shattering realization that communion with His Father was broken and He no longer could feel the warmth and strength of His Father's love. This separation began to crush out His life— as it will eventually for all who reject fellowship with the Source of life. In those awful moments the nature of God was revealed as supreme love. The third time He prayed the decision was made. He would continue to identify Himself with His creation at any cost.

What greater love could there be? It stands out in marked contrast to the selfish, self-seeking Satan. Then Jesus is condemned to death, and as His executioners do their fearful work, the universe stands in horror. Questions of estrangement are answered. Satan is completely unmasked. No link of sympathy remains between him and the angelic hosts. He stands at the judgment bar and is condemned as a murderer. He claimed that he would procure greater freedom for his minions. He asserted that God's law diminished freedom. He blamed God for evil. He pointed to God as unjust. Now none of the heavenly angels listen. They see only too clearly that, given the opportunity, Satan would destroy God and attempt to take by force God's creation. And this would be a disaster. It would be death. The freedom he promised was slavery to abject tyranny, injustice, and murder. Jesus died crying out, "It is finished." [4] The work He came to do, He had done. He demonstrated that man connected with God was free to fulfill his purpose and to rise above the determinism of sin. Then, He rose triumphant over the tomb. In all this—Incarnation, life and ministry, death, resurrection, and ascension—God revealed Himself, Creator-Redeemer. Satan revealed himself, author of rebellion and death.

Now the universe was secure against Satan. The work was not finished, however. The heavenly beings understood the nature of evil, but man was still in the estrangement of rebellion. God's purpose is to bring man into a complete at-one-ment with Him. This means to restore men to the image of their Maker—to make of them men

---

[4] Gospel according to John, ch. 19, v. 30.

who have reached a stage of character that reflects the divine. Through the gospel message God seeks to bring men into this relationship—a relationship that will find consummation when "we shall be like him; for we shall see him as he is." [5] John the revelator speaks of the last days of this gospel work.[6] At that time a group of men and women (one hundred forty-four thousand) will reach a special degree of Christian maturity. As Christ was a rebuke to Satan, so are they. Here, at the end of human history, God must be able to point to human beings who have chosen the way of righteousness and developed Christlike characters. This group answers other questions. God points to these as evidence of the power of redemption for all men who accept it. What a privilege, what a responsibility to witness thus before the universe!

Just before Christ comes the second time, says the prophet Daniel, each person who has a claim to salvation will be given attention. Angels, and those who were taken to heaven with Christ at His ascension, witness each claim. All are satisfied that each person chose freely the course of his destiny. It is seen that God offered salvation to each person. At the close of this investigation the universe is ready for Christ's glorious appearing, when "every eye shall see him." [7] Describing this event, Jesus calls it the time when at the sound of the trumpet "his elect" are gathered from all the earth.[8] These are accounts of a glorious, visible, audible coming, accompanied by the raising of the dead in Christ and the changing from mortality to immortality.[9] This, very obviously, is the first resurrection described by the apostle John.[10]

---

[5] First Epistle of John, ch. 3, v. 2.
[6] See Book of the Revelation, ch. 14, vs. 1-12.
[7] *Ibid.*, ch. 1, v. 7.
[8] Gospel according to Matthew, ch. 24, vs. 30, 31; Gospel according to Mark, ch. 13, vs. 26, 27.
[9] See First Epistle to the Corinthians, ch. 15, vs. 51-56.
[10] See Book of the Revelation, ch. 20.

With these events the apostle introduces a chronological sequence that brings the conclusion of the great controversy between Christ and Satan. In this eschatological sequence the last questionings of estrangement are answered, and the universe is brought into complete and eternal harmony with God.

This final sequence begins, then, with John's description of the second advent of our Lord.[11] To the rebellious sinners of earth Christ comes in overpowering glory as a judge and avenger, with fire and sword, to give final battle against the hosts of evil men. Overwhelming destruction could hardly be more graphically described than with John's pen. Not only does nature cooperate with an upheaval that changes the topography of the earth by shaking down the work of men's hands but also all organized opposition to God comes to a sudden end as men individually tremble before their Creator-Redeemer. John's description of the "brightness of his coming" ends with these words: "And the remnant [the remaining sinners] were slain with the sword of him that sat upon the horse, which sword proceeded out of his mouth." [12] The unrighteous who do not meet their end in these last-day upheavals are destroyed by the brightness of Christ's visible presence as He appears "in flaming fire taking vengeance on them that know not God." [13]

The scene changes and John sees thrones of judgment on which sit the "blessed and holy" ones who have part in the first resurrection.[14] "They came to life again, and reigned with Christ a thousand years." [15] Specifically, John sees the martyrs and those who have gotten the victory in these last struggles of the conflict join the "blessed and

---

[11] *Ibid.*, ch. 19.
[12] *Ibid.*, v. 21.
[13] Second Epistle to the Thessalonians, ch. 1, v. 8.
[14] Book of the Revelation, ch. 20, vs. 4-6.
[15] *Ibid.*, v. 4, R.S.V.

holy" ones who have part in the first resurrection, in a thousand-year reign with Christ in heaven. True, John's view of the righteous during the thousand years does not specify just where the reigning with Christ takes place. He says simply, "I saw thrones, and they sat upon them, and judgment was given unto them: . . . and they lived and reigned with Christ a thousand years." [16] But other texts do make this clear. Paul writes the Thessalonians that the righteous are to "meet the Lord in the air," "caught up" "in the clouds." [17] From this we conclude that Christ at His second advent does not touch the sin-polluted earth, but "he shall send his angels with a great sound of a trumpet, and they shall gather together his elect from the four winds, from one end of heaven to the other." [18] And the place to which the saved are taken at this time is indicated by the Saviour's own words of comfort to His disciples on the evening before His crucifixion. Said He, "In my Father's house are many mansions: if it were not so, I would have told you. I go to prepare a place for you. And if I go and prepare a place for you, I will come again, and receive you unto myself; that where I am, there ye may be also." [19] The place to which Christ takes His saints is described as "my Father's house," where there are "many mansions" (more properly, "dwelling places"). The unavoidable implication is that the destination of the righteous at the Second Advent is heaven—not the earth from which they are removed at the last trump.

Thus we have an explanation of what happens to the two classes on earth when the Lord comes. While one is left on the earth, dead, the other is taken, alive, to be forever with the Lord. Both the prophet Daniel and John the revelator describe the activities of the saved in heaven.

---

[16] *Ibid.*, v. 4.
[17] First Epistle to the Thessalonians, ch. 4, v. 17.
[18] Gospel according to Matthew, ch. 24, v. 31.
[19] Gospel according to John, ch. 14, vs. 2, 3.

They state that judgment was given to the saints, including the resurrected ones.[20] In the Revelation the word *judgment* is from the Greek, meaning generally "sentence," "verdict," or a "decision rendered." Here the word seems to mean the authority to pass sentence.

This work of judgment was alluded to by the apostle Paul when he wrote, "Do ye not know that the saints shall judge the world? . . . Know ye not that we shall judge angels?"[21] This work of judgment may well involve a careful investigation of the records of evil men and a decision regarding the amount of punishment due each sinner for his part in the rebellion against God. Thus, before the universe, more questions of estrangement will be answered.

The apostle John, along with other Bible writers, speaks of two resurrections one thousand years apart. The first resurrection of the righteous takes place at the second coming of Christ. The resurrection of evildoers, the second resurrection, follows the end of the thousand years of judgment by the saints in heaven. The first resurrection (of the righteous) is obviously in contrast to the second (of the wicked). The apostle Paul referred to the coming forth of "every man in his own order."[22] First came the resurrection of Christ, the first fruits; the resurrection of the saints was to come at the Second Advent. Then, at the close of the thousand years, the wicked come forth. There is definitely a resurrection of the just and of the unjust.[23] These resurrections are a thousand years apart—the first unto life and the second unto damnation.[24]

Thus, at the end of the thousand-year period the last scenes of the great controversy come to a gloomy world. The once-inhabited cities are in ruins. The wrecked pomp

[20] See Book of Daniel, ch. 7, v. 22; Book of the Revelation, ch. 20, v. 4.
[21] First Epistle to the Corinthians, ch. 6, vs. 2, 3.
[22] *Ibid.*, ch. 15, v. 23.
[23] See Book of Acts, ch. 24, v. 15.
[24] See Gospel according to John, ch. 5, v. 29.

and splendor of earth are only grim reminders of the teeming world that Satan had led in futile rebellion against God. Now Christ, accompanied by all the saints, descends to earth in awesome power, glory, and majesty to execute judgment upon the wicked. He bids the wicked dead to rise; and in answer to the summons the mighty host, numberless as the sands of the sea, responds.[25] Not only the "sea" but "death" and "hell"—grim receptacles of death's prey—deliver up their quota of the wicked dead. Raised with the same rebellious spirit that possessed them in life, they now make ready for the presence of the Eternal One.

They see the vast city of God, the New Jerusalem, which descends from God out of heaven.[26] Christ returns to the same Mount of Olives outside old Jerusalem[27] from which He ascended after His resurrection, when the angelic messengers gave assurance of His return from heaven.[28] Through the resurrection of the wicked Satan is thus "loosed" for "a little season."[29] His enforced idleness is past, after his thousand-year period of captivity. Desperate hope springs once again in his evil heart as he sees the innumerable hosts of the wicked of all ages. Then comes the last mighty struggle for supremacy. Deceiving the sinful hosts into thinking that they can take the city of God, he marshals the wicked hordes into frenzied battle array in a final, futile assault upon the "camp of the saints," the beloved city, in an endeavor to overthrow the kingdom of God. The wicked, who stubbornly refused an entrance into the city of God through the merits of Christ's sacrifice, now determine to gain admission and control by siege and battle.

The last act in the great conflict of the ages takes place

---

[25] See Book of the Revelation, ch. 20, v. 8.
[26] *Ibid.*, ch. 21, vs. 2, 3.
[27] See Book of Zechariah, ch. 14, v. 4.
[28] See Book of Acts, ch. 1, vs. 9-12.
[29] Book of the Revelation, ch. 20, vs. 3, 7-9.

as the entire human race meets face to face for the first
and last time. Satan's supreme attempt proves that he is
still in rebellion. And evil men show themselves to be
only evil. The final separation of the righteous from the
wicked is now irrevocably fixed. Then, from the great
white throne, the sentence of doom is pronounced upon
the wicked. The sentence is followed by immediate execution. Fire comes down from God out of heaven and de-
vours sin and sinners.[30] The very surface of the earth appears to melt, and becomes a vast, seething "lake of fire,"
for the judgment and "perdition of ungodly men." But
there, in the presence of God, the last questions of estrangement are answered. Righteous and wicked acknowledge
the justice of God. With all the facts of the great controversy in view, the whole universe, both loyal and rebellious,
with one accord declares, "Just and true are thy ways, thou
King of saints." [31] And out of the smoldering ruins of this
old earth springs forth "a new heaven and a new earth," [32]
wherein the redeemed find their everlasting inheritance
and dwelling place.

"The great controversy is ended. Sin and sinners are
no more. The entire universe is clean. One pulse of harmony and gladness beats through the vast creation. From
Him who created all, flow life and light and gladness,
throughout the realms of illimitable space. From the minutest atom to the greatest world, all things, animate and
inanimate, in their unshadowed beauty and perfect joy, declare that God is love." [33]

The work of salvation is completed, and the universe
is again at one with God.

[30] See Second Epistle of Peter, ch. 3, vs. 7, 10, 11; Book of the Revelation,
ch. 20, vs. 9, 10.
[31] Book of the Revelation, ch. 15, v. 3.
[32] *Ibid.*, ch. 21, v. 1.
[33] Ellen G. White, *The Great Controversy*, p. 678.

CHAPTER 22

The Family

WHENEVER A TOTALITARIAN group wants to take over an existing social structure, it strikes first of all at the home. It usurps for itself the education of the children and tries to minimize parental influence. This method worked for the ancient Greeks and Romans; it is still effective today. Ruin the home, and you will see society's bulwarks crumble into tyranny.

Those who set their minds to social studies will inevitably begin with the family. It is the primal institution in the order of Creation. The drama of Creation comes to a rising climax in the description: "So God created man in his own image, in the image of God created he him; male and female created he them. And God blessed them, and God said unto them, Be fruitful, and multiply, and replenish the earth, and subdue it." [1] Not until the family has been established can further social units evolve, such as the state, the church, culture, and economy.

No other level of life can equal the family in its closely knit structure. Lower animal life has been observed to bear some traits similar to those of the human family. For instance, it may show strong maternal and

---

[1] Book of Genesis, ch. 1, vs. 27, 28.

paternal attachments, but none of them compares with the human family as concerns moral purpose. Monkeys, dogs, and cats form a family that quickly disintegrates into one-being units. Within a few weeks a baby kitten is on its own and no longer needs parental care. But a human being is different. Over a period of years he is completely dependent on his parents or foster parents for his development, physically as well as mentally. This dependency forms a permanent relationship that would otherwise not exist.

Christians take the position that man is a combination of nature and spirit. This means that on the side of nature he is subject to biological laws and urges. For instance, we cannot deny the sex impulse as an urge toward procreation. The human race is perpetuated through the sex instinct. The old order dies, yielding place to the young in a progressive cycle. However, on the spiritual side, sex takes on far greater significance than a mere means to continue the human race. Spiritually, sex is the expression of an unswerving devotion, fidelity, and love.

This conception of the family has given Christianity its overwhelming impetus. Wherever Christianity has gone, the influence of the Christian family has had an undeniable impact on the community. Women have been raised from a very low estate—sometimes comparable to that of a household slave—to one of grace and influence. Children prior to the triumph of Christian principles were ofttimes very much like beasts of burden, to be shouted at and used as whipping posts. They have become essential members of a community that treats them with respect. The development of their character became, under Christianity, the parents' greatest challenge.

Moreover, where better than in the family can we learn morality—kindness, patience, obedience, self-control, purity, unselfishness, love, and all the other virtues that go to make Christianity? Here is the ideal place to begin to form, to model, to carve, all the splendid qualities that endear Christians one to another.

The importance of the family finds its chief support in the attitude of Jesus. Over the centuries what He had to say, but even more, what He could leave unsaid because His actions had clearly shown how He felt, have given us a clear picture of Christ's deep concern for the family and its salvation.

Critics of Christianity have contended that neither Jesus nor the apostle Paul considered the family sacred. After all, they declare, Christ experienced neither a love affair nor a marriage; and Paul deliberately chose celibacy as the highest mode of life. They remind us that Christ rebuffed His mother and brothers when they came desiring to speak with Him;[2] and that in His teaching, devotion to the kingdom was to take preference over attending the funeral of one's father.[3] They say that according to Jesus' own words, if one was to be a true disciple of His, this would involve hating one's family.[4] The Roman Catholic Church in particular has used these passages of New Testament Scripture in order to justify an ascetic life as the supreme devotion to God.

But certainly the above criticisms and viewpoints are neither reliable nor valid. How could anyone infer in any way from the Bible that celibacy was advocated by Christ as the highest pattern of life? Paul did advocate celibacy in his case and under the pressures of a task that clamored for laborers who could dedicate all their time and effort to it. In his understanding, Christ's kingdom was imminent, and there was so much to do to prepare mankind for this event that for him truly there was no other way than to remain single.

---

[2] See Gospel according to Matthew, ch. 12, vs. 46-50.
[3] *Ibid.*, ch. 8, vs. 21, 22.
[4] See Gospel according to Luke, ch. 14, v. 26.

Further, the stringent, costly requirements of the kingdom very evidently do at times take precedence over family life. There are times when ministers and other church leaders must leave the problems of their personal life while they attend to the more urgent problems of the church. This is not to say that a minister's family should be neglected; neglect in all its forms is wrong; but there are times when the shepherd is bound to care for his flock, due to the imperfect life conditions caused by sin. Jesus knew life and understood human nature so well that He realized the temptations presented by family ties would hinder the ministry for which He was pressed by time. Since the kingdom of God is the highest good, whereas the family is only a secondary good, He renounced the latter in order to dedicate Himself to the former.

Nevertheless, Christ's own words on the sacredness of marriage, linking it with the great act of Creation, form the base upon which a Christian marriage is built:

"Have you not read that he who made them from the beginning made them male and female, and said, 'For this reason a man shall leave his father and mother and be joined to his wife, and the two shall become one?' So they are no longer two but one. What therefore God has joined together, let no man put asunder." [5]

It is clearly seen from this message that Christ never meant marriage to be a matter of expediency, personal convenience, or sexual indulgence. To Him the family was a holy relationship, and marriage was a holy bond that was not to be accepted flippantly or arrogantly.

Never has this message been more apropos than today. Kinsey reports, newspapers, and legal transcripts indicate in plain terms that man seems to be moving toward an animal existence as far as the home relationships are con-

---

[5] Gospel according to Matthew, ch. 19, vs. 4-6, R.S.V.

cerned. Marriages have become a game. One partner is intrigued with the other so long as life with him is exciting, thrilling, full of artificial "kick." Once the glamour is gone, it's checkmate, the game is over—but not quite. Because soon he finds another pawn with whom he can swing another whirlwind romance. It is almost as if the individual involved were oblivious to the heartaches of those innocent parties who are forced to suffer on the side lines of his torrid relationships. This is not love. This is not marriage. This is merely sensational flirtation with one's own colossal ego.

Most sociologists rule that monogamy is the universal pattern and prototype of human marriage. They admit that a true marriage requires essentially two people, and two people only. Despite the occasional recognition of concubinage and other sexual irregularities in history, it is still true that monogamy has been recognized almost universally as the standard form of marriage and of sex relationship. On this point Albert C. Knudson states: "Neither anthropology nor history affords any support to the view that men and women are polygamous by nature to such an extent as to threaten the present monogamous type of marriage." Dean Knudson continues by saying that, "True marital love excludes the thought of being shared with more than one of the opposite sex." [6]

God has imposed on marriage a divine obligation to be faithful and true to one's mate. During the forty years of my ministry, as I have observed the shifting sands of emotion among people and have sat in counsel with husbands and wives on the brink of separation, I am convinced more than ever of the tremendous importance of fidelity in marriage, of abiding loyalty between husband and wife.

---

[6] Albert C. Knudson, *The Principles of Christian Ethics*, pp. 204, 205.

It would be impossible at this point to bypass the question of divorce. That we should have to consider it at all is a matter of deep regret. Divorce among Christians should be nonexistent. Speaking of the authorization Moses had given for bills of divorce, Jesus said clearly, "From the beginning, it was not so." Moses had suffered this deviation from the original plan "because of the hardness of your hearts." [7] In God's plan marriage was indestructible.

Then, in the New Testament we encounter this same permanency in the marriage bond. Only two exceptions are made. On the first, Jesus said: "Whosoever shall put away his wife, *except* it be for fornication, and shall marry another, committeth adultery: and whoso marrieth her which is put away doth commit adultery." [8] On the second, Saint Paul wrote to the Corinthians: "But if the unbelieving partner desires to separate, let it be so; in such a case the brother or sister [in the faith] is not bound. For God has called us to peace." [9]

Divorce and desertion were thus understood in the apostolic context. But the early Christian records indicate that as a rule, divorce was not the solution to an unhappy marriage. The Roman Catholic Church, of course, does not recognize divorce even in extreme cases. Her stand has been that marriage is a sacrament representing the union of God with the church. Since the latter cannot be dissolved, the former must not be dissolved either. This position was dogmatically affirmed by the Council of Trent. However, the Catholic Church has made numerous provisions for the annulment of marriages.

What, then, is the true Christian stand? Dean Knudson[10] suggests that divorce or separation is indicated when

---

[7] Gospel according to Matthew, ch. 19, v. 8.
[8] *Ibid.*, v. 9.
[9] First Epistle to the Corinthians, ch. 7, v. 15, R.S.V.
[10] See Knudson, *op cit.*

the union of husband and wife has lost its moral purpose and becomes revolting to both of them. This view may appear reasonable in the human setting, particularly if the decision is only for separation, temporary or permanent. However, in the Biblical setting the ties of wedlock are meant to be indissoluble. Sin and hardness of heart are such that two concessions are allowed: one for unchastity on the part of a spouse (divorce); the other for desertion (separation).

But let us return to the more positive side of wedlock. How can we build a successful marriage? I wish now to point out some bedrock rules that safeguard the joys of marriage. Every couple should be on the lookout for infractions of these rules, and should heed them before habitual neglect grows into a monster that will destroy their home.

1. Marriage must never be devised as the fulfillment of a *personal ambition.* A girl who calculatingly sets her cap for a minister, a lawyer, a doctor, or a millionaire, will not find the satisfaction she had hoped for if this is her main reason for a wedding. Marriages of ambition always try to take advantage of the opposite sex; while the Christian motive should be the joy that can come from sharing together in some joint achievement.

2. Marriage is not an *Olympic race.* Competition has no place here. Competition in marriage should be replaced by singleness of devotion to each other and to humanity.

3. Marriage is not the place for *psychological displacement.* In other words, you must not project your own inner conflicts upon your husband or wife. Before you accuse your mate of being unfaithful, hateful, sour, a brute, look into the recesses of your own heart and see what manner of attitudes you harbor. Do not yield to the temptation to pin your guilt on your marriage partner.

4. Marriage is not built on *surface values.* Married people who think that they can be unfaithful so long as

they are discreet about it are fooling themselves. Sooner or later their secret will appear in one form or another and the harm done may be irreparable. Nothing can take the place of a love limited to one's partner for eternity.

5. A happy marriage presupposes the *capacity* for a lasting relationship.

6. Abolish the *savior complex* in marriage. Many young people begin marriage with the idea that they are going to reform their mate. In a voice trembling with eagerness, they exclaim, "But I know he'll change. I'll *make* him change!" From then on, home life is the center stage for constant nagging and heckling. Romance soon vanishes. Hate takes its place. The best way to reform someone is to offer him acceptance and patience.

7. Do not think of marriage as a *utopia* which you have long deserved. So many couples live in a world of fantasy. They have the mistaken idea that marriage is *their* heaven on earth; therefore, everything must be ideal. They never face the reality of the husband's unstrung nerves after a grueling day at work; or of the wife's discouragement in trying to discipline three lively children; or of the thousand and one realities that have a way of creeping up on them in the form of overdrawn bank accounts, migraine headaches, and endless labor. Marriage becomes heaven on earth only when those involved think of heaven not as something that belongs to them by right, but rather when they try to make a little heaven out of their home for someone else.

8. Have *children*. A family without children is not really complete. Jesus always recognized the family—the father, the mother, the children—as the normal situation. Moreover, in the family without children the attitudes of both husband and wife more easily become warped and self-centered.

9. Apply these rules based on Christian conduct: Be

unselfish; have mutual confidence; keep no secrets from each other; be cheerful; never complain.

10. Find your happiness in home life. Work together and play together. A couple who spend their time *looking* for pleasure will not find it. When members of a family try to make one another happy, they will *be* happy.

11. *Tenderness* must be the quality on which everything in the home is built. But tenderness takes a strong spirit. Those who are weak will be more likely to use mental cruelty than tenderness in their marital approach. Those who are insecure will want to lord over their mate. They will be jealous, harsh, domineering. But the man and woman who understand the magnificent spiritual bond between them will evince tenderness in all their transactions.

To these practical rules on marriage I wish to add the law covering them all—that marriage is more spiritual than physical, and that love is the only perfect bond between members of a Christian family.

Thus, growing up and learning to love in a family can be life's most gratifying achievement, and a dimension in salvation.

CHAPTER 23

Health

$\mathcal{M}$OST PEOPLE have befuddled ideas on the relationship of religion and health. Either they snub their health completely, thinking that religion is of the spirit and has nothing to do with how you function physically; or they treat God as their personal magician who is to see to it that religion keeps them happy and well—free from moods of depression or discomfort, even though these be the direct result of their own wrong habits.

How differently the apostle Paul saw this relationship. In his letter to the Thessalonians he made an early plea: "May the God of peace himself sanctify you wholly; and may your spirit and soul and body be kept sound and blameless at the coming of our Lord Jesus Christ." [1] Paul drapes religion in its true perspective. According to him, redemption embraces the complete man—mind, soul, and body.

God's purpose is to make man whole. This process cannot be a one-dimensional project. You cannot have a full religious experience while your physical body is abused, debauched, and maltreated, just as you cannot

---

[1] First Epistle to the Thessalonians, ch. 5, v. 23, R.S.V.

have a full religious experience while your mind and your spirit are defiled, ravished, and prostituted. A thorough-going religious experience should tone up the body, illuminate the mind, and free the spirit—until all three move in one rhythmical, harmonious entity—free from disease, and sanctified.[2]

Of all the world's religions Christianity is the most materialistic. Shocking? Not when you understand what is meant. In other words, Christianity takes matter seriously, as indeed it should, for did not God speak the world into being and then look upon it, noting that what He saw was good? Matter is God-created and God-approved. Never try to dodge this great truth.

The central message of Christian faith deals with Christ's incarnation—God's redemptive invasion of mankind. Since the divine Word became flesh, then certainly flesh must not be set aside with disdain. We admit that man in his present condition needs salvage. His body is crippled. Sin has ravished him well, leaving him in pitiful condition—a mere spark of the glorious form he once was. That this happened, however, was not God's will. God no more wills the destruction of our body than He wills disease of our mind or soul. Bodily suffering, mental errors, cleavage of the soul, find their origin as far away from God as eternity is from the calendar on the wall. Even if such suffering eventually turns into good—still it was an evil in itself and God would have willed it differently.

The recuperative steps Jesus took in our behalf touch on every existing evil, not excluding the evil of physical disease. As a matter of fact, when He announced the kingdom of God to His disciples, He said, "As ye go, preach, saying, The kingdom of God is at hand. Heal the sick . . ." [3]

---

[2] See Ellen G. White, *The Ministry of Healing*, p. 130.
[3] Gospel according to Matthew, ch. 10, vs. 7, 8.

Part of the impact of the kingdom of God is upon the framework of man's health—his whole health.

We must not confine illness to viruses and bacteria. Exterminating all germs that destroy the body will never make man whole the way the Christian message proclaims. So much of man's disease is rooted in his thoughts and emotions. An American Medical Association statement revealed that about 50 per cent of diseases are rooted in wrong mental and spiritual attitudes, leaving only 50 per cent as the direct result of some physical cause. Sometimes the body grows ill and passes on its sickness to the mind and to the soul. Other times the mind and the soul become ill and pass on their sickness to the body.[4]

I remember well a physician friend of mine stating that the large portion of his patients did not need any medicine at all; they simply needed mental and moral healing. A member of the Mayo Clinic has said: "We can deal with 25 per cent of the people who come to us with the instruments of science, but we don't know what to do with the 75 per cent." This clinician meant that most of his patients needed to be cured of their mental and spiritual attitudes far more than they needed pills or surgery.

Probably one of the greatest revolutions in our generation is the discovery that people can either improve or impair their physical health by changing inner processes. This was not admitted in the Middle Ages. In those days a human being was treated as if he were made up of three separate, leakproof compartments. The body was in the physician's custody, the mind was under exclusive control of the educator, while the soul was entrusted to the ministry only. Each specialist was told, "Now you take care of your area."

But today, though we live in a highly specialized

---

[4] See Leslie D. Weatherhead, *Psychology and Life.*

era, we know that man is an unfragmentable unit, and must be treated *in toto*.[5]

Harold Shryock, physiologist at Loma Linda University's School of Medicine, gives the case history of a man in his early forties who consulted his doctor because of intermittent pain in the pit of the stomach. The pain had intensified with the passing of time, bringing fear that an ulcer of the stomach had developed that could be cancerous. The physician examined his patient carefully and became convinced that neither ulcer nor cancer were present. He found a clue, moreover, that the pain was of nervous origin. Some six months before the pain in the stomach became noticeable, the patient's seven-year-old foster daughter was returned by court order to her own mother. The disappointment was severe for the patient and his wife. Both had loved the girl like their own child. Six months later the wife became seriously ill and died. At this time the patient first noticed the pain in his stomach. He did not know the exact cause of his wife's death, but her principal complaint had been pain in the pit of the stomach. Then came the physician's careful appraisal of the case. The man finally understood that he did not have an ulcer or a cancer, and that his symptoms were the result of the emotional experience through which he had passed. The result was relief from anxiety. New interests were found and his emotional tensions disappeared. Then, after stressing the point that this man might have developed an actual stomach ulcer eventually had he not found a solution to his emotional problem, Doctor Shryock comments:

"Each individual has a certain tolerance for those experiences that produce nervous tension. When this limit is exceeded, the organs begin to function abnormally. This produces varied symptoms, for the stresses and pains of

---

[5] See Paul Tournier, *Medicine de la Personne*, Preface by Georges Bichel (Delachaux et Niestle, Paris).

life produce a different kind of illness in one person from
what they do in another. The particular organs that suffer
in response to nervous tension depend a great deal upon
traits inherent within the individual. In the case just cited,
symptoms suggesting stomach ulcer made their appearance.
In another case, high blood pressure may occur. In still
another, asthma may result every time the individual ex-
ceeds his tolerance for the stresses and strains of living.
These mischief-producing stresses result from failure to
provide certain of life's basic needs." [6]

A towering number of facts have come to light to
strengthen the view that man's physical, mental, and
spiritual make-up are dovetailed. A strong emotional impact, for instance, can change the heart rate; it can affect
the amount of salivary or gastric secretion; it can change
one's blood pressure.

A person filled with fear will have his adrenal gland
activated. His heart will beat faster, his breathing will be
more rapid, the glands in his gastro-intestinal tract will be
affected, his blood will shift to the peripheral muscles, and
his face will blanch.

People with great worries have been known to lose up
to 100 pounds within a few months. Some have eventually
died from nervous strain and psychic shock.

In my travels to primitive parts of the world, nothing
has been more indelibly imprinted on my mind than the
fact that members of certain tribes topple over and die
when they hear the witch doctor's pronouncement doom-
ing them to death. It seems obvious that they die from the
bodily injuries wrought by painful emotion.

Few things weaken a person as quickly as anxiety or
emotional conflict. They are the most common cause of
fatigue. Ulcers, heart disease, arthritis, even endocrine dis-

---

[6] Harold Shryock, *Highways to Health,* pp. 147, 148.

functions—all these can be caused by sickness of the mind and soul. The complexities of life, excessive strain, hostile impulses, hypertension, and sorrow are a tremendous drain on the human machinery.

All this does not mean that every disease is a figment of man's mental imbalance. Many diseases are of the tissues and they are real; just as other diseases, just as real, are of the mind or of the spirit. It does prove, however, the interdependence of the total man—body, mind, and spirit. When we speak of making man whole, we must include all three phases of him.[7]

The apostle Paul's counsel for the last-day church is that they invite the God of peace to sanctify them wholly —that their spirit, soul, and body be kept sound and blameless. How is this accomplished? Indeed, is it possible to improve the whole person? I think each of us can follow a definite program which will lead to better all-around health. Here are some vital steps:

1. *Self-surrender Is Absolutely Necessary.*

In order to find life, we must lose it. God must be allowed to step into the center of all our hopes and activities. As long as we reject God's rule in our lives, wholeness cannot come, because something of vital importance will be missing. We must recognize that everything we do finds its conclusion in Him. On this point Jesus said, "He that findeth his life shall lose it: and he that loseth his life . . . shall find it." [8] Self-surrender is the center of the human problem.

2. *Renounce Fear.*

Fear is our enemy number one. The late Dr. Jung of Switzerland said: "I no longer find the source of neurosis in the past, but in the present. What is the necessary task

---

[7] See Georges Liengme, *Pour Apprendre a Mieux Vivre* (Editions Victor Attinger, Paris).
[8] Gospel according to Matthew, ch. 10, v. 39.

which the patient will not accomplish? What's he afraid of? What's he running away from? What's the responsibility that he is refusing to take up?"

Our world spins in an atmosphere of fear. The present emphasis on overwhelming dangers, such as complete annihilation through atomic warfare, leads many to apathetic despair. What we need is a rational, creative hope—something that will be like a fresh breeze from the sky to keep us thinking positively. The antidote to fear is threefold: We must have a faith to live by, a self with which we can live, and a purpose for which to live. Only as we build these three cornerstones into our life edifice will it be possible for us to diminish the fears engulfing us.

3. *Exterminate Resentment.*

Resentments are poison—not symbolic poisons, but real poisons that affect the body. An outstanding psychologist recently found through extensive experimentation that if individuals thought pleasant thoughts, their eyesight was actually better, they could hear better, and their food tasted better. Conversely, those who harbored grudges and feelings of reprisal had duller senses. The wise man of the Scriptures said: "A tranquil mind gives life to the flesh, but passion makes the bones rot." [9]

One thing you cannot do and that is fool your nervous system. You may lie to those with whom you live while speaking with the tongue of an angel; but if you hate your fellow men, your body "takes a beating." If you despise the ground some people walk on, your nervous system registers it. Every time we are overcome with resentment, we are candidates for headaches, stiff necks, digestive upsets, and kindred ills.

4. *Keep a Clear Conscience.*

This is the secret to many a delayed illness. Those

---

[9] Book of Proverbs, ch. 14, v. 30, R.S.V.

who do not keep their conscience in line with what they know to be right are among the most miserable people on earth. They are indeed sick.

E. Stanley Jones has told the story of a businessman who went to a doctor because he could not sleep at night. After a thorough examination the doctor asked, "Is there something worrying you?"

"Now, look, Doctor," said the patient brusquely, "I came here to be treated medically, not to be grilled." And he left in a huff.

But the next day he returned, saying, "Doctor, there *is* something on my conscience. I defaulted a will and stole my brother's share of an inheritance." The doctor counseled, "Sit down and write that to your brother." The patient obeyed.

After the letter was written the doctor said, "I will go with you to mail it." He knew how hard it would be to mail that letter. So, together, the doctor and the patient went across the street and dropped the letter into a mail slot. Then the patient said, "Now I'm well." And he was. Guilt had functioned as a disturbance in his system. He never would have been a well man had he not expelled that guilt. Is it any wonder that the head of a medical college has said: "If you ministers cannot produce conversion, we doctors will have to, for life demands it"?

5. *Be an Optimist.*

Talk health and not disease. The moment you look at the dark side of life—moaning, groaning, and whining about your lot—that same moment is for you an open door to disease and poor health. Educate your mind to recall only the good things that have happened to you. Concentrate on the people who have been kind to you, then you will trust the future cheerfully.

6. *Commit Your Ways Unto the Lord.*

Keep the morning quiet hour. When the soul of the

day is just awakening and you are at your best, lift your heart to God, commit your will to His counsel, and get your directives from Him. Then you will go with His hand, not a chip, on your shoulder. Nothing can substitute for a strong, living faith in the God who created you, upholds the universe, and stands by to guide you along the way.

7. *Take Care of Your Body.*

In an effort to feed the spirit, do not starve the body. Follow a well-balanced diet. Eat only the best of what is available where you live. Breathe and drink properly, avoid artificial stimulants, and abstain from alcoholic beverages and narcotics. Do not allow the haste or hectic pace with which business needs to be accomplished influence you to wreck your physical resistance. Your energy is one of your most important assets. Guard it jealously. At night get a regular amount of sleep. During the day include some exercise in your schedule, even if it is only walking to work or to the store, or keeping up your premises. In case of persistent discomfort or lack of energy, consult a physician. Many a fatal illness might have been averted had proper medical care been obtained. Regular medical check-ups are not only commendable, but advisable.

A final thought must be added: No matter how close we live to God, nor how well we care for our bodies, nor how we strive for the right attitudes in life, disease may still inflict pain and even death. We have seen this happen in countless ways to people who apparently never deserved anything but joy. Ours is not to ponder the question "Why?" Suffice it to know that some diseases may have to wait that final cure. God has the power to heal. He does so through climate, education, and with His touch upon our bodies. He has worked, and will continue to work, miracles for the healing of men and women. But the time and place for these miracles are in His providence and in His alone.

The apostle Paul was never healed from his "thorn in the flesh." He asked God to heal him, but God said, "No, my grace is sufficient for you." Then Paul said, "I rather glory in my infirmities." [10]

One thing we know, God will heal the disease, or He will give power to use the infirmity as a steppingstone to a greater life. And one day we will experience the final and irrevocable healing—the "healing of the nations." [11]

---

[10] Second Epistle to the Corinthians, ch. 12, vs. 5-10.
[11] Book of the Revelation, ch. 22, v. 2.

CHAPTER 24

Charity

*C*OURTHOUSES ARE bulging with rules and regulations. Yet, no one has established the ideal community. Children still ignore "Stay Off the Grass" signs and adults try to evade income tax. Del Webb, the famous builder, has been praised for his so-called "ideal communities" for senior citizens. His genius has designed whole cities planned for retired people so that every detail suits their needs. Ideal? I wonder! Is it humanly possible to engineer a community ideal in all respects?

Someone says, "Of course it is possible, if people would only quit being so selfish. If everyone would abide by the golden rule, we could have many real utopian communities." The golden rule is certainly a virtuous precept. Kant thought so much of it that he called it the "categorical imperative." But a glutton or a sot or a libertine, though perfectly willing to treat others the way he would like to be treated, would be far from an ideal citizen.

Even the golden rule is not enough. It lacks an inward moral quality. In order for it to function in a moral way, it would need to say, "Do unto others as you *ought* to wish them to do unto you." In other words, the moral ideal must condition its application.

Inward morality is largely absent today. People as a

whole do not realize what is wrong. They are embarrassed to find themselves in a completely unsatisfactory world, after they have tried to do their duty toward elevating the tone of life. They have been proper; they have taught their children to be proper. They have donated substantial amounts to the Red Cross, the City of Hope, and the United Givers Fund. They have studied psychology in order to be better parents. Why, then, does the world remain a corrigendum? With all that concerned leaders have attempted, why can we not put an end to bloody racial riots, to theft on a giant scale, to mass plundering?

Let us go back to the ethical teachings of Jesus. "A certain man," said He, "was going down from Jerusalem to Jericho; and he fell among robbers, who both stripped him and beat him, and departed, leaving him half dead. And by chance a certain priest was going down that way: and when he saw him, he passed by on the other side. And in like manner a Levite also, when he came to the place, and saw him, passed by on the other side." [1]

Note that the story Jesus told was not a fable. It was an actual occurrence. As a matter of fact, both the priest and the Levite had listened to Christ's sermons before they encountered this distasteful episode. They knew the theory of charity. Intellectually they knew all about mercy, justice, love. But when it came to the moral inwardness that would compel them to apply the principle, they failed. They could not take the sight of someone whose face was disfigured and bloody from having been beaten by thugs. This bundle of filthy, smelly oppression and suffering grated on their sense of neatness. Rationalizations flowed freely. They passed by!

Fortunately, the story does not end here. Ellen G. White captures the sequel beautifully. She writes:

---

[1] Gospel according to Luke, ch. 10, vs. 30, 31, A.S.V.

"A certain Samaritan, in his journey, came where the sufferer was, and when he saw him, he had compassion on him. He did not question whether the stranger was a Jew or a Gentile. If a Jew, the Samaritan well knew that, were their condition reversed, the man would spit in his face, and pass him by with contempt. But he did not hesitate on account of this. He did not consider that he himself might be in danger of violence by tarrying in the place. It was enough that there was before him a human being in need and suffering. He took off his own garment with which to cover him. The oil and wine provided for his own journey he used to heal and refresh the wounded man. He lifted him on his own beast, and moved slowly along with even pace, so that the stranger might not be jarred, and made to suffer increased pain. He brought him to an inn, and cared for him through the night, watching him tenderly. In the morning, as the sick man had improved, the Samaritan ventured to go on his way. But before doing this, he placed him in the care of the innkeeper, paid the charges, and left a deposit for his benefit; and not satisfied even with this, he made provision for any further need, saying to the host, 'Take care of him; and whatsoever thou spendest more, when I come again, I will repay thee.' " [2]

The spirit of the story is unmistakable. The Samaritan was not following a rule book or doing his duty because he wanted to stack up credits on his reputation ledger. His mercy was the spontaneous overflow of a loving heart. His ethical system was foolproof because it was genuine. And this is the difference between a legalist and a true child of God.

This ethical conduct that Christ was teaching was nothing new. It had long been lost in the maze of do's and

---

[2] Ellen G. White, *The Desire of Ages*, p. 503.

don'ts set forth by the rabbis and Pharisees. At the time Christ talked about the Jericho road, the Jews acted as if charity consisted of so many ewe lambs as a burnt offering, so many gold pieces placed in the offering plate. As for their neighbor, they treated him in the spirit of a tooth for a tooth, an eye for an eye. There was no giving without first having received; no pardoning without first having an apology.

It had not always been so. Many, many years before, when God guided the children of Israel through the wilderness, He had taught them that merciful provisions of the law should extend even to the lower animals. The idea was that "if thou meet thine enemy's ox or his ass going astray, thou shalt surely bring it back to him again. If thou see the ass of him that hateth thee lying under his burden, and wouldest forbear to help him, thou shalt surely help with him." [3]

The God of Moses ever had been a God of lonely widows, of fatherless children, showing kindness and goodness to the weak, the poor, the downtrodden. All this the Jews had wiped from their consciousness in a grand sweep, so that Jesus had to remind them that from the social point of view, love must always come first.

Christ's teachings were not, as some have maintained, a new, revolutionary doctrine. Joseph Klausner, a distinguished Jewish scholar, says: "Throughout the Gospels there is not one item of ethical teaching which cannot be paralleled either in the Old Testament, the Apocrypha, or in the Talmudic and Midrashic literature near to the time of Jesus." [4] But the Jews, in their long history of estrangement, rapprochement, and re-estrangement from God, had

---

[3] Book of Exodus, ch. 23, vs. 4, 5.
[4] Joseph Klausner, *Jesus of Nazareth,* p. 384.

to the original depth of goodness. He swept away the cob-
webs of legalism and showed once again what godly ethics
were in depth and breadth. His teachings were unified,
and they concentrated on essentials.

This is what threw the Pharisees into a frenzied fury.
With Christ, a moral act was more than outward conduct.
A person could speak like an angel, but if his heart was
not in what he said, he was not moral. The motive alone
made an act either moral or immoral. How clear Christ
made this in His Sermon on the Mount! His indictment of
hypocrisy is more damning than that of any other sin.
Jesus minced no words in letting men know that the heart
is the seat of virtue.

Jesus' life embodied this genuine, free-flowing love.
His social contacts were warm. People who had never
known appreciation and who had been scorned and rebuffed all their lives found that they could depend on Jesus.
He was not exploiting them or playing a game. He was
simply there to help, to heal, to share. His good will was an
isle of verdure in a parched desert. His personal influence
finds no parallel in the history of religion.

The early Christian church was set on fire by Christ's
example. They had found in Him their champion. With
Him as their example they lived with purpose. The early
churches were vibrant in their faith; they were unflagging
in their ardor. For three full centuries they "turned the
world upside down." In word and deed they showed that
love was their ruling principle. The heathen took notice,
amazed at Christian joy in doing for others. No pagan
people had ever produced a way of life equal to it. The
Christian's love for humanity was not only more volumi-
nous but also more intense. They seemed to forget themselves while helping their fellow men who needed them.

The noblest qualities of man are brought out when by
acts of kindness he ministers to those less fortunate.

Their love did not end with solitary contemplation. It was a love of clothing the naked and feeding the hungry. With Minucius Felix they could say, "We do not *speak* great things; we live them."

What happened to the church? Why is our present world called an age void of love? It has been argued by certain scholars that the early Christian church was apocalyptically oriented. In other words, the Christians could live such a life of unselfish charity only so long as they felt Christ's return to be imminent. While they looked forward to this sudden, cataclysmic event, they did not get tired of lofty ethics. However, time passed, and the Lord did not return as they had understood. The church waxed cold in her ardor. Indifference took the place of involvement.

A number of religious thinkers accuse Christ of being an apocalyptic apostle, saying that He believed the present world order would come to an end soon and that this firm belief permeated all His ethical teachings. He told His disciples how they should act during the waiting period, but did not concern Himself with their way of life thereafter. Since the expected Advent did not occur, His teachings soon lost their appropriateness. His disciples lost purpose.

Such miss the nature and scope of Christ's teaching on the kingdom of God. His prophetic discourses not only proclaimed His return at the "end of the world" but outlined the events that would mark the advance of history during the intervening centuries. This we have seen.[5] Meanwhile, the majority of Christians did lose sight of this teaching. Likewise, they lost an essential part of the Christian motivation.

The majority of Christians today are a motley multitude of people enthralled with no great cause. To them life

---

[5] See Chapter 11, Time.

seems tragic—to many not worth preserving. But constitutionally and spiritually we were created to espouse
a great cause. God meant it to be that way.

Today we often speak of "the intrinsic worth of personality," or of "the essential dignity of man." These two
concepts have become clichés in the current parlance. They
are basically Christian concepts. Jesus declared over and
over again the supreme worth of every person to God. If
we could but come to terms with these concepts in a redemptive way, we would be on the right track.

But we must not talk about the dignity of man if we
are willing to let our neighbor starve. We must not
mouth platitudes about the worth of personality as long
as we refuse social contact with anyone below our social
status. A redeemed society, or church, must mean a community of persons responsive to the call of God in faith
and love. It does not mean a new set of social or political
institutions. Christ Himself had very little to say about
forms of government. He did, however, have much to say
about the attitudes and motives of men in their corporate
life. He was vehement in His accusation of those who
loved sin and who harmed others with their sin. Jesus'
concern with social wrongs burst forth in many of His sermons, such as the one about the victim of bandits on the
road to Jericho, cited at the opening of this chapter, or
the widow mistreated by an unjust judge,[6] or the poor folks
on whom publicans like Zacchaeus practiced extortion,[7] or
the destitute begging at the rich man's door,[8] or of prisoners unvisited and hungry people remaining unfed[9]—all
of these called out from Jesus a strong social message.

This social message, however, was not to be dependent
solely on a grand finale. You do not do for God on the

---

[6] See Gospel according to Luke, ch. 18, vs. 2-5.
[7] *Ibid.*, ch. 19, vs. 2-8.
[8] *Ibid.*, ch. 16, vs. 19-21.
[9] See Gospel according to Matthew, ch. 25, vs. 31-46.

basis that if you keep up the pace long enough and in-
tensively enough, He will then climax your efforts by fling-
ing back the curtains and ushering in an eternity of paradise. There is definitely a tension between this world and
the world to come—this the Christian would never deny;
but he will not be preoccupied with a conditional well-
doing. Rather, he will allow the final resolution to rest in
God's control, while he responds with obedience and faith
to God's rule. The true Christian will be so profoundly
God-centered that he will never fall prey to pessimism regarding this world's fate, nor to conceit regarding the fab-
ulous reward to come. His ethic will be that of charity—
a transformed heart overflowing for God, reaching out to
all fellow creatures, showing that it is a privilege to serve
and to minister. The hope for reward or the fear of punishment are forgotten; he is motivated entirely by love to fur-
nish the universe with a holy life such as God intended
life should be from Creation. The apostle Paul explains it
thus:

"The very spring of our actions is the love of Christ.
We look at it like this: if one died for all men then, in a
sense, they all died, and his purpose in dying for them is
that their lives now should be no longer lived for themselves
but for him who died and rose again for them. . . . For
God caused Christ, who himself knew nothing of sin, actually to *be* sin for our sakes, so that in Christ we might
be made good with the goodness of God." [10]

---

[10] Second Epistle to the Corinthians, ch. 5, vs. 14-21. From *The New
Testament in Modern English,* © by J. B. Phillips 1958. Used by permission
of The Macmillan Company.

CHAPTER 25

The Holy Spirit

ℛELIGIOUS WRITING in this "age of reason" has been reluctant to deal with the doctrine of the Holy Spirit. Individual writers have been satisfied to mention the Spirit, to acknowledge the Spirit's importance; few have dealt with the subject deliberately and systematically. Doubtless this hesitancy caused Prof. Stanley Romaine Hopper, of Drew University, to declare that "the doctrine of the Holy Spirit is at once the most central and the most neglected doctrine of the Christian faith." [1]

I suppose that the very term "Holy Spirit" evokes for many the magical, even the occult. Few persons have a clear concept of what the Holy Spirit represents. In many minds He is rather an extravagant medley of doves, winds, still small voices, and flames of fire; or, simply the catchall of God's unknown attributes. Whatever is not fathomed with respect to God is consigned to the Holy Spirit, in this way making Him a sort of genie whose work is prolific, whose influence is to be desired. Some fear the revolutionary effects of the Spirit in the Christian life. Yet others find it rather presumptuous to try to define or

---

[1] Quoted in "Holy Spirit," *A Handbook of Christian Theology.*

explain that which by its very appellation seems indefinite if not mysterious. The problem is compounded, because from all Biblical evidence the Spirit is something to be experienced rather than to be subjected to formal criteria. No matter how one tries to formulate a doctrine in descriptive words and sentences, the heart of understanding the Holy Spirit and His work remains in the realm of individual experience.

Now, this does not mean that we should ignore the subject, for its importance in the Christian faith remains primary. Bar the Holy Spirit from Christianity and what have you? A dull, paralyzed, lifeless philosophy, so brittle that it will crumble into bits at the slightest impact with earth's realities. God simply does not commune with this world without the Holy Spirit. Furthermore, man cannot be genuinely religious without the Holy Spirit.

The Bible attributes multiple connotations to the concept of "Spirit." The Old Testament, for instance, speaks of the Spirit as the life-giving breath of God, as the primal power of God in all things. In the work of Creation "the Spirit of God was moving over the face of the waters." [2] The Spirit differentiated man from his origin, the dust of earth's crust. Always, the Old Testament relates the Spirit to God's presence and power.

In the New Testament, Biblical teaching moves into sharper focus. The Holy Spirit's first appearance is in the form of a dove descending from heaven when John the Baptist [3] proceeded with Jesus' baptism. What a fitting symbol of the beginning of a new and important era, not only in Christ's life but in that of humanity! The descent of the Holy Spirit marked, in fact, the opening of Christ's battle against evil. He was the Prince of peace, yet His ministry would resemble the unsheathing of a sword.

---

[2] Book of Genesis, ch. 1, v. 2, R.S.V.
[3] See Gospel according to Matthew, ch. 3, vs. 13-17.

Christ had come to establish a kingdom directly opposed to the sort of power bloc the Jews had prayed for. It is almost ironical in a sense that the beginning of Christ's ministry was signified by a gentle dove; for the time would soon arrive when He would be hounded by an angry mob and put to death in a burst of fury. The might of God, however, would be the way of the Spirit.

Since the moment Christ received the Holy Spirit, His influence on every Christian has been of utter importance. Unbelievable acts of heroism and power are attributable to the Holy Spirit. The four Gospels credit Him with driving out demons, healing incurable diseases, and even forgiving sins. Many promises are made to those who follow Christ's example; but apparently all these benefits are epitomized in the gift of the Holy Spirit, for as Saint Luke says, "If ye then, being evil, know how to give good gifts unto your children: how much more shall your heavenly Father give the Holy Spirit to them that ask him?"[4]

No one can read the apostle Paul's writings thoughtfully and fail to recognize that with him the Holy Spirit occupied an exalted role, an awesome place. Paul believed in a "life-giving Spirit" who through the ages was the fountain of life to men. The Spirit is not a substance but a personality —a power which comes to man and delivers him from sin and death. The Spirit not only frees man from sin and death, but also He opens the way to a new life of freedom and joy, because along with forgiveness the Spirit brings those most excellent fruits which make living on earth a pleasant existence—namely, faith, righteousness, joy, peace, long-suffering, gentleness, goodness, faith, meekness, and temperance.[5] In all the Pauline literature the Holy Spirit is the vehicle through which God becomes the indwelling, dynamic principle of the Christian's life. He is

---

[4] Gospel according to Luke, ch. 11, v. 13.
[5] See Epistle to the Galatians, ch. 5, vs. 22, 23.

the divine power radiating from within every disciple, affecting the lives of millions who come within His radius. "In the Spirit" and "in Christ Jesus" are parallel expressions used to indicate the intimate union with God, which makes the Christian life an eternal life starting here in the midst of time, and to be consummated that glorious day when "we shall be like him; for we shall see him as he is." [6] Through the Spirit the divine Artist is at work on the canvas of every Christian's life. "We all, with unveiled face, beholding the glory of the Lord, are being changed into his likeness from one degree of glory to another; for this comes from the Lord who is the Spirit." [7]

Paul taught that the initiation into the Christian life —the baptism by which we die and rise again with Christ into newness of life—is "baptism in the Spirit." This is the true baptism, of which the immersion in water is the effectual sign.[8] They who receive this baptism become steeped, so to speak, in the Spirit. Paul understood that God would give such ones a spirit of wisdom and revelation in the knowledge of Him. This knowledge, Paul freely grants, is only partial. But, so far as it goes, it is real, personal knowledge— never complete or free from mystery, but a criterion for daily assurance and advance.[9]

Paul himself was possessed and directed by the Spirit. Some of his converts, however, were led to emphasize the more exciting and spectacular effects of the Spirit's ministry. A burst of sensationalism came, for instance, upon the church at Corinth. Paul never thought of denying that there was value in the visions of glory and the inspired utterances which men there attributed to the Spirit. He pointed

---

[6] First Epistle of John, ch. 3, v. 2.
[7] Second Epistle to the Corinthians, ch. 3, v. 18, R.S.V.
[8] See Epistle to the Romans, ch. 6, v. 3; Book of Acts, ch. 19, vs. 1-7; First Epistle to the Corinthians, ch. 12, v. 13.
[9] See First Epistle to the Corinthians, ch. 2; ch. 8, vs. 1-3; ch. 12, v. 8; ch. 13, vs. 9-12; Second Epistle to the Corinthians, ch. 10, vs. 3-6; Epistle to the Philippians, ch. 1, vs. 9, 10.

out, however, that these were manifestations of varying value. Speaking with tongues, for instance (which was recollective of Pentecost),[10] or uttering emotional cries that had no clear meaning, particularly in public and when there was no one to interpret, had far less value, according to him, than did clear insight into God's purposes through the prophetic gift. Greater than all these was the new creation that the Spirit brought through the experience of regeneration.[11]

Paul never attempted to define the Spirit or to interpret Him philosophically. He is perfectly content to describe the Spirit's operation. Perhaps this is because the moment one begins to speculate or postulate about the Spirit, the Spirit's image becomes distorted and marred. Let us beware, then, of treating this subject as if it were a building which we can put up block by block. Let us, like Paul, be content to describe the work of the Spirit, to accept this work rather than to dissect the Spirit as one might a corporeal being.

The apostle John identifies the Spirit as being truth. He exhorts his readers not to believe just any spirit, for apparently some spirits are of the devil. He commands them to "try the spirits whether they are of God: because many false prophets are gone out into the world."[12] With John, the Spirit and the truth are one. The heart of his message is that "it is the Spirit that beareth witness, because the Spirit is truth."[13]

Because the Spirit is truth we must take infinite care that we do not interpret the truth except with truth. No sin is worse than to lie against the Holy Spirit.

A rebellious creature, dishonestly claiming to use the Holy Spirit, becomes a despicable creature—a hellish de-

---

[10] See page 288.
[11] See First Epistle to the Corinthians, ch. 14.
[12] First Epistle of John, ch. 4, v. 1.
[13] *Ibid.*, ch. 5, v. 6.

mon. We can put it even more dramatically: Whereas we may be forgiven for sinning against Jesus Christ, to sin against the Holy Spirit is unforgivable. When we allow the Holy Spirit to use us, He becomes the seal of Christianity, the living water, the bridge between the spiritual world and the world of flesh. He becomes the power unto salvation and the energy toward good.

The work of the Holy Spirit in the Christian community was observed keenly by the author of the book of Acts. He portrays Christianity's triumphant march from Jerusalem to Rome and beyond as a direct result of the effusion of the Spirit at the Jewish Pentecost. For that occasion, representatives of many races and languages had gathered at Jerusalem. The disciples "were all with one accord in one place." [14] Without warning, Christ's promise of the Holy Spirit [15] was fulfilled gloriously. The Greek language used conveys the picture of an initial ball of fire that descends and divides itself into many small tongues, which settle on the members of the assembly. The figure of "tongues" was apt in view of the gift of speech the Spirit bestowed upon the believers. This gift was bestowed for the special purpose of qualifying the apostles to carry the gospel message into all the world. Pilgrims from the four corners of the earth were assembled for the feast. The Spirit communicated to the apostles the message and the utterance which led to the conversion of three thousand people in one day, and which spread to "every creature under heaven." [16] This was the "former rain" manifestation foretold by the prophet Joel.[17]

Such was the beginning. The whole story is a divine adventure. Human resources and personal ingenuity have

---

[14] Book of Acts, ch. 2, v. 1.
[15] *Ibid.*, ch. 1, vs. 2-4.
[16] Epistle to the Colossians, ch. 1, v. 23, R.S.V.
[17] Book of Joel, ch. 2, v. 23.

no place in the narrative. Personal-glory medals for out-standing performance gave place to the new age foretold by the prophet. Through him God had said, "I will pour out my spirit upon all flesh." [18] As a consequence, the speeches delivered so fervently were spoken under the in-fluence of the Holy Spirit: "Then Peter, filled with the Holy Spirit, said unto them . . ." [19] "But Saul, who is also called Paul, filled with the Holy Spirit, looked intently at him and said . . ." [20] The apostolic story makes it clear that sincere Christians are the only ones worthy to be associated with the Holy Spirit's action. "When Simon saw that the Spirit was given through the laying on of the apostles' hands, he offered them money, saying, 'Give me also this power, that any one on whom I lay my hands may receive the Holy Spirit.' But Peter said to him, 'Your silver perish with you, because you thought you could obtain the gift of God with money!' " [21]

In the victorious, westward march of Christianity it was always the Holy Spirit who directed the Christians' activities and showed them the way. In fact, it was the Holy Spirit who made Christianity possible. Under the influence of the Spirit, Philip explained the Bible to the Ethiopian eunuch. [22] Under the influence of the Spirit, Peter witnessed to Cornelius, the Jewish centurion. [23] Again, it was under the guidance of the Spirit that we find Paul and Barnabas sailing to Cyprus and setting out to evangelize the Mediter-ranean basin. [24] Paul's urgent call to Macedonia, also, was a call from the Spirit. [25] In fact, the book of Acts ends with a speech given by Paul under the influence of the Holy Spirit.

---

[18] *Ibid.,* v. 28.
[19] Book of Acts, ch. 4, v. 8, R.S.V.
[20] *Ibid.,* ch. 13, vs. 9, 10, R.S.V.
[21] *Ibid.,* ch. 8, vs. 18-20, R.S.V.
[22] *Ibid.,* vs. 26-40.
[23] *Ibid.,* ch. 10.
[24] *Ibid.,* ch. 13, vs. 1-5.
[25] *Ibid.,* ch. 16.

"Be it known therefore unto you, that the salvation of God is sent unto the Gentiles, and that they will hear it." [26]

Perhaps you feel that this review of the activity of the Spirit in Holy Scripture and the apostolic church is irrelevant in the present age where spiritual problems appear embroiled in psychology, politics, and socio-economics. Perhaps you would rather spend your time studying the stock market, or calculating how to make a stronger national community, or at a multitude of other occupations. To be sure, a thousand problems encroach upon our waking hours. In fact, the Christian who is not fully dedicated may soon find himself being swept up in questions pertaining only to his role in a materialistic society. So much so that before he realizes it, matters of the Spirit are relegated to a few minutes at the end of the week—if he happens to have them to spare.

Let us guard against this temptation. The work of God's Spirit is more appropriate and important now than it ever was. The Holy Spirit remains a basic dimension in salvation. Moreover, our need is more desperate, more intense, than in ages gone by. We need to be aware of the Spirit in all areas of life. He must become our comforter in sorrow, our strength in time of temptation, our teacher when we thirst for knowledge, our energy when action is demanded, our power when otherwise we would be weak, our guide when we have become lost among falsehoods, our illumination in darkness, our hope when we need grace. In other words, we cannot be Christians without the Spirit. Just as a light is not a light until it is lighted, so also we need God's Spirit in order to develop our God-given talents. We need God's Spirit in order to touch the hearts of hardened souls around us. We need God's Spirit in order to communicate with God, who otherwise would

---

[26] *Ibid.,* ch. 28, v. 28.

remain away out of our reach. Without the Spirit no amount of education can make of man a channel of light. He may know the intellectual content of the gospel, and he may be capable of brilliant recitations, but he cannot expect the seed he sows to bloom and bear fruit unless it is quickened into life by this dew of Heaven. It was not until after Christ's disciples had received the Holy Spirit that their enemies testified, "Ye have filled Jerusalem with your doctrine." [27]

Now, Christ did not limit the activity of the Holy Spirit to His twelve disciples. He promised the Spirit to the Christian church in all ages. In fact, the promise to us is for a "latter rain" manifestation that shall exceed any previous manifestation.[28] But this promise, like any other, is conditional.

We must be absolutely willing to be led by God. We must give up all preconceived theories and biased opinions, acknowledging divine management instead of self-management. "The Holy Spirit works with those who will be worked, moulds those who will be moulded, fashions those who will be fashioned." [29] Only to those who wait humbly upon God, who watch for His guidance and grace, and who are willing to step out and walk with Him in faith, is the Spirit given. This promised blessing claimed in faith brings all other blessings in its train. It is granted to supply every soul according to the *capacity* to receive.

Should you remain unconvinced of the importance of being filled with God's Spirit, then let us suggest what riches result through this indwelling power. Having God's Spirit provides deep insight, and who today does not need it? The problems we face cause our poor brains to whirl in confused attempts to understand the most perplexing

---

[27] *Ibid.*, ch. 5, v. 28.
[28] Book of Zechariah, ch. 10, v. 1.
[29] Ellen G. White, *Gospel Workers*, p. 274.

events. Only with the help of the Spirit can a human mind understand the great themes of Christianity and their far-reaching principles as they apply to our day. The Holy Spirit brings no outburst of fanaticism or false revivalism. He who receives the Spirit will be calm and steadfast, devoid of extravagance in thought, word, or deed. But, amid the confusion of delusive doctrines, he will be guided and shielded. Every voice except that which comes from Him who is the truth will be silenced.

How reassuring it is to know this, because contradicting doctrines and philosophies are being thrust upon us from every side. Scientists, historians, the man on the street—so many have lost sight of genuine godliness, have succumbed to the agony of living without God. So many consequently are without that vibrant power which fills the Christian's soul—the dynamic of the Holy Spirit. Today God calls the believer to work diligently in gathering up truth and keeping it complete in the framework of the everlasting gospel. This truth must now shine forth in the moral darkness of our world. Such is the task—an impossible one without the mighty workings of the Holy Spirit. With this power God's biddings are enablings.

We have been entrusted with an awesome gift, the gift of freedom. Through it we may either die in emptiness or we may reclaim all that sinful man ever lost. Under the guidance of the Holy Spirit let us use our freedom to find rather than to lose.

CHAPTER 26

Personal Involvement

MORE THAN a million people in the United
States have the capacity to be geniuses. Close
to 2,700 of them possess an intellect equal to that of the
greatest leaders in history. What a joint stock of unused
talent, intelligence, and skill! If it were used, we would
need fear no other power on earth. Our government would
soar to unbelievable heights of model administration. Its
citizens would live in a utopia.

Why are such rich resources left dangling in a vacuum?
The answer is that most of us could not care less, to use a
colloquialism. Finding people who are willing to get involved in something beyond their private vegetable patch
has become as arduous a task as digging for the proverbial
needle in a haystack.

Some time ago one of my friends refused to go to his
alma mater's reunion because he was afraid that if he
went to the meeting, they would elect him president—and
that would mean getting involved. The popular counsel is
against doing just that. If an accident happens in front of
your eyes, pass quickly by with closed eyes, lest you be
legally embarrassed. If a gang of youngsters decides to rob
a store, do not report them, because they may turn on you.
If an elderly man is treated disrespectfully by a young up-

start, keep still, for it is none of your business. In short, let life pass you by without touching you—that is your safest approach.

True, staying away from the heartbeat of life affords a measure of safety, but it is also morbid. Unless you take the trouble to risk yourself every day for the matters that mean something to you, you will have no rewards, no feeling of exuberance, and no inner satisfaction. The kiss of death will be on you. Andrew Marvell once observed:

> "The grave's a fine and private place,
> But none, I think, do there embrace."

Mr. Marvell, I believe, was hitting straight at the problem of noninvolvement, pointing out how embracing life and placing yourself in exchange in its currency is what keeps you breathing. I remember visiting the Egyptian mummies buried in the pyramids. They have lain there for thousands of years—clearly uninvolved, clearly dead.

Look back on your happiest days. Be honest. Were they not days when you were so completely lost and devoted in a dream, a scheme, or a project that the hours flew by? You even forgot to eat. Time had no bounds. You could not tear yourself loose from what you were doing. Strange that society should try to whisper in our ear, "Don't get involved. Let Mr. Smith do it. Stay out of it."

We as Christians have yet another consideration. We have been commissioned in unmistakable terms to go into all the world as a witness. Though these words are a direct injunction to us from Christ, we rarely take them seriously. Oh, we want to be religious, of course. Someday we hope to make it to heaven; but if this means getting too close to our fellow human beings, then what? We had not thought too much about that. We had hoped to practice our religion in some decently quiet and unostentatious manner. The ideal would be to avoid placing self in the compromising situation of trying to influence another. It is more cautious to keep one's faith as a personal and wholly private matter.

If this has been your view, then doubtless you will be deeply shocked to review Christ's teaching. For instance, read the Sermon on the Mount carefully. The very first commandment given by Christ was the commission to share in public witness. "Let your light so shine before men," said He, "that they may see your good works and give glory to your Father who is in heaven." [1] And then that command, "Go therefore and make disciples of all nations." [2]

Some today would accept almost any other terms than those of spreading their faith. If only Christ had said, "Give ten dollars to the church every week," or "Darn a dozen pair of socks for the poor," or "Bake a cake for the white elephant sale." This type of work they would dutifully perform; but getting involved with people? No. That is something else. That means sharing oneself.

How different were Christ's first disciples. They listened to the Master's words on the hillside, and they were not overawed. This order to take the gospel to the whole world did not strike them as an unreasonable utterance. They considered it neither impossible nor irrational. To them it was simply a work that had to be done and they never questioned the heavenly Authority that compelled them to go. They went. Later the apostle Paul could write to the church at Colosse that "the hope of the gospel" had been "preached to every creature which is under heaven." [3] Indeed, the apostolic believers had obeyed God's command. They carried the gospel to every nation of the then-known world in one single generation. With fire and

---

[1] Gospel according to Matthew, ch. 5, v. 16, R.S.V.
[2] *Ibid.*, ch. 28, v. 19, R.S.V.
[3] Epistle to the Colossians, ch. 1, v. 23.

untiring love they preached, they healed, and they lived a life of devotion before the men of their day. It was a golden time for Christianity.

Alas, with the passing decades men's zeal for witnessing slipped away. Building bigger and better cathedrals, pouring wealth into ecclesiastical treasuries became more important to them than saving people. The evangelistic urge was lost, and the church hushed its voice to a faint, introspective mutter.

That is the predicament into which the modern age was ushered. The job still ahead of us today is demanding; but it must not be ignored. Unnumbered countries, cities, and villages know little or nothing of God's Word. A black array of earthly powers holds sway over the lives and bodies of untold millions. Materialistic philosophies engulf imposing sections of the globe. Deeply entrenched religions hold people in the grip of idolatry. Populous centers are sated with extremes of sensual pleasures. This is our challenge. It must rein us up to a full appraisal of our mission and our resources. If we take Christ at all seriously, we cannot ignore the task before us, nor can we excuse ourselves politely from it. His words stand out in bold relief before us, silently waiting for our response.

1. *Everyone Must Go.*

Our Lord traces three features in the work assignment given to the "Church of the Remnant." First He says, "Go ye." This means *everyone.* In other words, evangelism is the task of every believer. It cannot be left with the minister or gospel team, or with a special race or breed of men. To be sure, men with special talents will be called to special phases of evangelism. But *all* will go—as did the apostolic believers. Then Christianity swept across the world like a fire bellowed by mighty winds. The reason for their dynamic evangelism is no secret. Clovis G. Chappell explains it thus in *When the Church Was Young:*

"The early church was blessed with some great preachers, but the fact that Christianity spread over that hard Roman world like a forest fire was due, not so much to great preachers, as to the personal testimony of ordinary men and women who went out to tell their friends the amazing difference that knowing Jesus had made in their lives."

The pattern has not changed since it was cut. Think of what we could accomplish today had we the same fervor as those first believers! With our advantage of living in a supermechanical age, no limits confine our spreading the gospel. But it will not be done unless we follow the same instruction of "Go ye"—all of you.

2. *The Witness Must Be Personal.*

The world is sick of hypocrisy and empty chatter. Primarily people want to know what God has done for individuals and what He will do for them. Those who have never had an encounter with God or who have fled from Him, are little interested in the latest theories about God. They long to see a revelation of God's character in us, so they can observe in a measurable way just what God has done for us and whether or not this is worth having.

The work of Jesus was a personal witness. He addressed Himself to men and women as individuals. No one was too unimportant or too soiled in character for Him to reach out His helping hand and pull the needy one to His love-filled heart. He listened to the widows' pleas, gave attention to men with communicable diseases, and spent long hours of counseling with men and women who had lost their way spiritually.

Personal witnessing remains the ultimate method of evangelism. Christians must step out into the world, not

afraid to get tired, dirty, or even abused. They must be unselfish in their effort to help, to give, to reflect godly qualities. If we just talk about God, we are spreading a message without a witness. Such a message will produce a lifeless cause made up of lifeless people.

When we go out, determined in mind and spirit to glorify God in deed as well as in word, then our influence will have its effect, for the influence of one who moves in harmony with God is irresistible. Even the most hardened unbelievers will be moved by it. Again Ellen White gives pertinent counsel:

"The followers of Christ are to shed light into the darkness of the world. Through the Holy Spirit, God's word is a light as it becomes a transforming power in the life of the receiver. By implanting in their hearts the principles of His word, the Holy Spirit develops in men the attributes of God. The light of His glory—His character—is to shine forth in His followers. Thus they are to glorify God, to lighten the path to the Bridegroom's home, to the city of God, to the marriage supper of the Lamb." [4]

Evangelism, then, is really the phenomenon of witnessing. The evangelist—layman or minister—cannot be just a zealot tracking down proselytes. Nor is he to be simply a recruiting sergeant enlisting soldiers for the army of the Lord.

Far more important, he will bear fruit from the abundance of his doctrine and the fragrance of his life. He can help finish God's work in the world because the work of God has been finished in him.

Personal witness carries Christianity to places where it seemed impossible to make any kind of penetration. The

---

[4] Ellen G. White, *Christ's Object Lessons*, p. 414.

Every Christian is included by the Saviour in the command to "Go," supported with the assurance "I am with you."

light shining out of a human life pierces darkness. This is as much a law of nature as the fact that a tiny candle will light up a dark room.

The Christian witness is given without thought to earthly gain and honor. God cannot use service if it flows from fear or from a sense of duty. Service given only because God has the power and means at His command to extract obedience might as well never be offered. God wants us to witness for only one reason—because we love Him so much that we cannot do otherwise; because our deep affection for Him compels us to give and to share and to go.

And how could we blame God for wanting service given in love? Surely you have felt the cold repulsion of "doing time" in a task for which you have no heart. You did it grudgingly because you had to. In this there is no beauty, no warmth, no joy. God knows about such service; it is weighed in the divine balances and found wanting.

3. *The Baptism of the Spirit.*

If information were the test of Christianity, how easy it would be for Christians to qualify for witnessing! The church program would be geared to providing members with proper instruction, then they would be on their way. Most humans like to talk and impress people with how much they know.

I knew a young man once who made an extensive and detailed study of the human voice. He knew just where to place a note so that it would sound clear and mellow, but the trouble with this young man was that he himself could not sing a note. Information is insufficient for voice training. It is insufficient for being a Christian too.

Something beyond information is needed. I believe this need is captured in Christ's own words, given to His disciples shortly before His ascension. He said: "Ye shall receive power after that the Holy Ghost is come upon you." [5]

Jesus did not come to this earth just to give information. He came to give power, just as He gave power to His disciples on the day of Pentecost. As they sat huddled in the upper room, there suddenly came a sound from heaven "as of a rushing mighty wind, and it filled all the house where they were sitting." [6] It was then that the church of information became the church of great deeds for God recorded in the Acts of the Apostles. That is why today we are thrilled as we read of the mighty miracles, the unbelievable deeds accomplished by these men once the Holy Spirit entered their hearts.

The same power is promised for our age of sophisticated error. The apostle Peter predicted a last spiritual "refreshing . . . from the presence of the Lord," [7] to take place immediately prior to the "restitution of all things" and the return of Jesus. The Scriptures call this great flash of divine power "the latter rain." [8] It will follow the work of the "former rain." True, the expressions "latter rain" and "former rain" are applicable to dispensations of the church. The former rain recalls the apostolic day, the seed-sowing time. The latter rain is applied to the gospel harvest. But these expressions have a definite application to the individual experience of the child of God. All must know the experience of the former rain, so that they can enter into the blessings of the latter rain.

Many times Christians fail to receive the "former rain" and the benefits therefrom that God provides. Such expect that somehow the lack will be supplied in the glorious "latter rain" experience. But this is not God's way. The

---

[5] Book of Acts, ch. 1, v. 8.
[6] *Ibid.*, ch. 2, vs. 1-8.
[7] *Ibid.*, ch. 3, vs. 19-21.
[8] Book of Deuteronomy, ch. 11, v. 14; Book of Jeremiah, ch. 5, v. 24; Book of Zechariah, ch. 10, v. 1; Epistle of James, ch. 5, v. 7.

work that He begins in the human heart through His light and knowledge must be continually going forward. We must advance daily in the exemplification of the active Christian virtues (the grace of the "former rain"), otherwise we shall not even recognize the manifestation of the Holy Spirit in the "latter rain." In fact, the last great "spiritual refreshing from the presence of the Lord" may fall on loving hearts all around us, and we shall not discern or receive it.

Strange? Yet this is God's way, and today He is adding His power according to plan. He is giving, we believe, the "latter rain" experience. According to His promise, He is pouring out His Spirit "upon all flesh."[9] There can be no mistaking this. We may not discern it or experience it, but thousands are proclaiming the virtues of God today. Thousands are revealing, according to pattern, the intense sacrificial giving and going of Pentecost.

People who lack God's Spirit always feel lonely, depressed, and rejected. To them life is ominous and threatening. They see only the bad in others and time itself for them has become a death knell. They expect the worst. Tension, strain, conflict, fatigue, and irritability constantly burden them, and because of this, they often try to make life equally miserable for others. But those who are filled with the power of God's Spirit, love every moment of the day. Friendliness and kindness flow freely from them. They believe that good will triumph; consequently they can live calmly and serenely amid stress. Rumors do not confound them, nor do threats frighten them. They are fully secure and courageous. They have self-control. Their life bespeaks such power as to amaze all with whom they come in contact.

Saint Paul gives away the key that unlocks this power.

---

[9] Book of Joel, ch. 2, v. 28.

He tells us that "when we cry, 'Abba! Father!' it is the Spirit himself bearing witness with our spirit that we are children of God, and if children, then heirs, heirs of God and fellow heirs with Christ." "We know that in everything God works for good with those who love him." [10]

Of course, all three of these features—the going, the personal witnessing, and the power—involve our taking a definite risk. Getting involved always means taking a chance. And the outcome may be painful. Who said that a true Christian witness invariably will succeed in the sense of popular success? Often it has led to shame, slander, and even death. To witness for Christ is a dangerous business. The needy one to whom you give your money may take advantage of you; the fallen friend whom you seek to lift may ruin your reputation; the orphan you adopt may break your heart; the drowning boy whose life you seek to save may pull you under with him. Of course; but only one thing is worse than being a witness and that is staying aloof—not being one. C. S. Lewis, in his book *The Four Loves,* says: "If you want to make sure of keeping it intact, you must give your heart to no one, not even to an animal. Avoid all entanglements, lock it up safe in the coffin of your selfishness. But in that casket—safe, dark, motionless, airless—it will change. It will not be broken; it will become unbreakable, impenetrable, irredeemable."

Today, upon your door sounds a knock like a clap of thunder. The summons is for you to be a witness for God. Then forget the warmth and comfort of the niche you have carved for yourself in an ivory tower far removed from the pitiful cries of those below. Descend to a desperate, dying humanity. Go without delay into all the world and preach the gospel to every creature under the sun.

---

[10] Epistle to the Romans, ch. 8, vs. 15-17, 28, R.S.V.

$\mathcal{H}$eaven on $\mathcal{E}$arth

$\mathcal{S}$ERIOUS PORTRAITS of life are sometimes found in ridiculous corners. Recently the "Post Scripts" section of the *Saturday Evening Post* was one such spot. My attention was drawn to a cartoon picturing a Christmas showcase exhibiting the year's most exciting new toy, a desk-sized world globe from which a cord led to a button. Next to the globe stood the inevitable big ad:

> Explode-A-Globe
> Press Button and Destroy the World!
> $4.50
> (Replacement globes 3 for $1.00)

This satire on Christmas giving in the nuclear age probably evoked many chuckles from readers. Whether or not we laugh at it, we admit the cartoon was created by the consciousness of man's precarious situation at the present time. But from laughter we are led to serious reflection. Is the world so bad that it might as well be blasted to powder? If it is not so bad, could it be better? If it could be better, then how do we go about making it better? This last question is the one that counts most. As a matter of fact, it is so important that nothing else matters much in the light of Creation and Christianity. The moment we declare ourselves Christians, our only excuse for being is to lift life toward its intended quality of existence.

Were the present life our highest hope, we should indeed soon wither like the desert flower that senses from afar the approaching simoom. This withering process is already fast at work in millions of people who as the days unfold become increasingly weary of life. They drift amid their years, a barren shell with a lost purpose. Why? As I have pondered the matter, it has become increasingly clear to me that the problem is basically a lack of vision. For such people the idea of ever attaining a blissful state has become a fantasy inconsistent with the fabric of human thought. They become confined to the gravitational field of the earth, not just physically but also spiritually. The straitness of this prison house makes it more and more difficult for them to envision lasting beauty or perfection. So accustomed to the dense fumes of hopelessness have they become that the most they expect from life is a few luxuries beyond the crust of bread necessary for survival. To my way of thinking this is piteous in the extreme, particularly so since God has promised so much more.

I should like to make a twofold proposal: first, that we can, by identifying our life and purpose with God's, live here and now in the atmosphere of heaven; second, that in God's own good time we can live eternally in a literal heaven to come. When Christ lived on earth He offered eternal life—that is heaven—to His fellow men on numerous occasions. One memorable statement was this: "And this is life eternal, that they might know thee the only true God." [1] This heaven was not restricted to a paradise thousands of years hence. It could begin in the present, and the eternal heaven would be an extension of the heaven begun on earth. At present I should like to take

---

[1] Gospel according to John, ch. 17, v. 3.

a look at this twofold heaven with a view to understanding how one interlocks with the other.

Perhaps we can simplify the problem by reviewing the ingredients of the heavenly life. What is heaven? When we think of living in heaven, what are the gifts that fill our imagination? According to the Bible, they are: perfect happiness, perfect relationships, perfect well-being, free from all pain and suffering, in a perfect world made new. I think most of us agree that we could never wish for more. Such a world sounds attractive. But presently men curl their lips and sneer because they see people weep heart-brokenly; they see people smile maliciously as they wedge the knife of slander into another's back. Perfect relationships? How seldom—if ever! As for pain and suffering, they strike everywhere, spreading their horrible misery among the rich, the poor, the old, the young. And the present world, though surpassingly beautiful in spots, appears to "wax old like a garment." [2]

Yet, I remain unshaken in my belief that heaven should *begin* right here in our world. As I search God's Word I cannot see it otherwise. In his book *Introduction to Religious Philosophy* Dr. Geddes MacGregor cites the Greek New Testament word *zōē* to describe a certain quality of life that is held out to those who wish to follow Christ's example. *Zōē* is the fullest life possible. Over and over again the New Testament presents *zōē* as a prize well worth seeking, not only in a life after death but as an immediate goal. John further records, "He who believes in the Son has eternal life." [3] This "eternal life" (*zōē*), then, implies that life varies in quality, and that the life the Christian tries to achieve is the very best, the highest quality of life. This concept of eternal life, you see, is quite different from eternal life simply as a means to survive.

---

[2] Book of Isaiah, ch. 51, v. 6.
[3] Gospel according to John, ch. 3, v. 36, R.S.V.

What is so remarkable about *zōē* is that it is timeless. When we consider the implications of the full life, we can see wisdom in Benjamin Franklin's counsel in *Poor Richard's Almanack:* "Wish not so much to live long as to live well." In other words, quite apart from an orientation for eternity, we have here on earth the opportunity to initiate "eternal life."

I am sure that it was this full quality of life that the rich young ruler sought when he asked Christ how he could inherit it.[4] He was asking not only for length of days, but for depth. He had tried obedience to the statutes conveyed to Israel through Moses. He had followed the rules; but none of this had given him a sense of living fully. He was seeking yet another dimension. Christ was willing to show him how to gain this added experience, but apparently the requirements were not appealing enough to the rich young man. He wanted this fullness of life. He looked for it; but when he could have attained it he somehow allowed his vision to fail.

The question for us is, How can we be enthusiastic in our pursuit of the fullest life when very obviously our destiny is, first of all, death and extinction? The answer to this is, of course, that Christ was victorious over death and made His victory available to all who believe in Him. Death, in such case, is not the taunting spirit that mocks our striving for good; rather, it is God's guarantee that in Christ life can be ours now and eternally. We shall concern ourselves with life in eternity later in this chapter. First, however, let us think of *zōē* as a possibility for the present existence.

In order to attain eternal life now, we shall need to reflect in present existence those attitudes and virtues that will identify our heavenly citizenship. We envision hap-

---

[4] See Gospel according to Luke, ch. 18, vs. 18-23.

piness, perfect relationships, and freedom from pain and suffering. How about happiness? Is it not almost fraudulent to speak of perfect happiness in a world in which unhappiness is part of the very air we breathe? And what about perfect relationships? How achieve them, when contracts are so easily broken and a man's word is often more a lie than a promise? And pain? A very brief look about us assures us that we cannot escape this monster. He bears seven heads, and no sooner is one chopped off than others grow in its place. Suffering, too, is a permanent guest. Try to rid yourself of him and he turns on you in fighting fury. If you fight back, he will soon engulf you.

True, we have no guarantee for total happiness and perfect relationships on this earth, nor against pain and suffering. But what we do have is the guarantee that heaven on earth can be actualized in part—an earnest of life in eternity.[5] Let me explain this by drawing a triangle:

In order to achieve the heavenly life, there would have to be a perfect relationship between all points in the above triangle; that is, love would have to connect all points, for love alone is the perfect relationship, its logical opposite being hate. First, let us see which relationship can be perfectly achieved. It is certainly not the Thou-God relationship, because I have very little to do with what you do with your God. I cannot force you to be on correct terms with God. You and God must work out your own problems. What about the I-Thou relationship? Well, at

---

[5] See Epistle to the Hebrews, ch. 2, vs. 7-9.

best it remains one-sided. I may love you, but you may not love me, and I cannot force you to love me, so there may exist an irremediable breach. But what of the I-God relationship? Here is hope. God already loves me. This I know with certainty. He has proved that amply. All I need to do is love Him in return, and the relationship is perfect. Once that line between God and me is unbroken, it goes a long way in fostering the full life which is a bit of heaven on earth. Being loved by God perfectly and loving Him with all my heart in return, I do not eliminate *all* pain and suffering, but I do annihilate that suffering and pain which stem from a lack of harmony with God. This is why Ellen G. White proclaims that "no earthly power or skill or learning can supply the place of God's abiding presence." [6]

Furthermore, heaven can be actualized in part even in the I-Thou relationship. Your neighbor may despise you and wish you evil, but you need not return this hate. You have the choice to love, even in the face of hate. Christ made this choice. The ideal of love matters infinitely in a world where altruism is rather out of style. Maurice Maeterlinck [7] once said, "There is no soul that does not respond to love, for the soul of man is a guest that has gone hungry these centuries back." The lack of understanding between persons is one of the most heartbreaking tendencies in modern life.

Nietzsche completely misunderstood the ideal relationship between members of the human race. He tried to convince men that whenever they showed so-called "love" toward another, they were basically doing it from a sense of weakness, hoping that in return for their good will they would receive reinforcement in the form of more good

---

[6] Ellen G. White, *Patriarchs and Prophets,* p. 328.
[7] Count Maurice Maeterlinck (1862-1949): Belgian dramatist; Nobel Prize for literature, 1911; made a member of French Academy of Moral and Political Science, 1937.

will. Nietzsche went so far as to deny the equality of men, saying that physical and intellectual capacity, material circumstances, and vocational gifts automatically make some men superior. This involved him in a scornful contempt of the notion of "neighbor." Instead of love for one's fellow men, Nietzsche would invite us to an enlargement of self-love, a concept totally out of harmony with the *zōē* that Christians seek. The premise on which Christian love operates is the exact opposite of what Nietzsche postulates. The Christian will love from a sense of fullness, not from a sense of weakness. Moreover, the natural self-love of the fallen man is inverted, not into an antimoral arrogance, but into a gracious neighbor love.

What you give to another in love may seem unappreciated or even resented, but in the interest of heaven on earth you must give it anyway. Those who hate you need your love most. Remember, when a rattlesnake is really angry he will bite himself. People who are angry pour poison into themselves. They are wretched. Disciples of Christ can avoid the pain and suffering that accompany man's hate for other men. This again goes a long way toward establishing heaven on earth.

The natural man seems to be instinctively repelled by the person who constantly tells others how to be a Christian. "Minding his own business" has become a trademark of the well-bred person. Yet, what else is the divine imperative, "Go thou into all the world . . ." if it is not exactly the opposite of minding one's own business? [8] Christianity demands that we take an active interest in the Thou-God relationship. This becomes our motive for service. Jesus spent His life trying to mend the relationship between men and God. He taught the concept of brotherhood among the races. He preached about having an experi-

---

[8] See Chapter 26, Personal Involvement.

ential religion, saying that works without love were worthless. He was concerned with men's physical health and with their attitude toward money. "Man shall not live by bread alone," He said, "but by every word that proceedeth out of the mouth of God." [9] Jesus knew that men would be unhappy as long as they broke God's commandments. He did not ignore their deliberate disobedience, but continually called His fellow human beings back to obedience to divine law. He spared no words in letting men know that strength, happiness, and success are all summed up in the exhortation, "Fear God, and keep his commandments." [10] I am my brother's keeper in the sense that Christ's example directs me to point out to my brother the steps that form the quest after the fullest life possible. In pointing out this high quality of living to my brother, I myself find a new and deeper level of happiness in my search for heaven on earth.

Now, the perfection of all three sides of the relationship triangle is the basis of Christian morality. Many persons believe that a moral life is simply a life in which certain values are upheld. Warner Fite[11] speaks of morality in four branches of values: *economics,* relating to wealth; *aesthetics,* relating to art and beauty; *ethics,* relating to human habits; *logic,* relating to knowledge and truth. The quality of man's life would equal the amount of morality he places in each of these branches. In other words, if he is moral in his outlook on politics, in his appreciation of beauty, in his conduct with other persons, and in his interpretation of truth, then he would be fully moral. I do not believe this is enough, because it leaves out the heart of morality, which is the I-God relationship. Man is incapable of perceiving what is moral in any phase of life without

---

[9] Gospel according to Matthew, ch. 4, v. 4.
[10] Book of Ecclesiastes, ch. 12, v. 13.
[11] See Warner Fite, *The Examined Life,* Indiana University Press.

having a deep personal experience with God. He may be an honest man, but he will not be a genuinely moral man until his relationship with God is established. Heaven on earth is not experienced until the triangle is complete.

Let us continue with a number of suggestions concerning attitudes. So much of inward happiness and content depends upon our attitudes toward the happenings of life. Heaven on earth means contentment and joy—not perfect contentment nor perfect joy, but the perfect rudiments, and as much of both as is possible within the framework of a rebellious world.

We might begin with the attitude of *cheerfulness*. I well remember a popular song which began, "Stay with the happy people." Half of our ills and worries seem to originate in our imaginations. Perhaps we are like the woman who was disgusted with her neighbor because she believed her to be a poor housekeeper. "Just look at the filthy laundry she has on the line," she confided to a friend. "Do you see those gray streaks up and down her sheets?" The friend walked over to the window, raised it, and looked out. "It appears," she said, "that your neighbor's clothes are perfectly clean. The streaks you see are on your window." Worry, fear, and anxiety hang like a soupy fog over the world. If you can evince cheerfulness and good will in the face of this depressing world, you have brought a bit of heaven to earth.

Hopefulness, akin to cheerfulness, is another important attitude. You can acquire hopefulness. You were not born into despair. It is when you look at the world in a narrow way that it indeed appears narrow. But when you look at the world in a hopeful way, with full confidence in God, the future looks cheering—bright as His promises. One day, years ago, a baby was born to a drunken father and a tubercular mother. Cynics and pessimists looking into the crude box which served as a cradle predicted a dark future for that helpless baby. But that baby grew up to compose some of the world's greatest music, for who does not love and admire Beethoven's Ninth Symphony? It is a most eloquent witness to man's faith in God.

Another suggestion is that you *live today in terms of tomorrow.* Thus is your future life established on the present patterns. If you are a good student today, you will probably reap rich rewards of knowledge tomorrow. If you are a good parent today, your chances are brighter for good sons or daughters tomorrow. If you are a good son or daughter today, you will probably be a good man or woman tomorrow. The person who treats his friends kindly today, need not fear a friendless tomorrow; but you cannot shun your friends today and be loved by them tomorrow. A man reaps the harvest he has planted.[12] Life proves this often.

However, if you have made mistakes in your relationship with God or your fellow men, then be not overcome by the thought of these mistakes. Failures of the past should be lost in repentance, forgiveness, and in a dynamic preoccupation with the worth-while present. Moaning and groaning over past sins or failures is like trying to saw sawdust. You can saw wood, but not sawdust.

Last, let me suggest that you need to *guard your ideals* so that you never lose them. Heaven on earth is an ideal. If you lose sight of it, it may disappear forever without having been realized in the least. Prof. William E. Hocking of Harvard once said, "There is a deep tendency in human nature to become like that which we imagine ourselves to be." If this is so, then keep the vision of heaven on earth before you always. Live the poetry you sing. People without ideals are tragic corpses. They are like Shakespeare's Hamlet, who cried out: "O God, I could be bounded in a nut-shell and count myself a king of infinite

---

[12] See Epistle to the Galatians, ch. 6, vs. 7, 8.

space, were it not that I have bad dreams." Contrast Hamlet's world weariness with Saint Paul's vibrant faith: "Our rejoicing is this, the testimony of our conscience, that in simplicity and godly sincerity, not with fleshly wisdom, but by the grace of God, we have had our conversation in the world." [13]

My thesis is that all human experience, so far as it is actual experience and not mere verbiage or even hallucination, can be of low or high quality—determined by what the individual does in terms of the triangle I already have set down. I am convinced that heaven on earth begins to exist only when this experience with God reflects our understanding of what our duty is, first of all to God, then to our fellow human beings. The Master summed it up thus: " 'Love the Lord your God with all your heart, with all your soul, with all your mind.' That is the greatest commandment. It comes first. The second is like it: 'Love your neighbour as yourself.' Everything in the Law and the prophets hangs on these two commandments." [14] And once this twofold duty is placed into operation, the results follow promptly and reliably. Heaven comes to earth.

Now to the second aspect of heaven on earth—that heaven which shall be established after Christ's cataclysmic return to earth. Some erroneous and highly unsatisfactory notions are postulated regarding this heaven. In my opinion the most unsatisfactory of all is a popular interpretation of Christ's statement, "Behold, the kingdom of God is within you." [15] This has convinced some that heaven is simply a state of being. Such reduce heaven either to thoughts about an eternity in which a physical body is totally irrelevant or to a vision of heaven in which ghosts swish

---

[13] Second Epistle to the Corinthians, ch. 1, v. 12.
[14] Gospel according to Matthew, ch. 22, vs. 36-40. *The New English Bible,* New Testament. © The Delegates of the Oxford University Press and the Syndics of the Cambridge University Press 1961.
[15] Gospel according to Luke, ch. 17, v. 21.

about, crossing one another as do currents of air. Neither of these views can be reconciled with the God of human history, nor with scriptural teaching. If Creation began with the creation of a world in which everything was called good, then physical proportions, the body included, must be highly relevant and important. By teaching the resurrection of the body in a glorified state, Christ and the apostles draw attention to heaven with respect to a bodily state and not merely a state of the mind or spirit.[16] God created man with the blood, the bones, the muscles, and the flesh of his organism. He created him to walk on the earth and to perceive the golden sun and the azure sky.

The reason why it is difficult for some to reconcile heaven as a spiritual life and heaven as a bodily life is that for centuries now the spirit and the body have warred within man. Yet, heaven must be the perfect reconciliation of the two, for if it is not, then our thoughts of heaven, by virtue of the way we have been created, will be disappointing. It is futile for anyone to tell us, "Never mind, you will not miss your bodily presence in heaven because you will have something so much better." The body is what we know. The few moments of ecstasy experienced from time to time have pressed us to desire the perfection of what we *are* and *have,* rather than the creation of something completely different from what we are now and here. When I read my Bible I find my deepest joy in picturing heaven as the kind of life I am living now, but brought to its superlative possibilities in all areas, both physical and spiritual. In other words, I find that the Bible opens with a perfect garden and it closes with a perfect city.[17] The final vision is that of the New Jerusalem coming down out of heaven, as a bride adorned for her

---

[16] See Gospel according to Matthew, ch. 22, vs. 23-33; First Epistle to the Corinthians, ch. 15; First Epistle of Peter, ch. 1, v. 3; ch. 3, v. 21.
[17] See Book of Genesis, ch. 2; Book of the Revelation, chs. 21, 22.

husband. Between the garden and the city is the long history of human failure retrieved by God's grace.

Here let us give closer attention to that city. According to one of the last books in the Bible "we have not here an abiding city, but we seek after the city which is to come." [18] The city for which we seek is the "city which hath foundations, whose builder and maker is God." [19] Now, let us see this city through the eyes of John the revelator, as it was revealed to him on the Isle of Patmos. [20] The city he saw was a city of inexplicable beauty, likened to a bride ready to meet her husband. It is a city ornamented with gold and every kind of precious stone. It is a city of happiness, where all tears are wiped away. There is no death to cast the slightest shadow of sorrow. In this city there is no need for a sun or a moon to shine, for God's glory is ample light within it. Nor is there need for a temple, because the Lamb Himself is the temple. These last two facts are of passionate interest to us, because they give us an insight into the government of this city—a city in physical form pyramidal, lying upon its base foursquare, a city with walls and streets. The government, of course, is a theocracy, with God the Supreme Ruler. All the life of that city is worship, because all the life is communion. That is how John envisioned it. The inhabitants of this city are those whose names are written in the "Lamb's book of life." [21] This means only those who have loved God. Those who have separated themselves from God and who have loved defilement are excluded.

The architect and builder of this city is none other than God Himself. He has fashioned it from measurements that will harmonize with the finest art. In short, this is the

---

[18] Epistle to the Hebrews, ch. 13, v. 14, R.V.
[19] *Ibid.*, ch. 11, v. 10.
[20] See Book of the Revelation, ch. 21.
[21] *Ibid.*, ch. 21, v. 27.

ideal city in search of which many pilgrimages have been made without success. It is the city that Abraham saw but never reached. It is the city which prophets, musicians, and poets have described, but none has entered. This city is now abuilding. It comes down from heaven only after all the awesome events of terrible judgment and sublime majesty at the end of the millennium are past.[22]

If you ask me, "Do you really believe that such a city will somehow someday descend from out of the sky?" I answer that I believe it firmly. Would you have me be so Sadducean as to assert that I believe only the things that I can see and handle today? How human and restricted such a view! Indeed, the vision of this splendor was given to me for my comfort and hope. I accept it as such, and look eagerly for its fulfillment. To be a citizen of this heavenly land is a supreme honor, for I believe it is only there that at last we shall see the consummation of the perfect triangle with which we concerned ourselves at the opening of this chapter. In the New Jerusalem we shall at last live in a three-way perfect relationship with man, his neighbor, and God. Perfect justice will prevail, perfect happiness, no pain, and no suffering. Is there anyone so crass as to deny that such a city is worth seeking, no matter what hardships on the way?

I do not wish to quarrel with those who think of heaven on earth primarily as a place where the climate is balmy, where the streets are paved with gold, where the fruit is delicious, and where everyone will skillfully play a harp. Personally, I see these aspects as a sort of fringe benefit above and beyond the most important part of heaven, which is the center where throughout eternity we shall fulfill our highest ambitions without encountering failure or frustration. Now, this for me is to develop one's talents

---

[22] See Chapter 21, Atonement.

forever, and never to feel the stress and strain of life the way it is today. That I long for with all my heart. Oh, I shall be pleased to garden some outside the city's walls on the earth made new, for I already take pleasure in planting.[23] But that will not be all. I shall engage in an endless variety of occupations that will be fully satisfying. The bliss of heaven is this: "Immortal minds will contemplate with never-failing delight the wonders of creative power, the mysteries of redeeming love. . . . Every faculty will be developed, every capacity increased. The acquirement of knowledge will not weary the mind or exhaust the energies. There the grandest enterprises may be carried forward, the loftiest aspirations reached, the highest ambitions realized; and still there will arise new heights to surmount, new wonders to admire, new truths to comprehend, fresh objects to call forth the powers of mind and soul and body."[24]

Here ends this book. I make no apologies for the hope I have and which I have endeavored sincerely to share with you. The evidence presented has been weighed as best I know. I am convinced that life must begin and end with God if it is to be worth while. I know that man's destiny is glorious if he will love God and believe in His Word. Such conduct involves, as we foresaw at the start of our search, a full commitment without any loopholes. Jesus so lived. His way was not to be broad, nor His gate wide. They who come to Him today, as then, must be transformed by the renewal of the mind, the cleansing of the soul, the submission of the body. Thus transformed they will be confident, serene, undaunted, through "the final age of this world."[25] And this is the way of an abundant life.

So, let us together dedicate our life purpose to a total experience in the deeper dimensions in salvation.

---

[23] See Book of Isaiah, ch. 65, v. 22.
[24] Ellen G. White, *The Great Controversy,* p. 677.
[25] Second Epistle to Timothy, ch. 3, v. 1, *The New English Bible.*

Bibliography

Amiot, François. *L'Enseignement de Saint Paul*. Paris: Librairie LeCoffre J. Gabalda, 1938.

Berkhof, Louis. *Systematic Theology*. Grand Rapids: Wm. B. Eerdmans Pub. Co., 1953.

Brightman, Edgar Sheffield. *Philosophy of Religion*. Englewood Cliffs: Prentice-Hall, Inc., 1940.

Bultmann, Rudolf. *Jesus and the Word*. New York: Charles Scribner's Sons, 1934.

Danielou, Jean. *God and the Ways of Knowing*. New York: Meridian Books, Inc., 1957.

Dictionary of Theology. Grand Rapids: Baker Book House, 1960.

Dictionnaire de la Bible. Paris: Letouzey et Ané, 1912-1962.

Divoire, Fernand. *L'Homme après la Mort*. Paris: Editions Montaigne, 1926.

Doctrinal Discussions. Washington: Review and Herald Publishing Assn., 1961.

Dodd, C. Harold. *The Meaning of Paul for Today*. New York: Meridian Books, Inc., 1958.

Enslin, Morton Scott. *The Ethics of Paul*. New York: Abingdon Press, 1957.

Feifel, Herman, ed. *The Meaning of Death*. New York: McGraw-Hill, 1959.

Froom, LeRoy Edwin. *The Prophetic Faith of Our Fathers*. 4 vols. Washington: Review and Herald Publishing Assn., 1954.

Gardner, E. Clinton. *Biblical Faith and Social Ethics*. New York: Harper & Brothers, 1960.

Griffith, A. Leonard. *Barriers to Christian Faith*. New York: Harper & Row, 1962.

Guardini, Romano. *Freedom, Grace and Destiny*. New York: Pantheon Books, 1961.

Halverson, Marvin, ed. *A Handbook of Christian Theology*. New York: Meridian Books, Inc., 1958.

Hanke, Howard A. *From Eden to Eternity*. Grand Rapids: Wm. B. Eerdmans Pub. Co., 1960.

Harkness, Georgia. *Christian Ethics*. New York: Abingdon Press, 1957.

Henry, Carl F. H. *Christian Personal Ethics*. Grand Rapids: Wm. B. Eerdmans Pub. Co., 1957.

Heschel, Abraham Joshua. *God in Search of Man*. New York: Farrar, Straus, & Cudahy, 1955.

Hocking, William Ernest. *The Meaning of God in Human Experience*. New Haven: Yale University Press, 1912.

Hutchinson, John. *Faith, Reason, and Existence*. New York: Oxford University Press, 1956.

Joad, C. E. M. *The Recovery of Belief*. London: Faber & Faber Limited, 1952.

Knudson, Albert C. *The Principles of Christian Ethics*. New York: Abingdon Press, 1943.

La Sainte Bible. Paris: Letouzey et Ané, 1935-1962.

Leclercq, Jacques. *Christ and the Modern Conscience*. New York: Sheed & Ward, Inc., 1962.

Lewis, C. S. *Miracles*. New York: The Macmillan Company, 1953.

Monsma, John Clover, ed. *The Evidence of God in An Expanding Universe*. J. P. Pitmans Sons, 1958.

Morgan, G. Campbell. *The Westminster Pulpit*. Los Angeles: Fleming H. Revell Co., 1954.

Pease, Norval F. *By Faith Alone.* Mountain View, California: Pacific Press Publishing Assn., 1962.

Phillips, J. B. *New Testament Christianity.* New York: The Macmillan Company, 1956.

Phillips, J. B. *The Young Church in Action.* New York: The Macmillan Company, 1956.

Pickett, J. Waskom. *The Dynamics of Church Growth.* Nashville: Abingdon Press, 1963.

Questions on Doctrine. Washington: Review and Herald Publishing Assn., 1957.

Ramm, Bernard. *The Pattern of Authority.* Grand Rapids: Wm. B. Eerdmans Pub. Co., Revised, 1957.

Schleiermacher, Friedrich. *On Religion.* New York: Harper & Brothers, 1958.

Sertillanges, A. G. (O.P.) *Dieu ou Rien?* Paris: Flammarion, 1933.

Tenney, Merrill C., ed. *The Word for This Century.* New Jersey: Oxford University Press, 1960.

Tillich, Paul, *Dynamics of Faith.* New York: Harper & Brothers, 1957.

Underhill, Evelyn. *Mysticism.* New York: Meridian Books, Inc., 1955.

Van Mierlo, S. *La Science, la Raison et la Foi.* France: University Presses, 1948.

Watson, Philip S. *Let God Be God.* Philadelphia: Muhlenberg Press, 1947.

White, Ernest. *Christian Life and the Unconscious.* New York: Harper & Brothers, 1955.

Wieman, Henry Nelson. *Man's Ultimate Commitment.* Carbondale: Southern Illinois University Press, 1958.

Youngs, Robert W. *What It Means to Be a Christian.* New York: Farrar, Straus, & Cudahy, Inc., 1960.